Method and Practice in Biological Anthropology

A Workbook and Laboratory Manual for Introductory Courses

Samantha M. Hens, Ph.D.
California State University, Sacramento

PEARSON

Prentice
Hall

Upper Saddle River, New Jersey 07458

Editorial Director: Leah Jewell
AVP, Publisher: Nancy Roberts
AVP, Director of Logistics, Operations, and Vendor Relations: Barbara Kittle
Director of Marketing: Brandy Dawson
Executive Marketing Manager: Marissa Feliberty
Operations Specialist: Ben Smith
Editorial Assistant: Lee Peterson
Full-Service Project Management: Babitha Balan, GGS Book Services
Production Liaison: Cheryl Keenan
Director, Image Resource Center: Melinda Lee Patelli
Manager, Rights and Permissions: Zina Arabia
Manager, Visual Research: Beth Brenzel
Image Permissions Coordinator: Jan Marc Quisumbing
Cover Art Director: Jayne Conte
Cover Designer: Kiwi Graphics

This book was set in 10/12 New Century Schoolbook by GGS Book Services and was printed and bound by Bind-Rite Graphics. The cover was printed by Bind-Rite Graphics.

For permission to use copyrighted material, grateful acknowledgment is made to the copyright holders listed on page 229, which is considered an extension of this copyright page.

Pearson Education LTD.
Pearson Education Singapore, Pte. Ltd
Pearson Education, Canada, Ltd
Pearson Education–Japan
Pearson Education Australia PTY, Limited

Pearson Education North Asia Ltd
Pearson Educación de Mexico, S.A. de C.V
Pearson Education Malaysia, Pte. Ltd
Pearson Education, Upper Saddle River, New Jersey

10 9 8 7 6 5 4
ISBN 13: 978-0-13-225006-1
ISBN 10: 0-13-225006-3

Contents

Guide for Instructors

This book complements a wide variety of introductory-level laboratory courses in biological anthropology. Few lab manuals are available, and the difficulty in choosing a lab manual that is right for a course lies in adapting it to the lab materials to which you may or may not have access. Some anthropology labs are well equipped with casts of fossil hominids and nonhuman primate remains, human skeletal elements, and models for genetics instruction. However, for many the lab is a vacant space, in which case the instructor struggles to provide meaningful lab-based exercises rather than simply straightforward lecture. This book is designed to fit into either situation. It easily functions with a well-equipped laboratory, or it may be used as a primary source of photos and/or exercises.

The book is divided into four sections, reflecting the typical design of introductory courses in biological anthropology: genetics and evolution, the human skeleton, the nonhuman primates, and our fossil ancestors. Each chapter has similar pedagogical elements, beginning with a list of chapter objectives, an array of topical lab exercises to choose from, a set of pre-lab questions, and post-lab questions. Most chapters contain more information than might easily be covered in a typical class period, thus the instructor may choose either which exercises are most relevant for their course or to cover a chapter over two or more class periods. The chapter exercises are designed to be worked on during class time and reviewed prior to the end of the class period. An assortment of exercises is included and can be used based on how well or poorly equipped an individual lab may be or on the instructor's choice. Instructors should choose the exercises that work best in their environment. It is unlikely that students will finish all the exercises in any one chapter. The pre-lab questions are designed to be considered prior to the start of a lab; they are one way to encourage students to read the chapters prior to class. I like to use them as a pre-lab pop quiz, which only takes a few minutes at the start of class. The pre-lab questions cover basic, essential information that all students can gain without necessarily assigning all of the exercises in any one lab and can help to supplement lecture notes when lecture time is diminished in the laboratory environment. The post-lab questions build on the information gleaned from that chapter's work. They are designed to be answered at home after the lab is completed and handed in at a later time, and they provide the students with an opportunity to assimilate the information learned in class and to work additional examples on their own.

Teaching an introductory laboratory course is a challenging assignment for any faculty member. It is my hope that this book will also help to make it a rewarding one.

Guide for Students

Welcome to the Introduction to Biological Anthropology Laboratory! This book is designed both as a laboratory manual and a workbook for introductory classes. At the beginning of each chapter is a set of objectives to guide you in learning the information. Each chapter contains several exercise, and it is unlikely that you will be able to accomplish all the exercises in one class period. Your instructor will guide you through the chapters and inform you which exercises are relevant for your class. You should read the chapters prior to class. Toward the end of each chapter is a set of ten pre-lab questions that you will be able to answer after reading the materials and prior to class. These questions are designed to test your recall of basic concepts and provide you with an understanding of what is expected throughout the class period. The post-lab questions are based on your lab experience. They are meant to review the in-class information and allow you additional opportunities to review what was covered in class and to work through additional exercises where relevant. They may or not be collected, depending on your instructor.

This term you will cover a vast amount of material; some may be familiar to you from other coursework, much will be brand new. It is my hope that your learning experience will be both fun and educational.

Acknowledgments

First and foremost, I thank the many students who have passed through my classroom. Their enthusiasm about the field of biological anthropology has inspired me to write this book. It is my hope that future students will have as much fun learning this material as I did so many years ago. Kathy Moore, my local Prentice Hall representative, was instrumental in talking me into this project and motivating me throughout the process. I appreciate the support and guidance of Nancy Roberts, anthropology editor at Prentice Hall, and LeeAnn Doherty, assistant editor for anthropology. I also would like to thank John Allen for his constructive comments in reviewing the text and Curt Nelson, Amanda Wolcott, and Autumn Cahoon for using a preliminary version of this text in their classrooms and providing essential feedback and student commentary.

About the Author

Samantha Hens is an associate professor of anthropology at California State University in Sacramento. Her research interests cover an array of topics in biological anthropology, including osteology and skeletal biology, skeletal growth and development, morphometrics, functional anatomy, human evolution, and forensic anthropology. She has published several journal articles on stature estimation in fossil hominids and sex estimation from the human pelvis and skull. Her most recent areas of study have focused on three-dimensional analyses of growth and the development of sexual dimorphism in orangutan crania and on comparisons of sexual dimorphism between the orangutan and the gorilla. Dr. Hens received the Outstanding Teacher Award in her college in 2006. She lives in northern California, where she actively enjoys the outdoors and practices yoga.

The Scientific Method

The Nature of Science

Science is a way of gaining knowledge through critical observation and experiment. Humans try in many ways to explain their universe, through music, art, literature, religion, philosophy and science, for example. While many of these approaches may provide answers that we seek, only one, science, is based on empirical tests about nature that can be repeated and verified.

All sciences—including physics, chemistry, molecular biology, geology, and biological anthropology—are based on three assumptions. The first assumption is **natural causality**, which states that all events in nature are due to natural causes. Thus, scientists assume that everything can be explained by natural means, without reference to a supernatural power or force. Scientific explanations, then, deal with *cause and effect*—the idea that one thing is the result of another, as opposed to *teleological* explanations, which believe that nature has a supernatural design and a purpose. The second assumption is **uniformity in space and time**, which states that all events occur in the same way wherever or whenever they may happen in the universe. Therefore, natural laws, such as gravity, do not change over time or distance. The third assumption is **common perception**, which states that all humans perceive events through their senses in the same way, although morals or ethics may vary. For example, all humans can perceive the color red in the same way through their visual system; however, in some societies red is the color of good luck or fortune, while in other cultures red may symbolize death.

EXERCISE 1

Some people claim that epileptic seizures are the result of a supernatural force being directed at a person for punishment of past behavior. Is this a statement of cause and effect or teleology? Does it violate any of the assumptions above? If so, which one?

_____

_____

_____

Others claim that epilepsy is the result of neurons misfiring in the brain of afflicted individuals. Does this statement represent cause and effect or teleology? Does it violate any of the assumptions above? If so, which one?

_____

_____

_____

The Scientific Method

The **scientific method** is a process for empirically testing possible answers to questions about natural phenomena in ways that may be _repeated_ and _verified_. The questions arise from our observations of the world around us. The answers that result from the testing are added to the body of knowledge we have about the natural universe. Scientific explanations are always subject to updates and modifications based on further testing (see Figure 1-1). The scientific method generally has the following steps (an example is provided for each step):

1. **Observation.** A researcher may make observations directly from nature with his or her own senses, or from the written words of other investigators who have published scientific articles that are available in university libraries. Either way, the observed phenomenon must be **repeatable**—something that can be observed more than once.

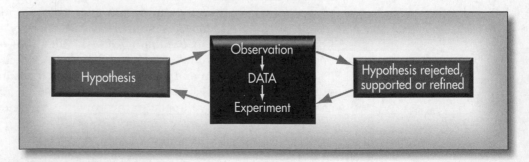

Figure 1-1 The Scientific Method.

- *Observation:* Historically, a scientist observed that maggots were found associated with spoiled meat.

2. **Formulate a research hypothesis.** A hypothesis is a proposed explanation for the observed phenomena (i.e., a general answer statement to the question).

   - *Hypothesis:* The maggots arise through spontaneous generation on spoiled meat.

3. **Experiment.** All hypotheses must be *testable*. The testing, or experimental, stage produces more information (data) about the original observation that may or may not support the hypothesis. This stage is often repeated multiple times, by different researchers, who may not have been involved in the original observations.

   - *Experiment:* Spoiled meat was placed into two containers, one with no lid and another with a tightly secured lid. Both containers were left in one room for several days. As the experiment proceeded, flies entered the room and laid eggs on the meat in the opened container. The eggs later hatched into maggots. The meat in the covered container was unaltered.

4. **Form a conclusion.** This may or may not support the original hypothesis. It is based on the data collected and tested in your experiment and has some validity, or support.

   - *Conclusion:* The hypothesis was wrong. Maggots do not appear via spontaneous generation but are the larvae produced by fly eggs.

Sometimes, countless experiments by numerous researchers working in many different countries all support the same conclusion and stand the test of time. In these cases, the validity of the results is not seriously doubted by the scientific community, and the conclusion may be considered a **scientific theory**. All scientific theories have been rigorously and exhaustively tested and are supported by a significant body of data. Often the lay public believes that theories are just hunches or not well-supported claims; however, this is a common misconception. Theories continue to be tested and may be modified in the light of new knowledge, especially as we advance technologically. Some examples of modern scientific theories include gravity, the germ theory of disease, heliocentrism, and evolution.

Experimental Design

Experiments test hypotheses. Specifically, they test the relationship between two (or more) variables. Does a change in one variable, cause a change in the other variable(s)? In any test, there are three kinds of variables. The **independent variable** is the condition or event under study. The **dependent variable** is the condition or event that may change due to the independent variable. The **control variables** are all the other conditions and events, which the researcher attempts to keep the same. Control variables are also independent variables, but they are held constant, whereas the independent variable may be altered in the experiment. It is not always easy to identify all the variables that may affect an experiment. Reading about other people's work is also important because it helps to familiarize us with what has already been done, helps us define the variables, and helps prevent us from repeating the same mistakes others have made.

- In the preceding maggot example, the dependent variable is the presence/absence of maggots; the independent variable that was altered is the open/closed container. The room temperature, humidity, amount of light, and so on are all independent variables that can be controlled in the experiment.

There are two types of experiments:

1. **Controlled experiments.** These occur when an investigator designs an experimental situation, usually in a laboratory. The researcher can alter one variable (the independent variable) and see what effect it has on the other variable (dependent variable). In all controlled experiments, one group should remain unchanged and unaltered in any way: the *control group* or *comparison group*. This control group is used as a baseline from which to compare the other group(s).

2. **Natural experiments.** The researcher has little or no control over any of the variables in natural experiments. Such experiments are common in animal behavior studies, where an investigator spends a considerable amount of time in the field observing subjects and taking careful notes of their observations. This type of experiment is common to some branches of the natural and social sciences.

EXERCISE 2

An experiment is done to test the effect of a new experimental drug for high cholesterol. Two hundred volunteers are separated into two groups of 100 each. Both groups are instructed to follow their regular diet and activities. Group 1 is given the experimental drug daily for 90 days, while Group 2 is given a placebo. The individuals in the groups do not know whether they are taking the new drug or the placebo. All participants are tested at the start of the study for their serum cholesterol levels. The average for Group 1 is 310 mg/dl, and the average for Group 2 is 302 mg/dl.

After 90 days, all participants' serum cholesterol is tested with a blood test. The average serum cholesterol level for Group 1 is 299 mg/dl, and the average for Group 2 is 300 mg/dl.

Using this information answer the following:

a. What is the hypothesis being tested?_____

_____

b. What is the dependent variable?_____

_____

c. What are the independent variables?_____

_____

d. Which variables are controlled?_____

_____

e. Which is the control group?_____

_____

f. Did the experiment produce data that supports the hypothesis?_____

_____

EXERCISE 3

An experiment is done to test the effect on mice of a high-fat diet. Fifty weanling mice are separated at random into two groups of 25 each. Group 1 is fed a normal diet with balanced amounts of protein, carbohydrates, vitamin supplements, and fat. Group 2 is fed the same amount of protein, carbohydrates, and vitamin supplements but is given a much higher fat content. The cages are cleaned and mice are given fresh food and water daily.

After six months, all mice are weighed. The average weight in grams for Group 1 is 8.2 g. The average weight for Group 2 is 12.6 g.

Using this information answer the following:

a. What is the hypothesis being tested?_____

_____

b. What is the dependent variable?_____

_____

c. What are the independent variables?_____

_____

d. Which variables are controlled?_____

_____

e. Which is the control group?_____

_____

f. Did the experiment produce data that support the hypothesis?_____

_____

EXERCISE 4

An experiment is done to test the effect of artificial light on geraniums. Seventy-five geranium seedlings are grown in a laboratory. The plants are separated into five groups of 15 plants each. The following table shows the groups, how much light each receives per day, and the average height of the plants after 180 days in the laboratory. All plants are fed the same amount of water and fertilizer daily. Group 4 receives as much light as all the other plants in the laboratory.

Group #	Sunlight Hours per Day	Height at 180 Days
1	3	5.0 cm
2	6	14.5 cm
3	12	29.2 cm
4	16	36.1 cm
5	24	25.4 cm

Using this information, answer the following:

a. What is the hypothesis being tested?_____

_____

b. What is the dependent variable?_____

_____

c. What are the independent variables?_____

_____

d. Which variables are controlled?_____

_____

e. Which is the control group?_____

_____

f. Did the experiment produce data that supports the hypothesis?_____

_____

EXERCISE 5

A series of observations that might be made by a biological anthropologist are listed at the end of this paragraph. Working in teams, choose one observation from the list, formulate a hypothesis, and roughly design an experiment to test your hypothesis. In your work, state your hypothesis, dependent variable, independent variable, and control variable(s).

a. Children from low-income households show evidence of malnutrition.

b. In most humans, the right humerus (upper arm bone) is larger than the left humerus.

c. Expectant mothers who smoke often have low-birth-weight babies.

d. People living on the island of Palau have the highest rates of schizophrenia in the world.

e. Orangutans living in zoos tend to be overweight when compared to their wild counterparts.

_____

_____

_____

_____

_____

_____

_____

_____

_____

The Research Article

The goal of the scientific community is to share information—the results of their experiments—with one another. Scientists are also highly competitive and critically examine and test the work of their colleagues. To this extent, scientists share their work by publishing research articles in scientific journals. Biological anthropologists publish their findings in numerous journals available in the university library and, sometimes, online. Some excellent journals are *The American Journal of Physical Anthropology, The Journal of Human Evolution, Current Anthropology,* and *The American Journal of Primatology.* For a helpful Internet resource that contains articles from both biologists and biological anthropologists go to www.PLOSBiology.org, which is a site sponsored by the Public Library of Science.

EXERCISE 6

Review an article from a copy of a typical biological anthropology journal. Then list the titles and functions of the various sections.

a. for example, Abstract—summary of paper

b. _____

c. _____

d. _____

e. _____

f. _____

In which section do you find the hypothesis being tested, or the study questions?

_____

Where would you look to find the details necessary to repeat this experiment?

_____

Science and Religion

As you should now understand, science is based on empirical observation of the natural world. Science's strength lies in its ability to continually test itself. Religious explanations of the world are based on the supernatural and the untestable, usually a spirit or deity. Such explanations provide a complete picture of the world and our place in it, and because this picture is complete, no further observations, hypothesis testing, compiling of data, or revisions of any sort are needed. Religion is one of the many ways of explaining the world around you, but it violates the assumption of natural causality and does not operate within the scientific method; thus, it cannot be scientific.

Despite these differences, for most people science and religion are compatible in today's world. Science may explain how or when we became human, but it leaves us wanting for answers to such questions as, What is the meaning of life? What does it mean to be a good person? These questions are often answered well by theologians.

Pre-Lab Questions

1. The idea that the universe is controlled by a supernatural force or deity is best described as a/an:
   a. empiricism
   b. cause and effect
   c. teleology
   d. scientific theory

2. The first step in the scientific method is:
   a. formulating a hypothesis
   b. observing an event
   c. setting up an experiment
   d. theorizing on the likely result

3. Scientific reports of experiments are usually reported by the investigators in:
   a. newspapers
   b. textbooks
   c. scientific journals
   d. magazines

4. The basic assumption in science that all humans experience events in the same way through their senses is called:
   a. uniformity in space and time
   b. natural causality
   c. cause and effect
   d. common perception

5. A scientific statement that is based on experimental data and has some validity is known as a/an:
   a. conclusion
   b. theory
   c. hypothesis
   d. explanation

6. The condition or event that may change in an experiment is the:
   a. independent variable
   b. controlled variable
   c. original observation
   d. dependent variable

7. **True or False:** The results of an experiment do not have to be repeatable.

8. **True or False:** An experiment wherein the researcher cannot control all the variables (which is common in animal behavior studies) is a natural experiment.

9. **True or False:** The variable that researchers try to keep the same for the experimental and control groups is the dependent variable.

10. **True or False:** Evolution is a popular hypothesis in biology, which needs further support to demonstrate its validity.

Post-Lab Questions

1. How does modern science differ from faith? How do these compare in terms of teleological or cause-and-effect explanations? _____

   _____

   _____

   _____

2. Describe the three assumptions all sciences are based on. _____

   _____

   _____

   _____

   _____

   _____

3. Describe the steps of the scientific method. _____

   _____

   _____

   _____

   _____

   _____

4. What does an experiment test? _____

   _____

   _____

   _____

5. Describe the differences among the independent variable, dependent variable, and control variable. _____

   _____

   _____

   _____

   _____

6. Using either Exercise 2, 3 and/or 4, can you identify any variables that were not controlled for in the study that could have been controlled?_____

   _____

   _____

7. Reviewing your team's answers to Exercise 5, can you think of an alternate test of your hypothesis? Was anything left out of your original experiment? _____

_____

_____

_____

8. Choose a research article from a physical anthropology journal online or in the library. Can you identify what hypothesis the author(s) is/are testing? Is the experiment designed in such a way that it might be repeated by another investigator? _____

_____

_____

_____

Chapter 2

Cell Biology and DNA

Objectives

After completing this chapter you should be able to:

1. describe and label the parts of the eukaryotic cell;

2. describe the types of cells found in the human body;

3. describe chromosome structure and identify human karyotypes;

4. describe the differences between mitotic and meiotic cell division;

5. understand the importance of crossing over and recombination;

6. describe DNA structure, DNA replication, transcription, and translation; and

7. calculate the sequence of bases in DNA or RNA when provided with the complementary strand, and translate the codons into amino acids using the chart.

Cells and Cell Structure

The **cell** is structurally and functionally the basic unit of life for all organisms. The term *cell* comes from Robert Hooke, who in the seventeenth century observed that cork was made up of small units, which reminded him of the "cells" or cubicles in which monks lived. All cells must arise from preexisting cells, and living organisms may be single-celled or multicellular in composition.

Cells may be classified into two types, depending on the presence of an internal, membrane-bound **nucleus**: (1) **prokaryotic** cells, which do not have

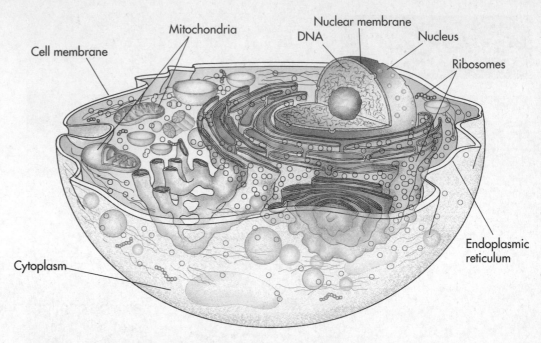

Figure 2-1 A typical eukaryotic cell.

a separate nucleus and are found in bacteria and cyanobacteria and (2) **eukaryotic** cells, which contain a true nucleus and make up all other forms of life. It is thought that the prokaryotic cells evolved first and that eukaryotic cells evolved from these simpler forms. All eukaryotic cells share certain structural features in common, including (1) a *plasma membrane,* separating the contents of the cell from the outside world; (2) *cytoplasm,* a gel-like or fluid-like matrix within the plasma membrane; (3) *organelles,* the various structures responsible for cell functions, such as metabolism and protein synthesis; and (4) genetic information, in the form of **DNA** (deoxyribonucleic acid), which is stored in the nucleus (Figure 2-1).

Two types of cells are found in humans: (1) **somatic cells** and (2) **gametes**. The somatic cells are those cells that make up the body of an organism—everything from hair and skin to lungs, liver, muscles, blood, and bone. Somatic cells are often referred to as *body cells.* In contrast, the gametes, or sex cells, are the sperm found in the male testes and the ova (or egg cells) found in the female ovaries. The gametes carry the genetic information required to make the next generation.

Chromosome Structure

Figure 2-2 Single-stranded and double-stranded chromosomes.

DNA and proteins are found on **chromosomes**. Chromosomes are located in the nucleus and are made up of long, threadlike material called *chromatin* that coils and condenses when a cell is about to divide, making the chromosome visible with a light microscope. Chromosomes are normally single stranded, but they become double stranded when DNA replicates itself, prior to cell division. Each strand is called a **chromatid**. When the chromosome is double stranded, the two chromatids are called *sister chromatids.* A constricted area, called the **centromere**, separates one chromatid strand into two "arms." Chromosomes come in different sizes and can be identified by size and position of their centromere. Centromeres may be in the middle of the chromosome, so that the arms are of approximately equal length, or they may be off center, making the arms of unequal length (Figure 2-2).

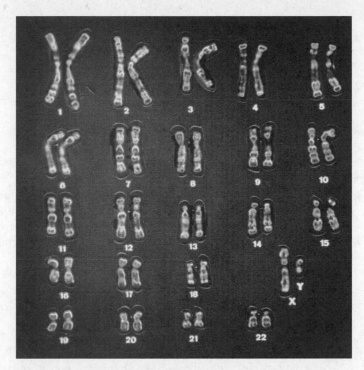

Figure 2-3 A human karyotype. Notice the autosomes, sex chromosomes, and basic chromosome structure.

Different species have a different number of chromosomes in their cells. Normal human body cells contain 23 pairs of chromosomes (46 chromosomes total). The chromosomes are numbered 1 through 23. In other words, there are two copies of number 1, two copies of number 2, and so on, until you reach the two copies of number 23. These are called **homologous pairs**. The members of each pair are similar in size, position of the centromere, and genetic information carried (always for the same traits) (Figure 2-3). This genetic information is distributed along the length of the chromosome as **genes**, segments of DNA that code for specific traits. **Alleles** are alternate forms of a gene; for example, the gene for eye color may have several alleles, such as brown, blue, and green. The first 22 pairs of chromosomes are called the *autosomes*. The final, 23rd pair, are called the *sex chromosomes*. Human females have two X chromosomes as their 23rd pair, while human males have one X and one Y chromosome as their 23rd pair. Human sex cells, or gametes, carry only one copy of each pair, so they have 23 chromosomes in each sperm or ovum.

EXERCISE 1

Can you think of any reason why the gametes have only 23 chromosomes, one of each pair? _____

_____

_____

Chimpanzees have 48 chromosomes in their somatic cells. How many chromosomes do you think are found in their sex cells? _____

_____

_____

_____

EXERCISE 2

When chromosomes are stained and photographed, the resulting image is called a **karyotype**. Chromosomes in a karyotype can be cut out and lined up. They may be arranged into pairs by matching their size and position of the centromere. The position of the centromere may be described as follows:

- **Acrocentric**—at one end, so arms are of unequal length
- **Metacentric**—in the middle, so that arms are of similar length
- **Telocentric**—all the way at one end, so that one arm is barely visible

Sometimes, an individual is born with the wrong number of chromosomes. This is caused by a **nondisjunction**, a failure of the chromosomes to segregate properly during cell division. In this case, you may have a different number of chromosomes in your karyotype due to a deletion or duplication of a chromosome. Some common abnormalities are:

- **Turner syndrome**—X0, deletion of a sex chromosome; these are females who tend to be shorter than average, with below-average intelligence, and are infertile.
- **Kleinfelter's syndrome**—XXY, an extra X chromosome; these males are taller than average, with below-average intelligence, and are infertile.
- **XYY**—an extra Y chromosome; these are males who may show a tendency toward aggressive behavior.
- **Down syndrome**—three copies of chromosome 21 (trisomy 21); these individuals are characterized by a suite of traits, primarily mental retardation.

Working individually or in pairs, you will be provided a copy of a standard human karyotype form and a human karyotype. Carefully, cut out the chromosomes and matching pairs, then glue or tape the chromosomes onto the form. When you have finished, answer the following questions:

a. Is the individual whose karyotype you have a male or a female? How do you know? _____

_____

_____

_____

b. Draw a circle around the sex chromosomes in your karyotype and label them. Do the same for the autosomes.

c. Are there any anomalies in the karyotype you have completed? If so, describe it. Be sure to highlight it and indicate the name of the syndrome on your karyotype. _____

_____

_____

_____

Cell Division

Cell division in eukaryotes requires two processes: division of the cytoplasm (*cytokinesis*) and division of the nucleus, **mitosis** or **meiosis**. Cytokinesis ensures that each end product (*daughter cell*) receives the cellular structures needed for life, such as cytoplasm and organelles. Mitosis and meiosis are different types of divisions and result in different numbers of daughter cells. Figure 2-4 provides an illustration of the two processes.

Mitosis. *Fertilization* is the fusion of egg and sperm nuclei, resulting in a single-celled **zygote**, or fertilized egg. This zygote then divides into two cells, which in turn divide into four, and so on. Eventually a multicellular organism is produced. During each cell division, each daughter cell receives a complete

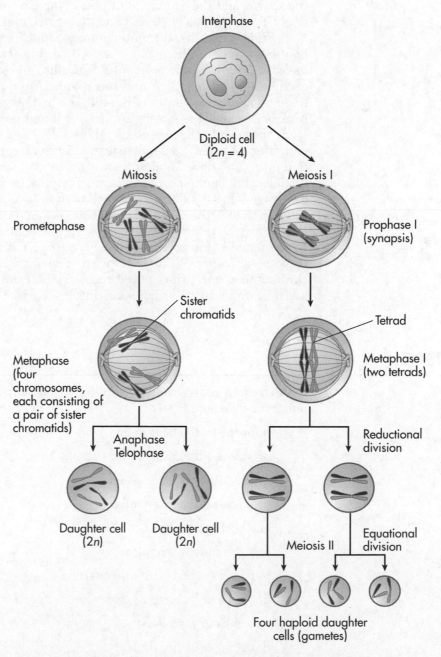

Figure 2-4 A comparison of the processes of mitosis and meiosis.

set of genetic information and the necessary cellular components. This cell division occurs during growth and later repair of body tissues.

Prior to the mitotic division, the chromosomes replicate themselves, that is, they become double stranded (in a human, this results in 46 double-stranded chromosomes). This is followed by one cell division wherein the sister chromatids separate from each other, with one strand going into each daughter cell. The end result is two daughter cells with 46 (single-stranded) chromosomes each. The full complement of chromosomes, 46, is called the **diploid** number. Thus, in mitosis, the cell begins diploid and ends diploid.

Meiosis. This process is more complicated than what occurs in mitosis. In meiosis, the genetic complement is cut in half so that the daughter cells each have half the number of chromosomes as the original cell. Because of this, meiosis is often called a *reduction division*. The genetic complement is now half the original, meaning one copy of each chromosome pair ends up in each daughter cell. This is the **haploid** number. This process produces the gametes, the sperm, and the ovum, and it takes place in the testes and ovaries, respectively. Two divisions, meiosis I and meiosis II, make this possible.

Prior to meiosis, the chromosomes replicate themselves, again becoming double stranded. Thus, there are 46 double-stranded chromosomes when meiosis I begins. During meiosis I, the homologous chromosomes pair with each other, join together, and intertwine. After the chromosome pairs have lined up across the center of the cell, the homologous chromosome pairs separate, one homologue moves toward one daughter cell, while the other homologue moves into the second daughter cell. The end result of meiosis I is two daughter cells with 23 double-stranded chromosomes each. In meiosis II, each daughter cell now divides, resulting in four daughter cells total. In the nucleus, the sister chromatids separate, with one strand going into each daughter cell. This division is similar to mitosis. The result is four daughter cells, with half the number of original chromosomes (23 each). In the male, this process is referred to as *spermatogenesis* and produces four sperm cells. In the female, this process is called *oogenesis* and produces one egg cell and three *polar bodies*. While the nuclear divisions provide all four cells with 23 chromosomes each, the egg cell receives all of the cell contents from the cytokenesis, while the polar bodies disintegrate.

EXERCISE 3

Compare and contrast mitosis and meiosis in the human with the following matching questions.

_____ happens in the body cells

_____ produces 4 daughter cells

_____ begins with 46 chromosomes

_____ produces 2 daughter cells

_____ one nuclear division

_____ one chromosome replication

_____ happens in the testes and ovaries

_____ daughter cells have 23 chromosomes each

_____ two nuclear divisions

_____ daughter cells are diploid

a. mitosis

b. meiosis

c. both mitosis and meiosis

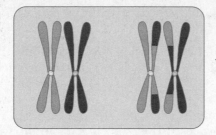

Figure 2-5 The process of recombination.

Recombination (Crossing Over)

During meiosis, an important event occurs that shuffles the genetic information around on the chromosomes. When the homologous chromosomes pair up and intertwine in meiosis I, the chromatids break and portions of chromatids bearing genes for the same trait are exchanged, or reshuffled, between homologous chromosomes. This is called **recombination**, or **crossing over** (Figure 2-5). The end result may be that the original chromatids are carrying different alleles at that location. Crossing over allows a great amount of variability to be incorporated into the chromosome.

EXERCISE 4

Draw a homologous pair of chromosomes. Use one color (e.g., pink) for one member of the pair and use a second color (e.g., blue) for the second member of the pair.

Next, draw the two chromosomes crossing over, so that the two colors are touching.

Third, draw the two chromosomes after the crossing over is completed and they have shuffled their gene pairs, exchanging genes (colors) between them. Have at least one exchange.

Compare your drawing to those of others in the class and see the amount of variation that might be possible.

DNA Structure and Function

In 1869, a chemist by the name of Friedrich Miescher found a substance in the cell nucleus that he called "nuclein." This substance became known as deoxyribonucleic acid, or DNA. In the 1950s, several researchers were attempting to discover the structure of DNA and exactly how it or some other molecule (e.g., proteins) might carry genetic information. In 1953, James Watson and Francis Crick proposed that the DNA molecule was composed of two strands that were twisted around each other in a **double helix** structure (like a twisted ladder). For their pioneering work, Watson and Crick were awarded the Nobel Prize in 1962 (Rosalind Franklin, who also worked on DNA structure, was also awarded the Nobel Prize that year; however, she died before the Nobel Prize was announced). It can be argued that the discovery of DNA as the genetic material and determination of its molecular structure are two of the most significant discoveries of the twentieth century. Understanding the function of DNA is essential for understanding life.

We now understand that DNA is made up of two chains of **nucleotides**. Each DNA nucleotide contains a phosphate, a sugar (deoxyribose sugar), and a base group. The phosphates and sugars make up the "sides" of the ladder-like structure. Each sugar is also connected to a base. The four possible bases are adenine (A), cytosine (C), guanine (G), and thymine (T). These bases join with each other in **complementary base pairs** to form the "rungs" of the ladder (Figure 2-6). The joining is very specific: A with T, C with G. Structurally and functionally, the base pairing lies at the heart of the DNA molecule. Because of

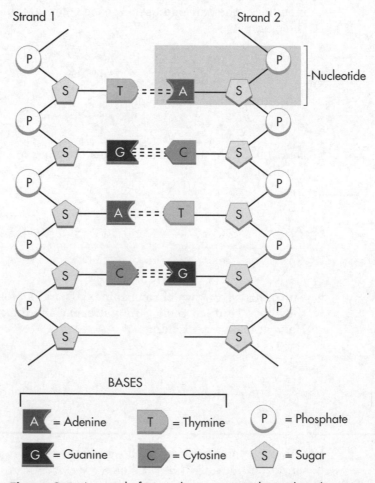

Figure 2-6 A strand of DNA demonstrating the nucleotide structure.

this strict base pairing, the sequence of bases in the DNA molecule is preserved when the molecule is replicating or being copied.

DNA has two main functions: (1) **self-replication**, which occurs when the cell is about to divide and (2) **protein synthesis**, or the formation of proteins. Proteins are structural molecules that are important for building all the cells of the body. Proteins also act as *enzymes,* allowing necessary chemical reactions in the body to take place.

DNA replication takes place just prior to cell division and results in the chromosomes replicating themselves. Replication begins when the DNA molecule "unwinds" and the strands separate, then "unzips" when the hydrogen bonds between the bases are broken. This results in two single strands of DNA with exposed bases. Free DNA nucleotides within the nucleus bond to the exposed bases, according to the base pairing rules, creating two new strands of DNA. Note that each new strand contains one original strand and one new strand. DNA replication is *semiconservative*: each parental strand remains intact, while a new complementary strand is formed.

EXERCISE 5

Practice DNA base pairing:

Consider the following DNA strand: A T C C T A G G T C A G

Identify the complementary bases: _____

Now, practice DNA replication. Consider the following double-stranded DNA molecule. Notice that the DNA bases are paired accordingly. Separate the strands and replicate them, identifying which strands are original and which are the new complementary strands.

T A C G G C A A C T G A G C T

A T G C C G T T G A C T C G A

_____

_____

Protein Synthesis. The sequence of the bases in the DNA chain codes for **amino acids**, which once linked together form proteins. The process of protein synthesis occurs in two stages: (1) **transcription**, and (2) **translation** (Figure 2-7). First, in transcription, the DNA must be copied into a form that is able to exit the nucleus of the cell. This is accomplished by the formation of another type of nucleic acid, **RNA** (ribonucleic acid). RNA is a single-stranded molecule, composed of RNA nucleotides linked together. An RNA nucleotide is composed of a phosphate, a ribose sugar, and a base group. Note that the sugar molecules in DNA and RNA are slightly different. There are also differences in the bases. RNA does contain A, C, and G, but it does not contain T. Instead, RNA has a base called *uracil* (U). The base pairing is similar: C with G and A with U. The process begins with the DNA molecule unwinding and "unzipping," wherein the DNA strands again become separated. One DNA strand will be the *template strand,* the strand that is copied. This time, free RNA nucleotides in the nucleus will pair up with the exposed DNA bases on the template strand, following the base pairing rules. The strand of RNA that is formed is called *messenger RNA* or **mRNA** because it carries the DNA "message" or code. The mRNA strand may now exit the nucleus and

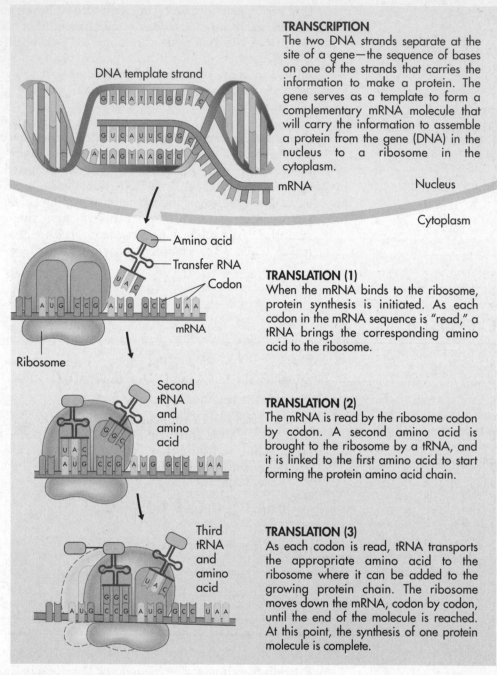

TRANSCRIPTION

The two DNA strands separate at the site of a gene—the sequence of bases on one of the strands that carries the information to make a protein. The gene serves as a template to form a complementary mRNA molecule that will carry the information to assemble a protein from the gene (DNA) in the nucleus to a ribosome in the cytoplasm.

DNA template strand

mRNA   Nucleus

Cytoplasm

Amino acid

Transfer RNA

Codon

mRNA

Ribosome

TRANSLATION (1)

When the mRNA binds to the ribosome, protein synthesis is initiated. As each codon in the mRNA sequence is "read," a tRNA brings the corresponding amino acid to the ribosome.

Second tRNA and amino acid

TRANSLATION (2)

The mRNA is read by the ribosome codon by codon. A second amino acid is brought to the ribosome by a tRNA, and it is linked to the first amino acid to start forming the protein amino acid chain.

Third tRNA and amino acid

TRANSLATION (3)

As each codon is read, tRNA transports the appropriate amino acid to the ribosome where it can be added to the growing protein chain. The ribosome moves down the mRNA, codon by codon, until the end of the molecule is reached. At this point, the synthesis of one protein molecule is complete.

Figure 2-7 Protein Synthesis.

head out to a specific organelle in the cytoplasm of the cell, called the **ribosome**, which is the site of protein synthesis. The DNA strands pair up again.

In the second stage, *translation,* the mRNA code is scanned through the ribosome, where it is "read" like a bar code in a supermarket. "To translate" means to change from one language to another. In this process, the mRNA code is translated into a strand of amino acids that will eventually form a protein. The mRNA strand is read three bases at a time. A series of three bases in RNA is called a **codon**. The *transfer RNA,* **tRNA,** carries an amino acid and sits at the ribosome, where the tRNA anticodons (codons found on the tRNA) will pair up with the mRNA codons. Each codon calls for one amino acid. Think of a codon like a three-letter word. As the codons are read by the tRNA, the appropriate amino acids are linked together in a long peptide chain. Many peptide chains linked together form a protein.

EXERCISE 6

The following chart lists all possible mRNA codons and the 20 amino acids they code for. Note that there is some redundancy in the code. Also note that some codons code for *start* or *stop*, which tells the cell where to start or stop making the protein. Using this information, fill in the blanks below the chart for the amino acid each codon calls for.

UUU Phenylalanine	UCU Serine	UAU Tyrosine	UGU Cysteine
UUC Phenylalanine	UCC Serine	UAC Tyrosine	UGC Cysteine
UUA Leucine	UCA Serine	UAA Stop	UGA Stop
UUG Leucine	UCG Serine	UAG Stop	UGG Tryptophan
CUU Leucine	CCU Proline	CAU Histidine	CGU Arginine
CUC Leucine	CCC Proline	CAC Histidine	CGC Arginine
CUA Leucine	CCA Proline	CAA Glutamine	CGA Arginine
CUG Leucine	CCG Proline	CAG Glutamine	CGG Arginine
AUU Isoleucine	ACU Threonine	AAU Asparagine	AGU Serine
AUC Isoleucine	ACC Threonine	AAC Asparagine	AGC Serine
AUA Isoleucine	ACA Threonine	AAA Lysine	AGA Arginine
AUG Start (Methionine)	ACG Threonine	AAG Lysine	AGG Arginine
GUU Valine	GCU Alanine	GAU Aspartic Acid	GGU Glycine
GUC Valine	GCC Alanine	GAC Aspartic Acid	GGC Glycine
GUA Valine	GCA Alanine	GAA Glutamic Acid	GGA Glycine
GUG Valine	GCG Alanine	GAG Glutamic Acid	GGG Glycine

Source: Laidlaw and Kopple (1987)

UCA _____   GUA _____

UGG _____   AGA _____

CUC _____   GCC _____

CAU _____   AUG _____

EXERCISE 7

The following is a template strand of DNA:

A C G G T T C A T G C A

What is the complementary mRNA strand?

_____

What are the complementary tRNA anticodons?

_____

Using the chart from Exercise 6, what is the sequence of amino acids for this peptide chain? Be sure to use the mRNA codons when reading the chart.

_____

_____

Pre-Lab Questions

1. Which of the following individuals was responsible for coining the term *cell*?
   a. Hooke
   b. Darwin
   c. Wilkins
   d. Watson

2. Prokaryotic cells are distinguishable from eukaryotic cells because prokaryotes do *not* contain:
   a. organelles
   b. a plasma membrane
   c. DNA
   d. a nucleus

3. Chromosome strands are called:
   a. centromeres
   b. alleles
   c. chromatids
   d. homologues

4. Alternate forms of a gene are called:
   a. alleles
   b. sister chromatids
   c. homologues
   d. replicated DNA

5. Sister chromatids separate during nuclear division in:
   a. mitosis
   b. meiosis I
   c. meiosis II
   d. both a and c

6. Who won the Nobel Prize in 1962 for identifying the structure of DNA?
   a. Hooke
   b. Meischer
   c. Watson and Franklin
   d. Watson, Crick, and Franklin

7. Which of the following is a possible base pairing in DNA?
   a. adenine-cytosine
   b. adenine-thymine
   c. cytosine-thymine
   d. thymine-guanine

8. Transcription in DNA:
   a. results in the formation of an identical DNA strand
   b. results in the formation of mRNA
   c. happens in the nucleus
   d. requires the assistance of tRNA anticodons

9. **True or False:** DNA replication occurs in the ribosome.

10. **True or False:** Crossing over is an important source of variability.

Post-Lab Questions

1. Describe the difference between the autosomes and the sex chromosomes. _____
   _____
   _____
   _____

2. How many chromosomes were there in your karyotype set? Was this the normal number for humans?
   _____
   _____

3. Referring to your lecture textbook, or the Internet, discuss the clinical symptoms associated with any
   anomaly you identified in your karyotype. _____
   _____
   _____
   _____

4. How do you determine the sex of an individual when examining his or her karyotype?
   _____
   _____

5. How are the different types of chromosomes identified for a karyotype? _____
   _____
   _____
   _____

6. If the chromosome number for an organism is 22 before mitosis, what is the chromosome number of each
   daughter cell after mitosis has taken place? _____
   _____

7. Why is the DNA replicated prior to mitosis? _____
   _____
   _____
   _____

8. What do you think might happen if a cell underwent mitosis but not cytokinesis? _____
   _____
   _____
   _____

9. If a cell in an organism had 16 chromosomes before meiosis, how many chromosomes would exist in each nucleus after meiosis? What is the diploid number? What is the haploid number? _____

_____

_____

_____

10. From a genetic standpoint, what is the significance of fertilization? _____

_____

_____

_____

11. Describe the differences between haploid and diploid cells and where are they found. _____

_____

_____

_____

12. Discuss the differences you observed when comparing your crossing over diagram to others in the class. How many different combinations did you see? _____

_____

_____

_____

13. What does it mean when we say DNA replication is semiconservative? _____

_____

_____

_____

14. Describe the differences in DNA and RNA structure. _____

_____

_____

_____

_____

_____

15. To transcribe means "to make a copy of." Is an exact copy of DNA made during the process of transcription? Why or why not? _____

_____

_____

_____

16. Where does transcription happen? What about translation? _____

_____

_____

_____

17. What amino acid would be produced if transcription took place from the DNA sequence CAT?

_____

- If a genetic mistake took place during replication and the new DNA strand has the sequence CAG, what amino acid would result? _____

_____

- What if the genetic mistake resulted in a DNA strand with the sequence GAT? _____

_____ _ _ _____

- Explain these results. _____

_____

_____

_____

Chapter 3

Principles of Inheritance

After completing this chapter you should be able to:

1. explain the difference between genotype and phenotype, homozygous and heterozygous, dominant and recessive;

2. determine the gametes produced from given genotypes and the genotypes formed from specific gamete pairs;

3. understand Mendel's Laws;

4. solve problems using Punnett squares involving monohybrid and dihybrid crosses, including the probabilities of offspring genotypes and phenotypes; and

5. understand the differences among complete dominance, incomplete dominance, codominance, and sex-linked inheritance.

The Basic Principles of Inheritance

Gregor Mendel was an Austrian monk who discovered the basic principles of inheritance that we use today. He studied mathematics, botany, and physics at the University of Vienna before beginning his experiments, breeding the common garden pea, in 1856. He published his work in 1865, but unfortunately the work was unrecognized and unappreciated at the time. Mendel was not the first person to study heredity in plants, but he was the first person to use statistics in his analyses. Working in the monastery garden, Mendel followed the inheritance of simple traits through several generations. He discovered that the information that controlled inheritance behaved like particles that were passed from one generation to the next. Today, we call these particles *genes*.

Mendel concluded that each pea plant contained two particles of information for each trait. Each parent plant contributed one particle of information for each trait to each of its offspring.

Can you explain this discovery using our modern understanding of cell biology and DNA from Chapter 2? _____

_____

_____

_____

The common garden pea has both male and female parts that can breed with each other in the same flower and also are able to self-fertilize. To begin his experiments, Mendel chose plants that were *true-breeders,* meaning that all self-fertilized offspring displayed the same traits as their parents. For example, if a true-breeding plant with round seeds self-fertilized, then all offspring also would have round seeds. In other words, the plant carries the same allele for the gene at each locus. When parents that are true-breeders for different traits are mated (e.g., round seeds and wrinkled seeds), the offspring are called **hybrids**. The offspring have alleles for both traits (e.g., round seeds and wrinkled seeds). The **genotype** is the genetic constitution of an organism, the actual alleles present. The **phenotype** describes the physical characteristics of an organism, the expression of its genes. Mendel was breeding plants, examining their phenotypes, and trying to infer the underlying genotypes.

When the transmission of one trait at a time is studied, it is called a **monohybrid cross**. When two traits at a time are studied, it is called a **dihybrid cross**. Beginning with the monohybrid cross, recall that somatic cells are diploid; they contain two copies of each chromosome arranged in pairs. These homologous pairs carry the same genes, although they may have different alleles. For one trait that has two forms (e.g., seed shape in pea plants has two forms: round seeds and wrinkled seeds), three combinations of alleles are possible. Different types of notation are used to represent the alleles; a common notation is used here. Using *R* to indicate the allele for round seeds, and *r* to indicate the allele for wrinkled seeds, if both chromosomes carry the *R* allele the plant is *RR*, while if both chromosomes carry the *r* allele the plant is *rr.* However, if one chromosome carries the *R*, while the other member of the pair carries the *r*, then the gene pair is *Rr.* Remember: sex cells are haploid and only carry one of these alleles.

EXERCISE 1

Mendel's pea plants carry two alleles for the flower color gene: *P* for purple flowers and *p* for white flowers. What three possible combinations might exist in any one plant?

_____

Mendel's pea plants also carry two genes for plant height: *T* for tall plants and *t* for short plants. Consider the genotypes in the following table and indicate the possible genotypes of the gametes (you may need to review meiosis to complete this exercise).

Diploid Genotype	Gamete Genotype
TT	
Tt	
tt	

Working in the opposite direction, during fertilization when the sperm and egg fuse, the haploid cells come together and form a diploid zygote. In the following table, provide the diploid genotypes that would occur by fusion of the following gamete genotypes.

Gamete Genotype	Gamete Genotype	Diploid Genotype
t	*t*	
T	*t*	
T	*T*	

In the preceding examples, there are two alleles for each gene. A plant whose genotype is *RR* or *Rr* has round seeds. *RR* and *Rr* are the genotypes, and "round" is the phenotype. This is the **dominant** condition. Dominance is the ability of one allele to mask or hide the expression of the other allele. In this case round (*R*) is dominant to wrinkled (*r*). The **recessive** allele is the allele that is not expressed, the one that is hidden, in this case *r*, wrinkled. A plant with two copies of the recessive allele, *rr*, would exhibit wrinkled seeds. The dominant gene is always written as a capital letter, while the recessive gene is written as a lowercase letter. These are cases of *complete dominance*. When both alleles are identical, the individual is said to be **homozygous** for that trait (*RR* or *rr*). When both copies are the dominant gene, the individual is *homozygous dominant*. When both alleles are for the recessive condition, the individual is said to be *homozygous recessive*. When the alleles are different (*Rr*), then the individual is said to be **heterozygous**.

EXERCISE 2

We know that purple flowers in pea plants are dominant to white flowers. Using the example for flower color in Exercise 1, identify the flower colors for plants that have the following genotypes. Label the homozygous and heterozygous conditions.

- *PP* _____
- *Pp* _____
- *pp* _____

Why? _____

_____

EXERCISE 3

In Mendel's pea plants, yellow seeds are dominant to green seeds. Using *Y* for yellow and *y* for green, list the three possible genotypes, followed by their phenotype (yellow or green), and label the homozygous and heterozygous conditions.

_____

_____

_____

Mendel's Laws of Inheritance

From the basic genetic principles already described, Mendel formulated two laws (or principles), which are described here using modern terminology:

- **Law of Segregation.** During meiosis, the chromosome pairs separate, so that each newly formed gamete receives one chromosome (that is, one allele of each pair).

- **Law of Independent Assortment.** During meiosis, the members of different pairs of alleles assort independently into gametes (especially so if they are on different chromosomes). In other words, the segregation of one pair of chromosomes does not influence the segregation of another pair of chromosomes in the same sex cells.

For example, we know that a pea plant with the genotype Rr produces the gametes R and r. If we consider an example where two traits are being compared at one time, and this same plant was also Tt, then all possible combinations of gametes would be RT, Rt, rT, rt.

EXERCISE 4

For this exercise, let's expand our practice to include three traits at once.

a. What gametes are produced from a plant that is Pp? _____

_____

b. What gametes are produced from a plant that is $PpTt$? _____

_____

c. What gametes are produced from a plant that is $PpTtYy$? _____

_____

Punnett Squares

The **Punnett square** is used to figure out all possible results of matings between individuals. In this way, we examine the gametes in all possible combinations. We are then able to determine the probabilities of offspring genotypes and phenotypes. To practice a Punnett square, start with the parental gametes along the top and left side of the square and then cross-multiply.

For example, the gene for seed color has two alleles, Y and y. Let Y stand for the yellow allele, and y stand for the green allele, where yellow is dominant to green. If one parent is homozygous dominant (YY) and the other parent is a heterozygote (Yy), a Punnett square is calculated with the alleles for one parent along the top, and the alleles for the other parent along the left side. The possible offspring may be calculated as follows:

	Y	Y
Y	YY	YY
y	Yy	Yy

The possible genotypes formed from the mating are *YY* and *Yy*. Of the offspring, 50% (2 out of 4) are homozygous *YY,* and 50% of the offspring are heterozygous *Yy* (2 out of 4). There are no homozygous recessives (*yy*) produced by this mating. All offspring produced from this mating are yellow, due to dominance. This is a simple monohybrid cross.

EXERCISE 5

a. Considering that purple is dominant to white, and using *P* for purple and *p* for white, draw a Punnett square crossing a heterozygous purple-flowered plant and a white-flowered plant.

b. What are the genotypes produced by this mating? _____

c. What are the phenotypes produced by this mating? _____

d. What percentage of the offspring is homozygous? _____

EXERCISE 6

a. We know that the allele for round seeds is dominant to the allele for wrinkled seeds. Using *R* for round and *r* for wrinkled, draw a Punnett square crossing two plants that are both heterozygous.

b. What percentage of the offspring is homozygous dominant? _____

c. What percentage of the offspring is homozygous recessive? _____

d. What percentage of the offspring is heterozygous? _____

e. What percentage of the offspring is wrinkled? _____

f. What percentage of the offspring is round? Why? _____

Incomplete Dominance, Codominance, and Sex-Linked Inheritance

The preceding examples illustrate complete dominance. Cases of incomplete dominance, codominance, and sex-linked inheritance also occur. **Incomplete dominance** describes a situation wherein one allele is not completely dominant over another. It generally allows a form of blending to occur. An excellent example is seen in the flower color of petunias. Red-flowered petunias are R^1R^1, white-flowered petunias are R^2R^2, and the heterozygote R^1R^2 plant has pink flowers. (Notice the different notation used here.)

In **codominance**, both alleles are fully expressed in the phenotype. One example is the coat color of shorthorn cattle. Red shorthorns are RR, while white shorthorns are $R'R'$. In this case the heterozygote $R'R$ has a reddish-gray coat and is called a roan. The roan color is due not to incomplete dominance or blending but to the animal having both red and white hairs.

EXERCISE 7

a. Calculate the Punnett square crossing two pink-flowered petunias. What percentage of the offspring is pink, white, and red?

b. Calculate the Punnett square crossing a roan shorthorn bull with a white cow. What percentage of the offspring has a roan coat, a red coat, and a white coat?

Recall that in many organisms, including humans, sex is determined by the sex chromosomes. Human females are *XX*, while human males are *XY* at their 23rd chromosome pair. The genes that occur on the sex chromosomes are considered **sex-linked**. The X chromosome is large and contains many genes, thus most sex-linked traits are located on the X chromosome. In humans there are two genes—color vision and hemophilia (a blood clotting disease)—that are found on the X chromosome and not on the Y chromosome, making them sex-linked.

Normal color vision is dominant over red-green color blindness (a situation in which red and green cannot be differentiated). Due to complete dominance, in order for a female to be affected by color blindness, both of her X chromosomes must carry the color-blind allele. A female carrying only one copy of the color-blind allele has normal vision and is called a **carrier**. However, a male only has one X chromosome. If his single X carries the allele for color blindness, he will be color-blind.

EXERCISE 8

a. Using X for normal vision and X^c for color-blind, calculate the Punnett square that would result from a carrier female mating with a color-blind male. *Hint:* The female genotype is X^cX and the male genotype is X^cY.

b. What are the chances that they will produce a color-blind son? _____

_____

c. What are the chances that they will produce a color-blind daughter? _____

d. Is there any way these parents might produce a daughter with normal vision? If so, how? _____

_____

_____

e. Is there any chance these parents might produce a son with normal vision? If so, how? _____

_____

Mendelian Traits in Humans

In the preceding pages, we have observed many examples of traits in the common pea plant that are inherited through a simple dominant/recessive relationship. Most human traits are very complex and are affected by several genes (*polygenic*). Examples of polygenic inheritance are hair color, eye color, intelligence, and musical ability. However, several traits have been identified in humans that represent simple inheritance as defined by Mendel. The *Online Mendelian Inheritance of Man* Web site is very helpful for identifying and describing those traits that are inherited in a simple fashion in humans (www.ncbi.nlm.nih.gov/entrez/query.fcgi?db=OMIM). The following is a list of ten common traits in humans that are inherited in a Mendelian (simple) fashion:

1. **Mid-digital hair:** Examine the middle segment of your fingers for the presence of hair, which is inherited as a dominant (*MM, Mm*). A complete absence of hair represents the homozygous recessive condition (*mm*).

2. **Tongue rolling:** The ability to roll the sides of the tongue up into a tube shape, inherited as a dominant (*TT, Tt*). Inability to roll the tongue is due to the recessive condition (*tt*).

3. **Earlobe attachment:** Most people have free earlobes, which hang down from the head and are inherited as a dominant (*FF, Ff*). Homozygous recessive individuals (*ff*) have earlobes that are attached directly to the head.

4. **Hitchhiker's thumb:** If you can bend your thumb back at an angle of greater than 45 degrees, you have the recessive condition (*hh*).

5. **Ability to taste PTC:** Phenyl-thio-carbimide is a bitter, synthetic chemical similar to a substance found in kale, turnips, and brussel sprouts. The ability to taste PTC is inherited as a dominant. About 70% of Americans can taste PTC.

6. **Darwin's tubercle:** This is a thickening, or projection, on the rim of the ear due to a thickening of cartilage. It is inherited as a dominant.

7. **Interlocking fingers and thumbs:** Placing the left thumb over the right is the dominant condition. Switching your thumbs feels awkward and uncomfortable.

8. **Earwax:** Flaky, grayish-white earwax is the recessive condition, while sticky, yellowish earwax is the dominant condition.

9. **Palmaris longus tendon:** The presence of two tendons on the inside of your wrist is inherited as a recessive. The dominant condition exhibits a third centrally located tendon (palmaris longus).

10. **Cleft (dimpled) chin:** The presence of a dimple in the chin is inherited as a dominant trait.

EXERCISE 9

For each trait in the following chart, list your phenotype. Using the information collected by everyone in your class, fill in the rest of the chart.

Trait	Your Phenotype Dom or Rec	# Dominant in Class	# Recessive in Class	% Dominant	% Recessive
Mid-digital hair					
Tongue rolling					
Earlobes					
Hitchhiker thumb					
PTC tasting					
Darwin's tubercle					
Interlocking fingers/thumbs					
Earwax					
Palmaris longus					
Cleft (dimpled) chin					

Dihybrid Crosses

All the examples and problems presented so far have demonstrated crossing one trait at a time. In this section, we will work with crossing two traits at once: a *dihybrid cross*. To make things easier, we are assuming that the traits are *not* carried on homologous chromosomes. Let's work with two of the traits previously listed: tongue rolling and cleft (dimpled) chin. Let T stand for the dominant condition and t for the recessive condition in tongue rolling, and let D stand for the dominant condition (dimpled) and d for the recessive condition (no dimple) for cleft chin.

EXERCISE 10

a. List all the possible genotypes for an individual with the ability to roll the tongue and a cleft chin. (Hint: Four combinations are possible.) _____

_____

b. List all possible combinations for an individual who cannot roll his or her tongue and has a cleft chin. _____

_____

c. List all possible genotypes for an individual who can roll his or her tongue and does not have a cleft chin. _____

_____

_____

d. What is the genotype for an individual who cannot roll his or her tongue and does not have a cleft chin? _____

_____

_____

e. Suppose an individual is heterozygous for both traits (tongue rolling and cleft chin). What is their genotype? _____

_____

_____

f. What are the genotypes of the gametes this person could produce? _____

_____

EXERCISE 11

Using the answer you determined for Exercise 10, question f, set up a Punnett square for a dihybrid problem, crossing two individuals that are heterozygous for tongue rolling and cleft chin. This square will have 16 boxes. Insert the parental genotypes on the top and left side of the following box, and calculate the possible offspring genotypes. When you are finished answer the questions below.

a. What are the chances of having a child that is:
  - *TTDD* _____
  - *TtDd* _____

- *TtDD* _____
- *ttDd* _____

b. What are the chances of having a child who has a cleft chin and cannot roll his or her tongue? _____

_____

c. What are the chances of having a child who does not have a cleft chin and can roll his or her tongue? _____

_____

d. What are the chances of having a child who cannot roll his or her tongue and does not have a cleft chin? _____

Ethics and the Future

Mendel's pioneering experiments provide the foundation for today's genetic research and technology. Many diseases have a genetic basis—for example, cystic fibrosis, Huntington's disease, sickle-cell anemia, and familial hypercholesterolemia, among many others. Modern genetic research is treating diseases that were once thought to be incurable. Insulin and human growth hormone are now produced through genetic engineering techniques. The latest in cancer research hopes to remove cells from the bodies of cancer patients, genetically alter them to enhance their tumor resistance, and then reinsert them into the body of the patient. Genetic engineering is also common in agricultural products—for example, many crops are genetically engineered for resistance to disease, drought, and/or pests. Considerable controversy surrounds these modern techniques. Some groups strongly oppose bioengineering and any "tinkering" with the genome. To be a responsible member of our society, it is important that you are able to make an educated decision about these issues. That understanding begins here, with the material covered in this chapter.

EXERCISE 12

Cystic fibrosis is the most common metabolic error in European-derived ("white") populations, with about 1 of every 1,600 being a carrier. Individuals born with cystic fibrosis are lacking an enzyme that allows them to break down thick mucus in the lungs and makes them susceptible to serious and often fatal lung infections. With aggressive treatment, most individuals may reach adulthood; otherwise death from pneumonia is likely in childhood. There is no cure; however, genetic engineering offers promise for these affected individuals. Cystic fibrosis is inherited as a recessive, and individuals with one copy of the gene are carriers of the disease. The gene has been located on chromosome 7.

a. What percentage of the gametes of a heterozygote individual will contain the recessive allele? _____

_____

b. Draw a Punnett square crossing two individuals who are heterozygous for this trait.

c. What percentage of the offspring will be affected with cystic fibrosis?
_____

d. What percentage of the offspring will be normal? _____
_____

e. What percentage of the offspring will also carry the trait? _____
_____

f. Is it possible for an affected child to be born to one healthy parent and one carrier? _____
_____

Pre-Lab Questions

1. Mendel published his works in:
    a. 1965
    b. 1956
    c. 1776
    d. 1865

2. In a dihybrid cross:
    a. only one trait is considered
    b. the parents are always heterozygous
    c. two traits are considered
    d. all offspring must be heterozygous

3. When all self-fertilized offspring display the same traits as their parents, we know that the parents are:
    a. hybrids
    b. heterozygous
    c. codominant
    d. true breeders

4. The physical characteristics of an organism are referred to as the:
    a. dominant allele
    b. gametes
    c. phenotype
    d. genotype

5. An individual who is carrying two of the same alleles for a gene is known as:
    a. homozygous
    b. heterozygous
    c. dominant
    d. a hybrid

6. The allele that is masked or hidden in the genotype is the:
    a. heterozygote
    b. recessive allele
    c. dominant allele
    d. true breeder

7. When both alleles are fully expressed in the phenotype, this is called:
    a. incomplete dominance
    b. codominance
    c. sex-linked
    d. recessive

8. **True or False:** Sex-linked traits are often located on the X chromosome.

9. **True or False:** Mendel's Law of Independent Assortment states that during meiosis, the chromosome pairs separate, so that each newly formed gamete receives one chromosome from each pair.

10. **True or False:** Numerous traits in humans are inherited in a simple Mendelian fashion.

Post-Lab Questions

1. Distinguish between incomplete dominance and codominance. _____

   _____

   _____

   _____

2. What does it mean when we say that a trait is sex-linked? _____

   _____

   _____

   _____

3. How might the Law of Independent Assortment be violated if two traits were on the same chromosome?

   _____

   _____

   _____

4. Mendel's pea plants carry two alleles of the gene for seed shape: R for round seeds and r for wrinkled seeds. Consider the genotypes in the following table, and indicate the possible genotypes of the gametes.

Diploid Genotype	Gamete Genotype
RR	
Rr	
Rr	

5. In the following chart, provide the diploid genotypes that would occur by fusion of the following genotypes.

Gamete Genotype	Gamete Genotype	Diploid Genotype
r	r	
R	r	
R	R	

6. For the following, state whether the genotype is homozygous or heterozygous and whether the plant would have round or wrinkled seeds.

   • RR _____

   • Rr _____

   • Rr _____

7. Considering that the allele for tall plants is dominant to the allele for short plants, and using T for tall and t for short, draw a Punnett square crossing a heterozygous tall plant and a short plant.

- What percentage of the offspring is homozygous dominant? _____

    _____

- What percentage of the offspring is heterozygous? _____

    _____

- What percentage of the offspring is homozygous recessive? _____

    _____

- What percentage of the offspring is tall? Why? _____

    _____

    _____

- What percentage of the offspring is short? Why? _____

    _____

    _____

8. Working with the dihybrid cross you did in Exercise 11, answer the following questions:

- What are the chances of having a child who is *ttdd*? _____

    _____

- What are the chances of having a child who is *ttDD*? _____

    _____

- What are the chances of having a child who is *Ttdd*? _____

    _____

- What are the chances of having a child who has a cleft chin and can roll his or her tongue?

    _____

9. Using the following chart, copy your personal phenotype information collected in class in the first column and ask or examine your parents for their phenotype for each trait. Try to determine your genotype. (If you are unable to determine your parents' phenotypes, you may ask a friend or relative for their information.)

Trait	Your Phenotype Dom/Rec	Mom's Phenotype	Mom's Possible Genotype	Dad's Phenotype	Dad's Possible Genotype	Your Genotype
Mid-digital hair						
Tongue rolling						
Earlobes						
Hitchhiker thumb						
Darwin's tubercle						
Interlocking fingers/thumbs						
Earwax						
Palmaris longus						
Cleft (dimpled) chin						

Chapter 4

Human Variation

Objectives	After completing this chapter you should be able to:
	1. determine the type of inheritance observed in pedigree analyses;
	2. determine the genotypes of individuals in a pedigree diagram;
	3. describe the phenotypes and genotypes in the ABO blood group system and their inheritance;
	4. compute Punnett squares to determine possible paternity using blood types; and
	5. understand how DNA fingerprinting works and in what contexts it is used.

Pedigree Analysis

The basics of genetic inheritance incorporating modern terminology and concepts were introduced in Chapter 3. Without modern DNA sequencing technology, we may not know whether a person is homozygous or heterozygous or if they are carrying a recessive allele for a trait. This may be critical information for a family that has an inherited condition, such as the disorders mentioned at the end of Chapter 3, such as cystic fibrosis, Huntington's disease, sickle-cell anemia, and familial hypercholesterolemia, among many others. One way to discover this information is to trace the family history by conducting a **pedigree analysis**. A pedigree analysis is a diagram that shows family relationships (matings, offspring) over several generations, which allows the transmission of a genetic trait to be traced. Pedigree analyses work best for traits that are transmitted in a simple, Mendelian fashion. Using our understanding of dominant, recessive, and sex-liked inheritance, and our ability to compute Punnett squares, we are able to establish the mode of inheritance.

Some simple guidelines should be remembered when tracing the inheritance of genetic traits.

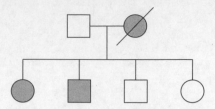

Figure 4-1 Basic pedigree diagram.

■ When examining a trait that is inherited in a dominant fashion, the individual who expresses the trait *must* have at least one parent who also shows the trait. Thus the trait will not skip generations.

If one parent exhibits the trait, then the individual must be heterozygous.

When one parent is affected, approximately half of the offspring will be affected.

■ If the trait is inherited in a recessive manner, and neither parent shows the trait, then both parents *must* be heterozygous carriers. Thus, the traits will appear to skip generations. Affected children are born of "normal" parents.

Usually less than half of the offspring are affected.

If both parents exhibit the trait, then *all* children must exhibit the trait.

Pedigree diagrams use standardized symbols (Figure 4-1). Males are represented by squares, and females are represented by circles. A horizontal line connecting a male and a female indicates a mating. Offspring are indicated by a vertical line descending from the parents. Multiple children, or siblings, are connected by horizontal lines above the symbols. Individuals affected by the trait in question are shown with a shaded symbol. Deceased people have a line drawn through them.

EXERCISE 1

Practice drawing this simple pedigree: Sharon and John are married. They have three children—two boys (Justin and Ian) and one girl (Dana). Justin is married with one daughter. Dana is married with one daughter. Sharon is affected by a dominant trait, which is also seen in Justin and his daughter. No other family members are affected. Write the genotypes for each member of the family above their symbol.

EXERCISE 2

Familial hypercholesterolemia, a condition causing high cholesterol that may lead to heart attack and stroke, is inherited as a dominant trait. Thus, affected individuals only need one copy of the allele to exhibit the condition. The homozygous recessive individual will not have any chromosomes affected with the trait. Using *H* to indicate the dominant condition and *h* to indicate the recessive condition, individuals who are *HH* or *Hh* will show high cholesterol, and individuals who are *hh* will be normal.

The following is a sample pedigree for familial hypercholesterolemia. Note that all affected individuals have at least one parent who is also affected by the disease. Working in groups, or guided by your instructor, determine the genotypes for each individual in the pedigree. You may write the answers below the symbols.

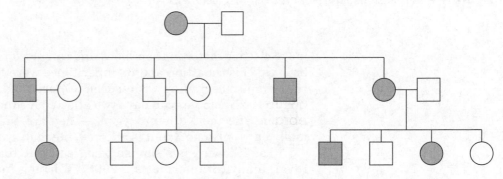

EXERCISE 3

Albinism is a metabolic disorder wherein affected individuals exhibit a lack of pigment in the skin, eyes, and hair. This disorder is inherited as a recessive. Thus, two copies of the affected allele are needed to express the trait. Using the letters *A* and *a* to describe the trait, in this case, *AA* and *Aa* individuals are phenotypically normal, while individuals who are *aa* are albinos.

The following is a sample pedigree for a family affected by albinism. Note that most affected individuals have parents who are phenotypically normal and that the parents must be carriers of the trait. Working in groups, or guided by your instructor, determine the genotypes for each individual in the pedigree.

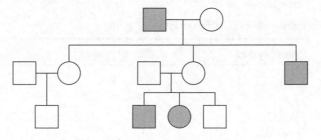

EXERCISE 4

As noted in Chapter 3, sex-linked traits are carried on the sex chromosomes, although most are found on the X chromosome, making them X-linked traits. Tracing their inheritance can be quite tricky! Hemophilia is an X-linked condition that is inherited as a recessive. People afflicted with this disease do not

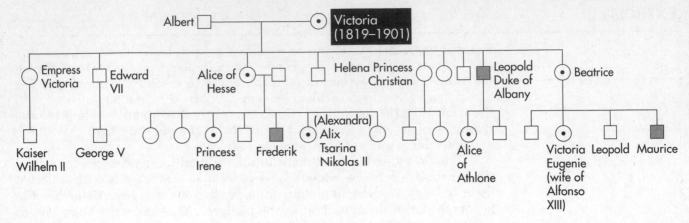

Figure 4-2 A sample pedigree for the family of Queen Victoria.

make clotting factor in their blood and can bleed to death from minor cuts and bruises. This condition and its inheritance were made famous by the British royal family, beginning with Queen Victoria and Prince Albert in the 1800s (Figure 4-2). Females can have two affected X's (homozygous) or one normal X and one affected X (heterozygous—they are carriers). Males, though, normally have only one X; if it is affected, the males are considered **hemizygous**.

The following is a sample pedigree exhibiting hemophilia in the British royal family (Stanford et al., 2006). Working in groups, or guided by your instructor, determine the genotypes for each *named* individual in the pedigree. Remember to label the females as XX and the males as XY. Affected X chromosomes may be notated as X^h.

Blood Types and Blood Typing

The ABO blood group system aptly demonstrates the relationship between genotype and phenotype. It is a multiple allele system located on chromosome 9 and has three possible alleles—A, B, and O—but, of course, each individual has only two alleles (one on each chromosome of the homologous pair). A and B are codominant, and both are expressed in the phenotype. A and B are both dominant to O. Considering these relationships, four blood types (phenotypes) and their associated genotypes are possible (see Table 4-1).

Table 4-1 The four blood types

Phenotypes	Genotypes
Type A	AA or AO
Type B	BB or BO
Type O	OO
Type AB	AB

EXERCISE 5

Can you list which of the genotypes above are homozygous? _____

_____

_____

Can you list which of the genotypes above are heterozygous? _____

_____

_____

The letters A, B, and O refer to the proteins (**antigens**) found on the surface of red blood cells. There are two different types of antigens: A antigen and B antigen. Type A blood has the A antigen. Type B blood has the B antigen. Type AB blood has both antigens, and type O blood does not have any antigens. Certain antibodies will react to these antigens and cause **agglutination**, or clotting of the red blood cells. In the past, before our understanding of this blood group system was complete, some individuals would die from blood transfusions due to receiving the wrong blood type.

Anti-A antibodies will react with the A antigen. Likewise, anti-B antibodies will react with the B antigen. So type A blood will react negatively to blood that is type B or AB. On the other hand, type B blood will react negatively to blood that is type A or AB. Because type AB blood has both A and B antigens, it does not make any antibodies and will not react negatively to any other blood from this system. Individuals with type AB blood are considered **universal recipients**: they *may receive* blood (in a transfusion) from any other blood type. However, they can only give to other AB individuals. Because persons with type O do not have any antigens on their red blood cells, they make antibodies against both the A and B antigen; thus, they *cannot receive* transfusions from anyone except another type O person. Yet because they do not have any antigens that might react with another blood type, type O individuals *can give* their blood to anyone and are considered **universal donors**. Table 4-2 summarizes this information.

Table 4-2 Blood type antigens

Blood Type	Antigens (Proteins)	Can Donate Blood To	Can Receive Blood From
A	A	A or AB	A or O
B	B	B or AB	B or O
AB	A and B	AB	Any type
O	None	Any type	O

EXERCISE 6

a. Can a person with type A blood receive a blood transfusion from a person with type O? _____

_____

b. Can a person with type B blood receive a blood transfusion from a person with type AB? _____

_____

c. Can a person with type O blood donate blood to a person who is type AB?

_____

d. Can a person with type B blood donate blood to a person who is type O?

_____

EXERCISE 7

You will be given a sample of artificial blood. Use the kit provided to determine the blood type of your sample and answer the following questions.

a. What is the blood type of your sample? _____

_____

b. What are the possible genotypes for this sample? _____

_____

Determining Parentage

The ABO blood group system is regularly used to assist in determining parentage, especially paternity in a court of law. If a woman sues a man over paternity, blood types are one of the first lines of evidence. (Today DNA typing is also common, but it is much more expensive.) Consider the following example: a woman has blood type A and her child has blood type B. The man has blood type O. To determine if he can be the father of the child, consider that the woman with type A blood may be either AA or AO. Her child is type B and may be either BB or BO. Thus, the woman must have the genotype AO and must have handed down the O allele to her infant, who also must be BO. The child cannot inherit a B allele from the mother. The child must have inherited the B allele from the father. The man is type O, which has the genotype OO. There is no way he can be the father of this child.

EXERCISE 8

A woman who is blood type B gives birth to a child who is blood type O. Using this information, answer the questions and fill in the genotypes and phenotypes in the following table (part e):

a. What is the mother's genotype? _____

_____

b. The mother claims a certain man who is blood type B is the father of this child. Is this possible? If so how, if not, why not? _____

_____

_____

c. This woman has a second child who is blood type A. Is it possible that the same man is the father of this child? _____

_____

_____

d. There is a third child in the house whose blood type is AB. The woman claims this is her sister's child, also fathered by the same man. Her sister's blood type is O. What does this suggest to you? _____

_____

_____

_____

e. These two sisters have a brother who is blood type O. Based on the information you have about these three siblings, determine the possible blood types of their parents.

	Genotype	**Phenotype**
Mother		
Sister		
Brother		
Child #1		
Child #2		
Child #3		
Proposed father		
Grandmother		
Grandfather		

DNA Fingerprinting

You should now understand that the DNA is the same in all the cells of your body and that DNA is unique to each and every living thing. Oak trees are different from us, not in their DNA but in the order of their DNA base pairs. In other words, each living thing differs from another in the sequence of their base pairs. In that way, each individual's DNA is like a fingerprint, unique to them and no one else. Determining an individual's particular sequence of base pairs is a way to identify them and is called **DNA fingerprinting**.

DNA fingerprinting is commonly used for determining parentage and has largely replaced the older methods based on blood tests. DNA fingerprinting is also used to identify crime suspects, and even to clear someone's name. DNA evidence is sometimes brought into a trial, which may help to convict or exonerate a suspect. Each individual contains millions of base pairs and a unique sequence.

To identify each and every base pair in a person is possible, but it would take a lot of time. Instead, scientists use a different method that compares segments of DNA to identify a person. These segments are known to vary among individuals. This will not determine an actual DNA fingerprint, but it will determine whether or not two samples of DNA are from the same person, related people, or unrelated people. First, the DNA is cut into pieces using *restriction enzymes,* bacteria that cut apart DNA at certain base pair sequences. Then the DNA is poured into a gel where an electrical charge is applied, causing the cut DNA segments to move toward the positive charge. This stage is called *gel electrophoresis*. The smaller pieces of DNA move faster than the larger pieces, and the DNA segments become size sorted in the gel with the smaller pieces at one end and the larger pieces at the other end of the tray. The next step is to *denature* the DNA, which involves either heating or chemically treating the DNA fragments so that they are all single stranded instead of double stranded. Finally, a *Southern blot* test is completed, in which a sheet of nitrocellulose paper is applied to the gel and baked, whereby the DNA becomes permanently attached to the paper with the pattern of size-sorted fragments permanently recorded.

A fun DNA fingerprinting exercise can be found on the NOVA website at: www.pbs.org/wgbh/nova/sheppard/analyze/html.

Pre-Lab Questions

1. Individuals with a disorder that is inherited as a recessive will express the trait if they carry:
   a. two copies of the allele
   b. one copy of the allele
   c. the allele on their sex chromosome
   d. the allele on the X chromosome

2. In dominant inheritance, when one parent expresses the trait and the other does not, the affected individual must be:
   a. homozygous dominant
   b. homozygous recessive
   c. heterozygous
   d. a female

3. Females expressing sex-linked recessive traits like red-green color blindness:
   a. are heterozygous
   b. must carry the trait on both of their X chromosomes
   c. only need to have one x affected to express the trait
   d. express the trait when their only x is affected

4. When a male's single X chromosome is affected by a sex-linked trait, that male is considered:
   a. homozygous recessive
   b. homozygous dominant
   c. heterozygous
   d. hemizygous

5. An example of codominance in the ABO blood group system is:
   a. AO
   b. BB
   c. AB
   d. OO

6. Type A blood has:
   a. A antigens
   b. B antigens
   c. neither A nor B antigens
   d. O antigens

7. Type O blood has which of the following possible genotypes?
   a. AO
   b. BO
   c. OO
   d. none of the above

8. **True or False:** Under the ABO blood group system, a universal donor may give blood to anyone.

9. **True or False:** It is possible for dominant traits to skip a generation.

10. **True or False:** Individuals affected with a recessive condition may have phenotypically normal parents.

Post-Lab Questions

1. Practice drawing a simple pedigree using the family from Exercise 1. In this example, Sharon is affected by a recessive trait, which is also seen in Justin and his daughter. No other family members are affected. What are the genotypes for each member of the family? Compare your two pedigrees, which individuals are different?

2. Examine the following pedigree. Determine the genotypes for all individuals in the chart. Is the trait inherited as dominant, recessive, or sex-linked?

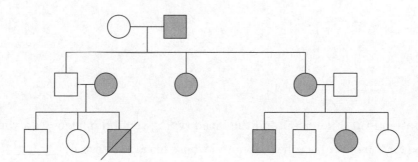

3. Examine the following pedigree. Determine the genotypes for all individuals in the chart. Is the trait inherited as dominant, recessive, or sex-linked?

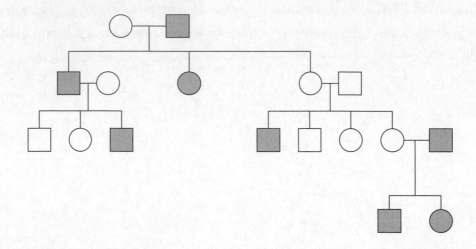

4. Examine the following pedigree. Determine the genotypes for all individuals in the chart. Is the trait inherited as dominant, recessive, or sex-linked?

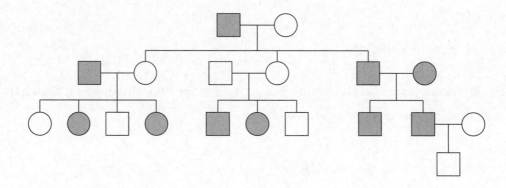

5. Using the information from Exercise 7 and the blood typing you did in class, can you determine at least a partial genotype for the parents of the individual whose blood you tested? _____

_____

_____

6. While inline skating with his friend Paul on a rural section of the local bike path, James was attacked by a mountain lion. When they arrived at the hospital, Paul offered to donate blood to his friend. Paul has blood type O. James has blood type A. Will James be able to accept blood from Paul? Why or why not?

_____

_____

7. Considering question #6, how might the situation be different if Paul had blood type AB?

_____

_____

8. Dolores is suing John for paternity. Dolores has blood type O, and her child is blood type A. John has blood type AB. Could he be the father of this child? What is the child's genotype?

_____

_____

9. John was also sued recently by a woman named Helen. Helen has blood type A, and her child is blood type B. Could he also be the father of this child? Does it matter if Helen is a homozygote or a heterozygote for type A blood? Why or why not? _____

_____

_____

_____

_____

_____

Chapter 5

The Hardy–Weinberg Principle: Genetics of Populations

After completing this chapter you should be able to:

1. define population, Hardy–Weinberg, equilibrium, evolution, natural selection, fitness, mutation, genetic drift, founder effect, population bottleneck, gene flow, and nonrandom mating;

2. describe the effects on populations of gene flow, genetic drift, mutation, and natural selection;

3. determine the allele frequencies for a gene in a population;

4. calculate the expected ratios of genotypes based on the Hardy–Weinberg formula; and

5. determine if a population is in equilibrium or evolving according to the Hardy–Weinberg formula.

Evolution, Populations, and the Hardy–Weinberg Principle

The previous chapters in this book have introduced concepts of basic genetics in individuals. We examined the structure and function of DNA, the formation of gametes in meiosis, the growth of the individual through mitosis, and the basic principles of inheritance of traits. Chapter 4 allowed us to expand our knowledge to practical situations involving human variation in blood types and tracing the inheritance of traits through generations. Now that you have an understanding of how genetics works in the individual, it is time to expand your knowledge to include how genetics works in groups, or populations of individuals. A **population** is a potentially interbreeding group of individuals within a species. Rather than look at the genotype of an individual or the individual's offspring, we will now look at the genotypes of all the individuals of a population so that we may calculate the frequency of certain alleles or genotypes in the group.

The **Hardy–Weinberg Principle** states that heredity alone cannot cause changes in the frequency of alleles in a population. The frequency of alleles that make up a population will remain constant, generation after generation, so that the population remains in **equilibrium**,—in other words, it is not evolving, and allele frequencies do not change over time (Hardy, 1908). Thus, **evolution** may be defined as a change in allele frequencies in a population over time. For the genetic makeup of a population to change over time (evolve), forces (sometimes referred to as *evolutionary agents*) must act to disrupt the Hardy–Weinberg equilibrium.

For example, we know that two alleles exist for tongue rolling in humans, which is inherited as a dominant. Using T for the dominant allele and t for the recessive allele, we know that TT and Tt individuals can roll the tongue, while tt individuals cannot roll the tongue. We can use p to represent the frequency of the T allele and q to represent the frequency of the other allele t. If the allele for tongue rolling is present 70% of the time, then the alternate allele for non-rollers must be present 30% of the time, because $p + q = 1.0$. Note that we are discussing the frequency of *alleles* in the population, not genotype frequency. So if T is present 70% of the time, the allele would be found sometimes in homozygotes (TT) and sometimes in heterozygotes (Tt). Similar logic holds true for the t allele.

Using this same example for tongue rolling, we could also work in the other direction and start with the *genotype frequencies* to determine the number of alleles. We could survey 50 college students for tongue rolling and find that 10 students are TT, 25 students are Tt, and 15 students are tt. Note that $10 + 25 + 15 = 50$ and that each student has 2 alleles, for a total of 100 alleles. If 10 students are TT, then there are 20 T alleles and 0 t alleles in these individuals, while if 25 students have Tt, there are 25 T alleles and 25 t alleles, and in the last scenario 15 students are tt, indicating that they have a total of 30 t alleles and 0 T alleles. If you add up all of these alleles, $20 + 0 + 25 + 25 + 30 + 0 = 100$ alleles total.

The Hardy–Weinberg formula for a two-allele system is as follows:

$$p^2 + 2pq + q^2 = 1.0$$

In this equation, p^2 is the frequency of the homozygote dominant condition, $2pq$ is the frequency of the heterozygote condition, and q^2 is the frequency of the homozygote recessive condition in the population.

The Hardy–Weinberg formula can now be used to determine the *genotype* frequency of homozygote dominant individuals (TT), heterozygotes (Tt), and homozygote recessive (tt) individuals according to the equation. Since $p = 0.7$, then $p^2 = (0.7)^2 = 0.49$. Thus 49% of the individuals in the population are homozygous for tongue rolling. The number of heterozygotes is calculated with $2pq = 2(0.7)(0.3) = 0.42$, or 42% of the population can roll their tongue due to the heterozygous condition. Finally, the number of nonrollers is calculated with $q^2 = (0.3)^2 = 0.09$, so 9% of the population is homozygous recessive and cannot roll their tongue. All these frequencies must total 1.0 (100%), so always check your work.

$$p^2 + 2pq + q^2 = 1.0$$

$$0.49 + 0.42 + 0.09 = 1.0$$

EXERCISE 1

The allele for PTC tasting is inherited as a dominant. Use T for tasters and t for nontasters and answer the following questions:

a. What genotype(s) are able to taste PTC? _____

_____

b. What genotype(s) are unable to taste PTC? _____

_____

c. If the T allele is found in 60% of the population, what is the frequency of the t allele? _____

_____

d. Using the Hardy–Weinberg formula, calculate the frequency of the homozygote dominant, heterozygote, and homozygote recessive individuals in the population. _____

_____

_____

_____

EXERCISE 2

Freckles are inherited as a dominant. Use F for freckles and f for no freckles, and answer the following questions:

a. What genotype(s) will have freckles? _____

_____

b. What genotype(s) will not have freckles? _____

_____

c. If the allele for freckles (F) is found in 20% of the population, what is the frequency of the f allele? _____

_____

d. Using the Hardy–Weinberg formula, calculate the frequency of the homozygote dominant, heterozygote, and homozygote recessive individuals in the population. _____

_____

_____

_____

EXERCISE 3

Let's use a slightly different format now where you are provided the number of individuals with a certain genotype but not the allele frequencies. In this case, you are interested in the frequency of people who are PTC tasters on a college campus. TT and Tt represent tasters, and tt represents nontasters. You collect genotype information on 100 students: 10 students have the TT genotype, 43 students are heterozygous, and 47 are nontasters. This information is provided in the following chart. Now calculate the number of T and t alleles and fill in the rest of the chart. *Remember:* Each student has 2 alleles on his or her chromosome pair, so there are 200 alleles total.

Phenotype/Genotype	# of Students	# *T* Alleles	# *t* Alleles	Total # Alleles
Tasters/*TT*	10			
Tasters/*Tt*	43			
Nontasters/*tt*	47			
Totals	100			200

Now you can calculate the *observed allele frequencies* (how often the allele occurs in the population). Take the *total* number of that allele in the population and divide by the total number of alleles at that locus. *Remember:* $p + q = 1$

Observed Allele Frequencies for College Students (These should total 1.0.)

T alleles = _____
t alleles = _____

Then calculate the *observed genotype frequencies*. This is the total number of *people* with that genotype divided by the total number of *people* in the population.

Observed Genotype Frequencies for College Students (Again, these should total 1.0.)

Tasters/*TT*   _____
Tasters/*Tt*   _____
Nontasters/*tt*   _____

Is the population in equilibrium for that trait? Calculate the *expected genotype frequencies* using the Hardy–Weinberg principle to determine it.

$$p^2 + 2pq + q^2 = 1$$

Compare the *expected* genotype frequencies you got from the Hardy–Weinberg principle to the *observed* genotype frequencies you got from the college students. Are they similar? If so, the population is in equilibrium; if not, the population is evolving.

EXERCISE 4

In this exercise, you are interested in the frequency of people with freckles on a college campus. *FF* and *Ff* individuals have freckles, and *ff* people do not have freckles. Assume that you have examined the genotypes of 200 college students. Your study reveals the following information: 20 students have freckles and are

Phenotype/Genotype	# of Students	# *F* Alleles	# *f* Alleles	Total # Alleles
Freckles/*FF*	20			
Freckles/*Ff*	30			
No Freckles/*ff*	150			
Totals	200			400

the homozygous condition, 30 students have freckles and are heterozygotes, and 150 students do not have freckles. Fill in the following chart, calculating the number of *F* and *f* alleles in each box. *Hint*: The total number of alleles is 400, because each person has 2 alleles on their chromosome pair.

Now you can calculate the observed allele frequencies (how often the allele occurs in the population). Take the *total* number of that allele in the population and divide by the total number of alleles at that locus. *Remember*: $p + q = 1$.

Observed Allele Frequencies for College Students (These should total 1.0.)

\# *F* alleles = _____

\# *f* alleles = _____

Then calculate the *observed genotype frequencies*. This is the total number of *people* with that genotype divided by the total number of people in the population.

Observed Genotype Frequencies for College Students (Again, these should total 1.0.)

Freckles/*FF*　　　　_____
Freckles/*Ff*　　　　_____
No freckles/*ff*　　　_____

Now, is the population in equilibrium for that trait? Calculate the *expected genotype frequencies* using the Hardy–Weinberg principle.

$$p^2 + 2pq + q^2 = 1$$

Compare the *expected* genotype frequencies you got by using the Hardy–Weinberg principle to the *observed* genotype frequencies you got from the college students. Are they similar? If so, the population is in equilibrium; if not, the population is evolving.

Forces of Evolution (Evolutionary Agents)

The idea of a population at equilibrium is a theoretical construct. Populations are always evolving. Five forces or agents act on the gene pool of a population and cause changes in allele frequencies through generations: natural selection, mutation, gene flow, genetic drift, and nonrandom mating. When observed genotype frequencies do not correspond to expected genotype frequencies calculated with the Hardy–Weinberg formula, we know that one or more of these forces are acting on the population.

Natural selection is often defined as differential reproductive success, which means that some individuals have certain variations that allow them to survive and reproduce more than other individuals, thus perpetuating more of their genes in the population. These individuals have higher **fitness** than those who have fewer offspring or no offspring. Thus, selection is sometimes referred to as "survival of the fittest." Individuals with higher fitness (i.e., more offspring) will pass on more genes to the next generation, thus increasing the frequency of their genes in the population. Natural selection acts on the individual, although the population evolves.

Mutation represents an actual change in the genetic material of an organism, at the DNA or chromosome level. DNA bases, genes, or entire chromosomes may be altered, added, or deleted. Many mutations are harmful to the organism and are later eliminated by natural selection; however, most mutations are neutral and remain in the DNA of an individual, where they may be passed on to offspring. Some mutations are beneficial. Mutations do not cause evolution, but they provide raw material upon which the other evolutionary forces act. Sickle-cell anemia is a recessive disorder caused by a mutation in the DNA base sequence of the hemoglobin gene. Individuals who carry two copies of the affected gene have misshapen red blood cells that are unable to transport oxygen to the tissues; without treatment, this causes death at an early age. However, mutations are the only way to introduce new genetic material into a population from within.

Allele frequencies in a population are also changed by **gene flow**, which is the immigration of new members into the population from outside or the emigration of existing members of the population. This gene flow due to migration is a powerful evolutionary force. New members add genetic variation to the group when they interbreed with existing members.

Genetic drift represents a shift in gene frequencies due to chance. It is usually related to small population size. Populations often become small when they have undergone a **population bottleneck**, or a loss of their genetic variation. This is often due to such extraneous factors as war, famine, drought, or disease that decimate the population.

Founder effect occurs when a new population is being founded by a small, nonrandom sample that is separated from the larger population. This could be due to a small number of individuals being separated somehow from the larger group and unable to join them or to a population suffering a bottleneck. A population with only a few founders, or members to breed the next generation, greatly reduces genetic diversity and increases the chance of inbreeding and recessive alleles.

The effects of genetic drift and small population size are studied by geneticists on populations that are near the brink of extinction, such as cheetahs and elephant seals, and in island populations, which are usually separated from the parent population on the mainland. Drift is also commonly studied in the peopling of the Americas and in human populations who choose to mate within a smaller geographic and/or cultural area, often due to religious choices. Many scientists believe that drift was a very important human evolutionary force because most of human history was spent in small band or tribal-size societies that may have been heavily influenced by drift.

For equilibrium to be maintained, individuals must mate randomly—that is, they must have an equal probability of mating with any adult in the group. This is rarely the case. **Nonrandom mating** occurs when individuals show a strong preference for certain mates over others, sometimes choosing mates with similar genetic makeups.

EXERCISE 5

This exercise demonstrates the effects of natural selection on a population. To begin, working in groups, count out 70 red beans and 30 pink beans for a total of 100 beans. The red bean represents the allele for normal hemoglobin, which carries oxygen on the surface of the red blood cells. The pink bean represents the sickle cell gene, which has a mutation that damages the hemoglobin and causes distortion of the red blood cell and an inability to carry oxygen. Sickle-cell anemia is a recessive disorder. Therefore, in this population there is strong selection against the homozygote recessive.

Red/Red—homozygous dominant (healthy)

Red/Pink—heterozygous (healthy)

Pink/Pink—homozygous recessive (anemia)

1. Put all beans in your can and mix them together.

2. Without looking in the can, randomly pull out pairs of beans until the can is empty. Place each pair separately on your desk. These represent the genotypes of the 50 individuals you are studying (50 individuals, 100 alleles).

3. Record the number of each type of bean pair in the generation 1 row, and record the frequency of the 2 alleles.

4. Because your pink/pink individuals have sickle-cell anemia, they have a higher chance of not surviving to the next generation. To demonstrate this, remove 90% of the pink/pink pairs from your gene pool.

5. Place all the remaining beans in the can and mix them thoroughly.

6. Repeat steps 2 through 5 three more times. In the following table, record for each generation the number of each genotype and the frequency of each allele.

7. When you are finished, answer the questions that follow the table.

	Red/Red	Red/Pink	Pink/Pink	Frequency Red	Frequency Pink
Generation 1					
Generation 2					
Generation 3					
Generation 4					

a. What happens to the frequency of the red bean allele? _____

_____

_____

_____

b. What happens to the frequency of the pink bean allele? _____

_____

_____

_____

c. If you continued this exercise for another ten generations, do you think you could eliminate the pink bean allele from the population?

_____

_____

_____

_____

EXERCISE 6

This exercise demonstrates the effect of genetic drift on a population. To begin, working in groups, count out 70 red beans and 30 pink beans for a total of 100 beans. The beans represent an allele found in mountain gorillas that has a 2-allele system. Due to human encroachment and habitat loss, the mountain gorilla now numbers about 600 individuals in the wild. The recent war in Rwanda put these remaining individuals in even greater danger of extinction.

1. Put all the beans in the can and mix them together.

2. Without looking in the can, randomly pull out pairs of beans until the can is empty. Place each pair separately on your desk. These represent the genotypes of the 50 gorillas you are studying (50 individuals, 100 alleles).

3. Record the number of each pair in the prewar row of the following chart.

4. Assume the war in Rwanda resulted in the *random* loss of some mountain gorillas. To demonstrate this, randomly pull out 20 allele pairs, or 40% of the population.

5. Without mixing up the beans/alleles again, count the remaining allele pairs and record their frequencies in the postwar row in the following chart. Then answer the questions that follow the table.

	Red/Red	Red/Pink	Pink/Pink	Frequency Red	Frequency Pink
Prewar					
Postwar					

1. What happened to the frequency of the red allele? _____

_____

_____

_____

2. What happened to the frequency of the pink allele? _____

_____

_____

_____

3. How does this differ from what you saw in Exercise 5? _____

_____

_____

_____

Pre-Lab Questions

1. A change in allele frequency in a population over time is:
   a. the Hardy–Weinberg equilibrium
   b. evolution
   c. genetic equilibrium
   d. natural selection

2. If a population is in the Hardy–Weinberg equilibrium and $p = 0.8$, then:
   a. $q = 0.8$
   b. $q^2 = 0.8$
   c. $q^2 = 0.64$
   d. $q = 0.2$

3. If a population is in equilibrium over several generations, allele frequencies:
   a. will approach 0.5 over time
   b. are influenced by evolutionary agents
   c. cannot be predicted
   d. will stay the same

4. Genetic drift results in:
   a. a loss of genetic diversity in a population
   b. an increase in genetic diversity in a population
   c. gene frequencies approaching 0.5
   d. population bottleneck

5. Mutation is important because:
   a. it decreases variation in the population
   b. it is the only way to add new genetic material from within a population
   c. it results in abnormalities
   d. it is very common

6. Two ways new alleles can be added to a population are:
   a. selection and genetic drift
   b. genetic drift and gene flow
   c. gene flow and mutation
   d. mutation and selection

7. **True or False:** $p^2 + q^2 = 1.0$.

8. **True or False:** Natural selection acts on the individual.

9. **True or False:** A population bottleneck reduces the number of individuals in a population.

10. **True or False:** Genetic drift has a pronounced effect on large populations.

Post-Lab Questions

1. In the formula $p + q = 1$, what do p and q represent? _____
_____

2. In the formula $p^2 + 2pq + q^2 = 1$, state what is represented by each of the following:

   • p^2 _____

   • $2pq$ _____

   • q^2 _____

3. A population has the following genotype frequencies: $AA = 15\%, Aa = 35\%, aa = 50\%$.

   a. What is the frequency of the A allele? _____
   _____

   b. What is the frequency of the a allele? _____
   _____

4. The allele for sickle-cell anemia is inherited as a recessive. Using the letters A and a to represent the gene, answer the following questions:

   a. What genotype(s) will be normal? _____

   b. What genotype(s) will have sickle-cell anemia? _____

   c. If the allele for sickle-cell anemia is found in 5% of the population, what is the frequency of the A allele? _____
   _____

   d. Using the Hardy–Weinberg formula, state the frequency of each of the following:

      • homozygote dominant

      • heterozygote

      • homozygote recessive

5. Using the information from Exercise 5, what would happen to this population, if a medical breakthrough became available that saved the lives of many pink/pink children, so that now only 10% of them failed to survive to adulthood? What would be the effect on the population of this change in selective pressure?

_____
_____
_____
_____

6. With your understanding of the natural selection and genetic drift exercises in this chapter, can you deduce how the allele frequencies might change in the mountain gorilla population if gene flow were operating on the population? How might the allele frequencies change if a new gorilla troop moved into the area? How might the allele frequencies change if several original members were stolen from the troop and taken to zoos? _____

_____

_____

_____

7. As a budding anthropological geneticist, you are interested in the frequency of tongue rolling in a Central American village. You know that tongue rolling is inherited as a dominant, and you use R to represent the gene for rollers and r to represent the gene for nonrollers. Your study of the village reveals the information in the following chart:

Phenotype/Genotype	# of People	# R Alleles	# r Alleles	Total # Alleles
Rollers/RR	80			
Rollers/Rr	20			
Nonrollers/rr	100			
Totals	200			

a. Fill in the rest of the preceding chart.

b. Calculate the observed allele frequencies of the R and r alleles using the formula $p + q = 1$.

c. Calculate the observed genotype frequencies for each of the three genotypes.

d. Calculate the expected genotypes according to the Hardy–Weinberg formula.

e. Comparing your observed genotype frequencies to your expected genotype frequencies, is the population in equilibrium?

Introduction to the Human Skeleton

After completing this chapter you should be able to:

1. list the main functions of the skeletal system;

2. describe the difference between cartilage and bone structure;

3. describe the three types of joints;

4. be familiar with the terms used to describe bony markings;

5. define the parts of a long bone and a cranial bone;

6. identify the main bones of the skeleton, differentiating between axial and appendicular elements; and

7. describe anatomical position, planes of the body, directional terminology, and body movements.

Introduction

Biological anthropologists have long studied the skeleton for the clues it contains about the identity of individuals when they were alive. The skeleton can reveal a plethora of information about the individual including sex, ethnicity, age at death, health, and trauma. When multiple individuals from a population are studied, information may be gleaned about populations, such as mortality profiles, health, and disease. Interpretation of the skeletal remains of our ancestors helps us to determine their relationship to us. Skeletal studies are also carried out on our primate cousins, assisting us in understanding their growth and development, health, body size, and evolution, to name a few specifics. To carry out skeletal research, one must become familiar with the basic anatomy of the human skeleton. Chapters 6–9 begin this process. Although the information is quite in depth, your instructor will assist you in identifying the information that is appropriate for your lab. This chapter introduces basic bone chemistry and anatomy, joint structure, and orientation terminology. Chapters 7 and 8 provide considerable detail on the skeletal anatomy of humans; ask your instructor to help you pick out the information relevant to your lab. Chapter 9 introduces the concepts of human variation, measurement, and forensic anthropology.

The Skeletal System

The skeletal system is involved in several functions: supporting and protecting the body, storing lipids and many other minerals (especially calcium), providing a site for blood cell formation, and providing a system of levers that the muscles use to move the body. The skeleton is made up of two types of connective tissue: bone and cartilage.

As connective tissues, the few cells in bone and cartilage are suspended in a large amount of extracellular matrix, which contains elastic fibers called *collagen*. **Cartilage** has a poor blood supply and has more collagen and elastic fibers than bone does. **Bone** has an excellent blood supply and is highly mineralized with fewer collagen fibers, which gives bone its characteristic rigid structure. In embryos, the skeleton is composed almost completely of cartilage that is later replaced by bone during the growth period. Adults retain cartilage in some areas of the skeleton including the bridge of the nose, the ear, the larynx, the trachea, the surface of some joints, and parts of the rib cage.

The bones of the skeleton meet at **joints**, which are also known as articulations. You are probably most familiar with the joints found in the limbs, such as the hip, knee, ankle, shoulder, elbow, and wrist. However, many other joints are found throughout the body.

Three types of joints are described by the type of tissue that connects the bones: **fibrous joints** are connected by short, tough fibrous tissues and are immovable; **cartilaginous joints** are connected by cartilage and are slightly movable; and **synovial joints** are freely movable joints that are surrounded by a fibrous capsule lined with a synovial membrane, which secretes a lubricating synovial fluid (Figure 6-1).

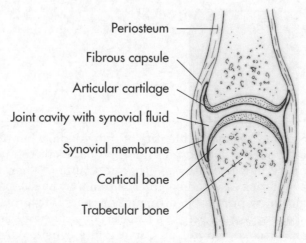

Periosteum

Fibrous capsule

Articular cartilage

Joint cavity with synovial fluid

Synovial membrane

Cortical bone

Trabecular bone

Figure 6-1 Structure of a synovial joint.

EXERCISE 1

Examine the articulated (reassembled) skeletons in the lab. If your lab is not equipped with a skeleton, feel free to examine the illustration in Figure 6-3. Can you identify an example or two of each type of joint?

Fibrous

_____

_____

Cartilaginous

_____

_____

Synovial

_____

_____

Bones are held together at some articulations by **ligaments**, which are tough, straplike tissues that connect bones to each other. The muscles of the skeleton are attached to the bones by tough, fibrous tissues called **tendons**. You can see and feel several of your own tendons—for example, the tendons on the inside of your wrist and the Achilles tendon at the back of your ankle. Tendons, and sometimes ligaments, will leave a mark at their point of attachment on the skeleton. Thus, the surface of bones is not smooth and uniform; rather, it is scarred by bumps, ridges, holes, and grooves that represent where tendons and ligaments were attached and where blood vessels and nerves passed through the bone. Table 6.1 lists some of the common terms that refer to the types of bone markings on the skeleton.

Table 6.1 Bone markings

Process	Projection or protuberance of bone
Tubercle	Small, rounded projection
Tuberosity	Larger projection, roughened surface
Trochanter	Large projections on the femur
Condyle	Smooth, rounded articular surface
Spine	Long, narrow, pointed projection
Line	Small, low, narrow ridge
Torus	Thick, prominent ridge
Crest	Narrow ridge, not as thick as a torus
Fossa	Depression, hollow, or cavity
Foramen	Hole
Sinus	Cavity lined with mucous membrane
Canal	Passageway, longer than a foramen
Meatus	Canal-like passageway
Facet	Small, smooth, nearly flat articular surface

Bone Structure

Two basic types of osseus (bony) tissue comprise the bones of the skeleton. **Compact (cortical)** bone is the smooth and homogeneous bone on the outside surface. **Cancellous** bone is the porous bone beneath the hard surface, composed of small **trabeculae** (bars) of bone that resemble a framework of steel bars; the trabeculae are very strong yet allow bone to remain lightweight.

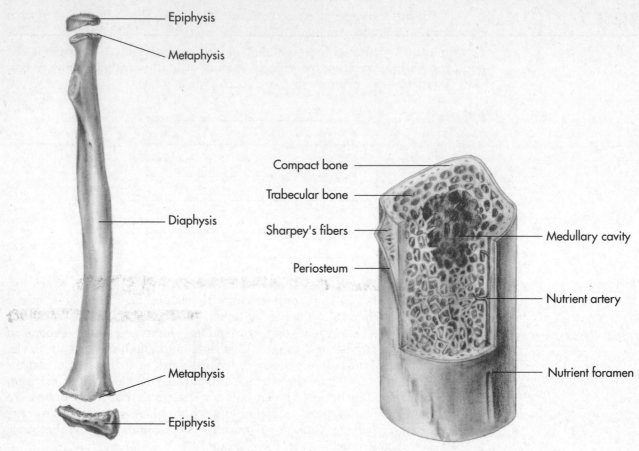

Figure 6-2 Structure of a long bone.

The **long bones** of the limbs have a typical structure with the following elements (also see Figure 6-2):

■ **Diaphysis**—shaft of the long bone, the smooth surface is composed of compact bone

■ **Epiphysis**—ends of the long bone, a thin layer of compact bone with cancellous bone underneath

■ **Epiphyseal plate (line)**—a thin area of cartilage between the diaphysis and the epiphysis that provides for longitudinal growth, sometimes called a *growth plate*

■ **Marrow/medullary cavity**—central hollowed-out region, containing yellow (lipids) and red (blood cells) bone marrow

■ **Periosteum**—a tough membrane surrounding the outside of the bone shaft but not the articular ends

The bones of the skull have a different arrangement:

■ **Outer table**—smooth compact bone on the outer (*exocranial*) surface

■ **Inner table**—smooth compact bone on the inside (*endocranial*) surface

■ **Diploe**—cancellous bone separating the inner and outer tables

EXERCISE 2

Examine the long bone that has been cut in half lengthwise. Identify the compact bone, cancellous bone, and marrow cavity. Next examine the cranial fragments and identify the inner and outer tables and the diploe.

The adult human skeleton contains 206 bones. The skeleton is subdivided into two regions: the **axial skeleton** (the bones of the skull, thorax/chest, and vertebral column) and the **appendicular skeleton** (the bones of the pectoral/shoulder girdle, upper limbs, pelvic girdle, and lower limbs). Figure 6-3 labels the major bones of the body.

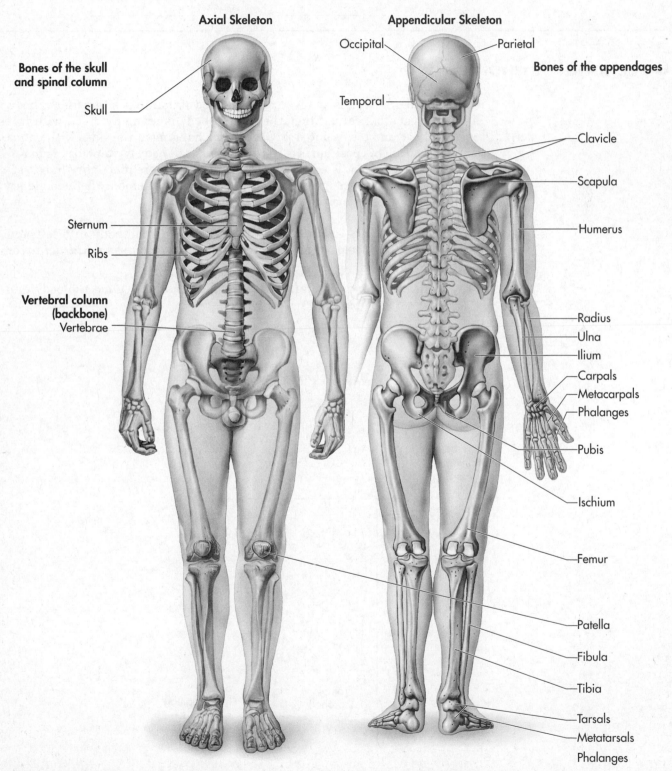

Figure 6-3 The bones of the human skeleton, anterior (*left*) and posterior (*right*) views.

EXERCISE 3

Examine an articulated skeleton in the lab or in a photograph, and identify the following bones with their correct names:

Fingers	_____	Shin	_____
Breastbone	_____	Hip	_____
Shoulder blade	_____	Thigh	_____
Upper arm	_____	Ankle	_____
Collarbone	_____	Wrist	_____

Directional Terminology

Anatomical position is a universally accepted standard position for the body. In Western anatomical position, the human body is standing erect, with feet together, head and toes pointed forward, arms hanging at the sides with palms facing forward. This position is essential because all body terminology is in reference to this position. The major **planes** of the body are imaginary lines, sections, or cuts drawn through the body wall. The three commonly defined planes are at right angles to each other (see Figure 6-4).

- **Sagittal plane**—runs longitudinally, dividing the body into left and right parts. If the parts are equal, then it is referred to as a *midsagittal* or *median plane.*

- **Frontal or coronal plane**—runs longitudinally, dividing the body into front and back parts.

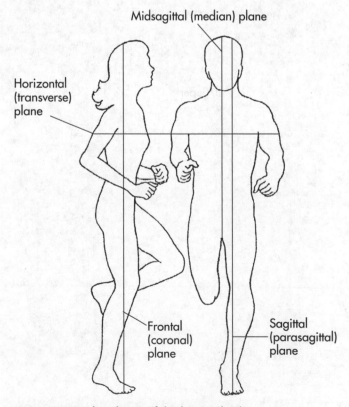

Figure 6-4 The planes of the human body.

■ **Transverse plane**—runs horizontally, dividing the body into top and bottom, or upper and lower, parts.

Directional terminology may differ, depending on whether you are examining a human or a four-legged animal (quadruped), such as a monkey. The following paired terms have slightly different meanings in reference to humans and to quadrupeds. Figure 6-5 illustrates the differences.

■ **Superior/inferior** (above/below)—Refers to placement along the long axis of the body; for example, in humans the chest is superior to the abdomen, the mouth is inferior to the nose.

■ **Anterior/posterior** (front/back)—In humans, the face, chest, and abdomen are anterior to the back, shoulder blades, and buttocks; the back, shoulder blades, and buttocks are posterior to the face, chest, and abdomen.

■ **Medial/lateral** (toward the midline/away from the midline)—The big toe is medial to the little toes; the ears are lateral to the nose.

The next set of terms is more absolute. These terms do not differentiate between a two-legged and a four-legged animal:

■ **Cranial/caudal** (toward the head/toward the tail)—In humans these terms are interchangeable with superior and inferior, but in four-legged animals they are interchangeable with anterior and posterior.

■ **Dorsal/ventral** (back side/belly side)—In humans these terms are interchangeable with anterior and posterior, but in four-legged animals they are interchangeable with superior and inferior.

■ **Proximal/distal** (toward the trunk/away from the trunk)—These terms generally refer to directions along the limbs; the wrist is distal to the elbow, the hip is proximal to the ankle.

■ **Superficial/deep** (toward the surface/external, away from the surface/internal)—The skeletal muscles are deep to the skin; the ribs are superficial to the heart.

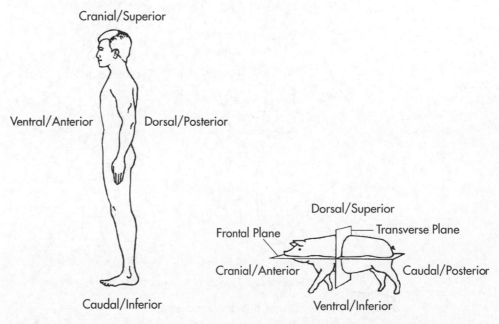

Figure 6-5 Directional terms on the human body and the four-legged animal body.

Body Movements

The skeletal muscles are attached to bone at two points: the *origin* (the stationary or less movable attachment) and the *insertion* (the movable attachment). When the muscle contracts across a freely movable synovial joint, the muscle fibers shorten and the insertion moves toward the origin, moving the bone and associated body part. Many joints allow more than one type of movement. The following are some of the more common body movements (also see Figure 6-6):

■ **Flexion/extension**—Flexion decreases the angle of a joint, brings ventral surfaces together; extension increases the angle of a joint, moving ventral surfaces apart.

■ **Adduction/abduction**—Adduction is movement toward the midline; abduction is movement away from the midline.

■ **Pronation/supination**—Pronation is movement of the palm downward; supination is movement of the palm upward.

■ **Inversion/eversion**—Inversion turns the sole of the foot inward (toward the midline); eversion turns the sole of foot outward (away from the midline).

■ **Dorsiflexion/plantarflexion**—Dorsiflexion is movement of the ankle joint so that you are standing on your heels; plantarflexion is movement of the ankle joint so that you are pointing your toes.

■ **Rotation**—Movement of a bone around its vertical axis (e.g., turning the arm inward or outward, shaking the head "no").

■ **Circumduction**—Movement of a bone so that the proximal end is stable but the distal end outlines a circle; circumduction involves flexion, extension, adduction, and abduction.

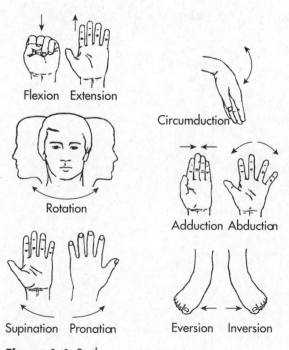

Figure 6-6 Body movements.

Pre-Lab Questions

1. Freely movable joints are called:
   a. fibrous joints
   b. cartilaginous joints
   c. synovial joints
   d. articular processes

2. Tendons connect:
   a. bone to bone
   b. skeletal muscle to bone
   c. skeletal muscle to ligaments
   d. ligaments to bones

3. A hole in bone is referred to as a:
   a. foramen
   b. tubercle
   c. trochanter
   d. torus

4. The two kinds of bone tissue are:
   a. compact and loose
   b. compact and cancellous
   c. cancellous and trabecular
   d. compact and medullary

5. The shaft of a long bone is called the:
   a. epiphysis
   b. periosteum
   c. diploe
   d. diaphysis

6. Which of the following is part of the trunk of the body?
   a. femur
   b. patella
   c. vertebra
   d. humerus

7. Which of the following is part of the limbs?
   a. radius
   b. vertebra
   c. rib
   d. mandible

8. A directional term indicating toward the midline of the body is:
   a. proximal
   b. superior
   c. medial
   d. lateral

9. **True or False:** Bone has a poor blood supply.

10. **True or False:** The knee is proximal to the ankle.

Post-Lab Questions

1. Match the bony marking to its definition.

    _____ meatus   a. large projections on the femur

    _____ line   b. thick, prominent ridge

    _____ fossa   c. canal-like passageway

    _____ trochanter   d. depression or hollow

    _____ torus   e. small, narrow ridge

2. Describe the differences among fibrous, cartilaginous, and synovial joints.

    _____

    _____

    _____

    _____

3. Draw a simple long bone that has been sawed in half lengthwise. Label the diaphysis, epiphysis, epiphyseal plate, compact bone, cancellous bone, and marrow cavity.

4. Which of the following are torso elements? Which are limb elements?

    Ribs   _____   Sternum   _____

    Radius _____   Tarsals   _____

    Ulna   _____   Ilium   _____

    Skull   _____   Femur   _____

5. Match the following bones to their location in the body.

_b__ ulna   a. thorax (chest)

_d__ pubis   b. upper limb

_____ sternum   c. lower limb

_____ fibula   d. pelvic girdle

_____ carpal   e. pectoral girdle – *shoulder*

_____ metatarsals

_____ ischium

_____ scapula

6. Label the bones indicated on the following illustration.

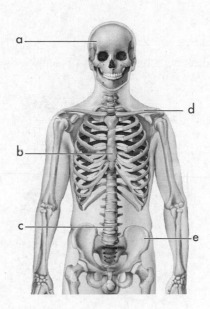

7. Match the following movement with its opposite:

_____ pronation   a. inversion

_____ extension   b. abduction

_____ eversion   c. supination

_____ adduction   d. flexion

8. Using the directional terminology, identify the term that belongs in the blank space.

   a. The wrist is _____ to the shoulder.

   b. The chest is _____ to the abdomen.

   c. The sternum is _____ to the shoulders.

   d. The thumb is _____ to the little finger.

   e. The hips are _____ to the chest.

   f. The abdomen is _____ to the back.

   g. The tongue is _____ to the teeth.

   h. The knee is _____ to the foot.

9. Label the bones shown in the following illustration:

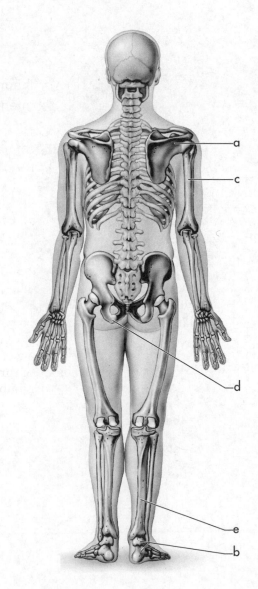

Chapter 7

The Appendicular Skeleton

Objectives

After completing this chapter you should be able to:

1. identify the major bones of the limbs and girdles;

2. identify the major landmarks on the bony elements;

3. understand the articulation of the bony elements; and

4. determine whether the bone is from the left or right side of the body.

Introduction

The appendicular skeleton is composed of 126 bones of the upper and lower limbs and the pectoral (shoulder) and pelvic girdles. The bones of the upper and lower limbs have different functions, but you will see that they share a similar basic plan. Each limb is made up of three segments that are connected by synovial joints. The girdles connect the limbs to the axial skeleton, or trunk of the body. The pelvic girdle also functions to support and protect the lower abdominal organs and organs of reproduction. Examine the bones described in this chapter and the landmarks or bony markings that your instructor identifies as the most important for your lab. The markings will assist you in *siding*, which is determining whether the bone is from the left or right side of the body. As you will see in Chapter 9, the bones of the appendicular skeleton are very helpful for determining sex, age at death, and stature (height) of individuals. The limb bones are also a source of valuable information on the biomechanics of locomotion.

The Pectoral Girdle

The pectoral girdle connects the upper limb to the trunk of the body and is an attachment point for many muscles of the trunk and neck. This girdle is very light and allows a wide range of movement. The pectoral girdles are paired (one is on the left side and one is on the right side of the body) and each is composed

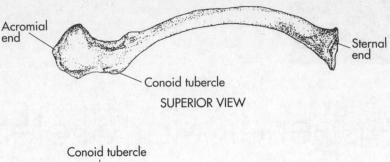

SUPERIOR VIEW

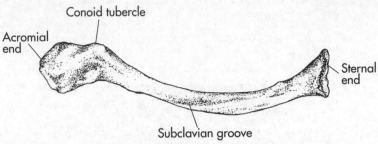

Figure 7-1 Left clavicle, inferior view.

of two bones: the anteriorly located **clavicle** (collarbone) and the posteriorly located **scapula** (shoulder blade).

The **clavicle** (Figure 7-1) is a gently curved bone with two ends that functions to hold the upper limb away from the chest while providing stability to the shoulder joint. The *sternal* (medial) end attaches to the sternum while the *acromial* (lateral) end attaches to the scapula. The sternal end is rounded, oval, or triangular in cross-section, and the acromial end is flattened in cross-section. Some important landmarks to identify are the *conoid tubercle,* which is an attachment point for a ligament on the postero-inferior surface, and the *subclavian groove,* a shallow depression on the inferior surface for the subclavian blood vessels.

EXERCISE 1

Examine a clavicle: either a picture or a model from the classroom. How would you describe the differences in the sternal and acromial ends?

_____

_____

_____

_____

The **scapula** is a roughly triangular-shaped bone with a flattened body and three edges: the *vertebral* (medial) *border,* the *axillary* (lateral) *border,* and the *superior border* (Figure 7-2). A prominent ridge running along the dorsal surface of the bone toward the superior end is known as the *spine* and is very helpful for siding. Two major projections are the *acromion* at the end of the scapular spine, which is where the lateral end of the clavicle attaches, and the *coracoid process,* which is an attachment point for muscles of the upper arm. Another prominent landmark is the *glenoid fossa* (or cavity), a shallow socket that attaches to the humerus to create the *shoulder joint.*

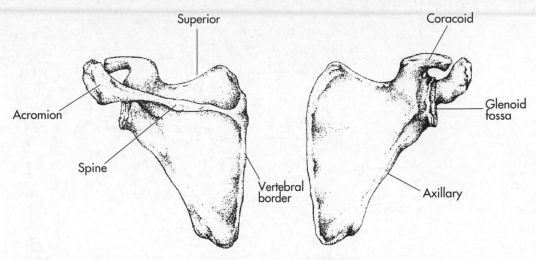

Figure 7-2 Left scapula, posterior (*left*) and anterior (*right*) views.

EXERCISE 2

In your own words, describe the differences between the dorsal and ventral surfaces of the scapula. Which features do you think would be most helpful for determining left from right?

_____

_____

_____

_____

_____

_____

The Upper Limb

The upper limb has three segments: the arm, composed of a single bone, the humerus; the forearm, which is composed of two bones, the radius and the ulna; and the wrist and hand, which are composed of numerous bones. The **humerus** is a typical long bone (Figure 7-3). At the proximal end is the rounded *head,* which fits into the glenoid fossa of the scapula. The head is separated from the shaft by the *anatomical neck* and is further constricted at the *surgical neck* (so-called because it is likely to fracture at this location). Also on the proximal end, lateral to the head, are two prominences, the *greater tubercle* and the *lesser tubercle,* separated by the *intertubercular (bicipital) groove.* Muscles of the rotator cuff attach on these tubercles, and the tendon of the biceps muscle lies in the groove.

As you move down the shaft of the humerus, you will find the roughened *deltoid tuberosity* on the lateral surface. The deltoid muscle attaches here. At the distal end are two projections, the one that resembles a spool of thread is the *trochlea,* and the small rounded projection just lateral to it is the *capitulum.* The trochlea articulates with the ulna, and the capitulum articulates with the

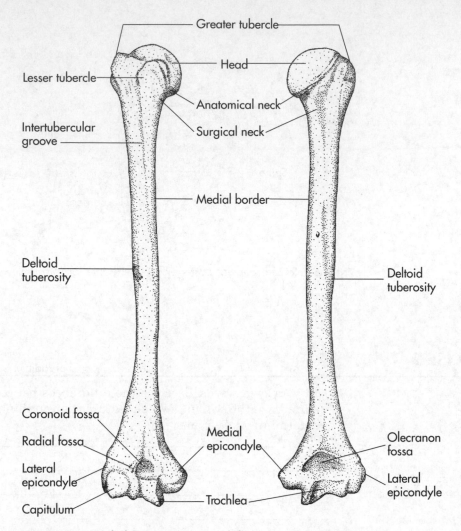

Figure 7-3 Right humerus, anterior (*left*) and posterior (*right*) views.

radius. Three depressions lie just above the trochlea; on the anterior surface are the shallow depressions called the *coronoid fossa* and the *radial fossa*, and on the posterior surface is a deeper depression called the *olecranon fossa*. The projection on the distal medial end is called the *medial epicondyle,* and the projection on the distal lateral end is the *lateral epicondyle.* These epicondyles are attachment sites for muscles of the forearm.

EXERCISE 3

Examine the glenoid fossa of the scapula and the head of the humerus together. Do you think it would be easy to dislocate this joint? Why or why not?

_____

_____

_____

_____

_____

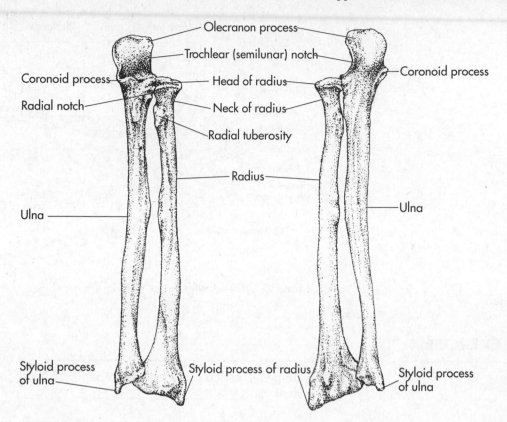

Figure 7-4 Left ulna and radius, anterior (*left*) and posterior (*right*) views.

In anatomical position, the radius is located on the lateral side of the forearm, and the ulna is located on the medial side of the forearm. The radius and the ulna are parallel to one another (Figure 7-4).

The proximal end of the **radius** has several important landmarks: the *head,* which attaches to the capitulum of the humerus; the constricted *neck,* just distal to the head; and the *radial tuberosity,* which projects anterolaterally and is the attachment site for the biceps muscle. The pointed styloid process of the radius is found on the distal–lateral end.

The **ulna** resembles a wrench. At the proximal end is the *olecranon process,* which fits into the olecranon fossa of the humerus; the *coranoid process,* which fits into the coranoid fossa of the humerus; the *trochlear notch,* which encloses the trochlea of the humerus when the bones are connected; and the *radial fossa,* located laterally and articulating with the head of the radius. The ulna also has a small pointed *styloid process* on the distal end.

The **carpals** are the eight small bones of the wrist that are bound together tightly by ligaments. They are arranged into proximal and distal rows with four bones in each. Moving lateral to medial, in the proximal row lie the scaphoid, lunate, triquetral (triangular), and pisiform, and in the distal row are the trapezium, trapezoid, capitate, and hamate. The hand is made up of two types of bones: the **metacarpals** in the palm, numbered 1 to 5, with the thumb being the first metacarpal; and the **phalanges** (singular: phalynx), or fingers. Each hand contains 14 phalanges. Each finger has 3 phalanges arranged into proximal, middle, and distal rows, while the thumb has only 2 phalanges, proximal and distal (Figure 7-5).

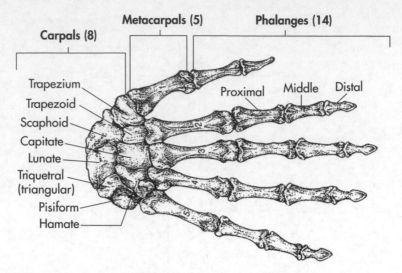

Figure 7-5 Bones of the hand, anterior (palmar) view.

EXERCISE 4

Four bones articulate with the humerus. List them and describe where they articulate. _____

_____

_____

_____

_____

The Pelvic Girdle

The pelvic girdle or hip is formed from two **coxal bones (os coxae)**, which are sometimes referred to as *innominates,* although many consider this term incorrect. The sacrum also contributes to the bony pelvis; however, it is considered to be part of the axial skeleton, and its anatomy is discussed in Chapter 8. The bones of the pelvic girdle are heavy and massive and are attached securely to the axial skeleton at the sacroiliac joint and to the lower limb at the hip joint, where strong ligaments hold the femur (thigh bone) tightly in the hip socket. All the weight of the upper half of the body is transmitted through the hip joint, making stability an important component of that joint.

Three bones come together and fuse during adolescence to form the coxal bones: the *ilium,* the *ischium,* and the *pubis* (Figure 7-6). The **ilium** is the large, flaring, superior portion of the bone. It may be easily palpated on your own body simply by placing your hand on the sides of your pelvis just below the waist. The **ischium** is the thick, inferior portion of the bone upon which you sit. The **pubis** is the most anterior portion of the bone composed of the two slender rami, which come together anteriorly superior to the genitals.

EXERCISE 5

Color in the different bones of the os coxae in Figure 7-6.

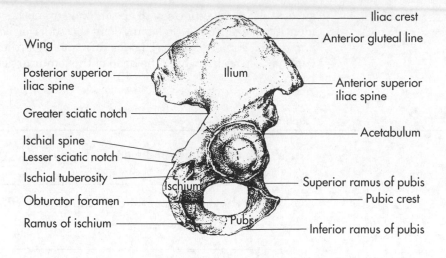

Iliac crest

Anterior gluteal line

Wing

Ilium

Posterior superior iliac spine

Anterior superior iliac spine

Greater sciatic notch

Acetabulum

Ischial spine

Lesser sciatic notch

Ischial tuberosity

Ischium

Superior ramus of pubis

Obturator foramen

Pubic crest

Ramus of ischium

Pubis

Inferior ramus of pubis

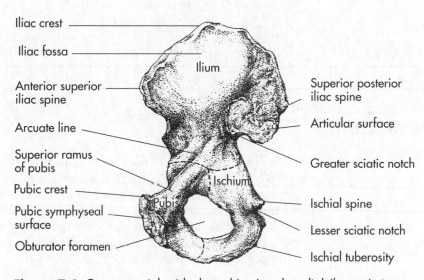

Iliac crest

Iliac fossa

Ilium

Anterior superior iliac spine

Superior posterior iliac spine

Articular surface

Arcuate line

Greater sciatic notch

Superior ramus of pubis

Ischium

Pubic crest

Pubic symphyseal surface

Pubis

Ischial spine

Lesser sciatic notch

Obturator foramen

Ischial tuberosity

Figure 7-6 Os coxae, right side: lateral *(top)* and medial *(bottom)* views.

The pelvis has numerous landmarks that act as sites of muscle attachment and are helpful in determining age and sex from a skeleton. First, on the ilium is the *auricular surface,* an ear-shaped region that articulates with the sacrum to form the sacroiliac joint. This joint changes its surface features during life, making it an area we can examine to determine how old a person was when they died (see Chapter 9). Just inferior to the auricular surface lies a large notch, the *greater sciatic notch,* so-called because the sciatic nerve passes through this region. The *iliac crest* runs along the superior rim of the ilium and terminates at each end at a bony prominence, ending anteriorly in the *anterior superior iliac spine* and ending posteriorly at the *posterior superior iliac spine.* The shallow *iliac fossa* lies on the internal surface, and the *arcuate line* demarcates the pelvic inlet. On the inferior portion of the ischium is a rough surface known as the *ischial tuberosity,* which is a site of attachment for the hamstring muscles. Superior to this tuberosity is the prominent *ischial spine,* which demarcates the *lesser sciatic notch.* The *ischial ramus* curves anteriorly to connect to the *inferior ramus of the pubis.* Together with the *superior ramus of the pubis,* these rami enclose the *obturator foramen,* a large opening that blood vessels and nerves pass through on their way from the pelvic cavity to the lower limb. Anteriorly, the left and right pubic bones meet in the midline of the body at the *pubic symphysis,* a cartilaginous joint. This joint surface also changes form with age, making it another pelvic area that is useful for identifying age from a skeleton. Along the superior edge of the pubic bones is the *pubic crest*. Finally, all three bones fuse and form the *acetabulum* ("little vinegar cup"), a deep socket where the head of the femur articulates to form the hip joint.

EXERCISE 6

a. Which three bones make up the pelvis? _____

_____

b. When they fuse together in the adult, what feature do they form?

_____

_____

c. Which two areas of the os coxae are useful for age determination?

_____

_____

The Lower Limb

The lower limb, like the upper limb, has three segments: the thigh, which has the largest bone of the body, the femur (thigh bone); the lower leg, which is composed of two bones: the thick, strong tibia (shin) and the slender fibula; and the ankle and foot.

The **femur** (*plural:* femora) is a large, heavy, and strong bone (Figure 7-7). At the proximal end is a ball-shaped *head,* which articulates with the acetabulum of the pelvis to create the hip joint. On the head of the femur you will notice a

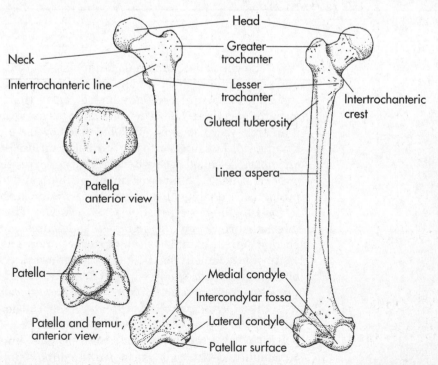

Figure 7-7 Left femur and patella, anterior (*left*) and posterior (*right*) views.

small pit, the *fovea capitis,* from which the short, strong ligament of the head of the femur runs into the acetabulum and assists in keeping the femur in place. The *neck* is just inferior to the head and creates an angle by which the proximal end is connected to the shaft of the bone. The neck is a common site for fractures, especially in the elderly (referred to as a "broken hip"). Where the neck meets the shaft are two large projections: the *greater trochanter* and the smaller, and posteriorly located, *lesser trochanter.* These are separated posteriorly by a large *intertrochanteric crest* and anteriorly by the small, faint *intertrochanteric line.* On the posterolateral surface is a roughened area called the *gluteal tuberosity,* a site of attachment for the gluteal muscles. As the femur runs inferiorly to articulate at the knee, it angles medially to bring the knees together in the midline. Along the length of the femur shaft, on the posterior surface, is the *linea aspera,* a raised line or ridge that anchors the hamstring muscles. At the distal end of the femur are the *medial* and *lateral condyles:* large projections with a smooth inferior surface that articulate with the tibia below. The condyles are separated posteriorly by the large *intercondylar notch* and anteriorly by the smooth surface of the *patellar surface.*

EXERCISE 7

Which landmarks do you think would be especially helpful for siding the femur? Why? _____

_____

_____

_____

EXERCISE 8

Describe how the ball-and-socket joints for the shoulder and hip differ. Would it be easy or hard to dislocate the femur? Explain your answer.

_____

_____

_____

_____

The **patella** (kneecap) is a small, slightly triangular bone that lies just in front of the distal femur at the patellar surface (Figure 7-8). The inferior edge is shaped into a slight point, the *apex.* The posterior surface is smooth and composed of two *facets,* medial and lateral.

The **tibia** is the larger bone of the lower leg and is located medially and anteriorly to the fibula (Figure 7-9). At the proximal end, the tibia has two large articular surfaces that articulate with the femoral condyles: the *medial* and *lateral condyles,* separated by the *intercondylar eminence.* On the anterior surface is the *tibial tuberosity,* a large, roughened surface that is the attachment site for the quadriceps muscle of the anterior thigh via the patellar ligament. You can feel the patellar tendon on your own knee, just below (inferior to) the patella. Along the anterior surface is the *anterior crest,* which is easily palpated along the front of your own tibia because it is not covered by muscle. At the distal end is the projecting *medial malleolus.*

The **fibula** is the lateral lower leg bone and is not involved in forming the knee joint, although it does form the outside bulge of the ankle. On the proximal end is the *head* and on the distal end is the pointed *lateral malleolus.*

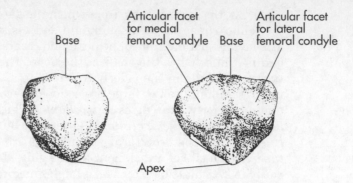

Figure 7-8 Right patella, anterior (*left*) and posterior (*right*) views.

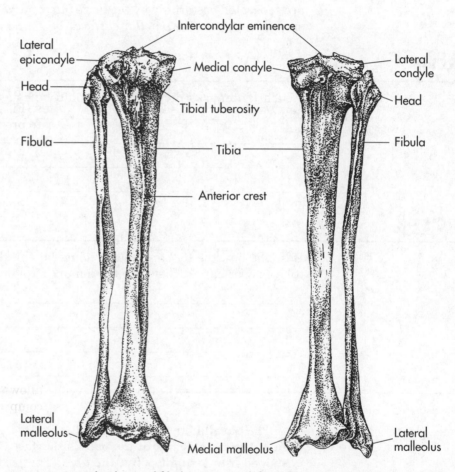

Figure 7-9 Right tibia and fibula, anterior (*left*) and posterior (*right*) views.

EXERCISE 9

a. Which three bones articulate with the femur? _____

_____

b. Which three bones articulate with the tibia? _____

_____

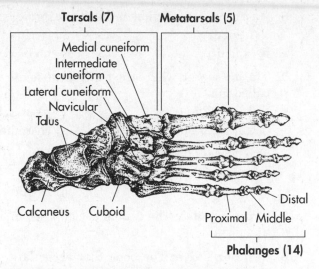

Figure 7-10 Right foot, superior (dorsal) view.

The foot is composed of 7 **tarsal** bones, 5 **metatarsals** (numbered 1 to 5, medially to laterally), and 14 **phalanges** (Figure 7-10). The foot phalanges, like the hand phalanges, are organized into proximal, middle, and distal rows, except for the first digit (the big toe, or **hallux**), which has only proximal and distal phalanges. The weight of the body is carried through the largest of the tarsals, the **talus**, which articulates with the tibia to form the ankle joint, and the **calcaneus**, which lies inferiorly to the talus and is the heel of the foot. The other tarsals include the medial, intermediate, and lateral cuneiforms; the cuboid; and the navicular. The human foot has two strong arches: the longitudinal arch, which runs from heel to toes, and the transverse arch, which runs from medial to lateral. Strong ligaments hold the foot together and maintain the arches. If these ligaments are weakened, one experiences flat feet or fallen arches.

Pre-Lab Questions

1. The clavicle:
   a. acts to stabilize the shoulder joint
   b. has vertebral and axillary ends
   c. allows the upper limb to compress onto the torso
   d. is part of the pelvic girdle

2. Which landmark of the humerus attaches to the scapula?
   a. spine
   b. glenoid fossa
   c. head
   d. capitulum

3. The medial bone of the forearm is the:
   a. radius
   b. humerus
   c. tibia
   d. ulna

4. How many bones make up the wrist?
   a. 7
   b. 8
   c. 5
   d. 14

5. The portion of the os coxae that you sit on is called the:
   a. ischium
   b. ilium
   c. pubis
   d. sacrum

6. An important function of the pelvic girdle is:
   a. flexibility
   b. stability
   c. circumduction
   d. abduction

7. The hip socket, where the head of the femur articulates with the pelvis, is called the:
   a. acetabulum
   b. auricular surface
   c. glenoid fossa
   d. sacroiliac joint

8. The lateral bone of the lower leg is the:
   a. radius
   b. femur
   c. tibia
   d. fibula

9. **True or False:** The thumb is composed of only two phalanges: proximal and distal.

10. **True or False:** The bone that articulates with the tibia to create the ankle joint is the calcaneus.

Post-Lab Questions

1. Fill in the blanks with the correct terms to complete the statement.

   a. The proximal bone in the lower limb is the _____ .

   The proximal bone of the upper limb is the _____ .

   b. The medial bone of the forearm is the _____ and the lateral bone of the forearm is the

   _____ .

   c. The two large, roughened projections on the proximal end of the femur are the _____

   and the _____ .

   d. Medial and lateral _____ are found on both the femur and the tibia.

   e. The small bone of the knee is the _____ .

   f. The two digits that only have two phalanges each are the _____ and the

   _____ .

   g. The _____ of the humerus articulates with the _____ of the scapula,

   while the _____ of the femur articulates with the _____ of the pelvis.

   h. The vertebral, superior, and axillary borders are found on the _____ .

   i. There are _____ bones in the wrist called the _____ , but there are

   _____ bones in the ankle called the _____ .

   j. The roughened surface of the ischium that you sit on is called the _____ .

2. Draw the humerus and label the following parts: head, deltoid tuberosity, capitulum, trochlea, and medial epicondyle.

3. Draw a femur and label the following parts: head, neck, medial and lateral condyles, greater trochanter.

4. Consider the muscle markings on the humerus, especially the deltoid tuberosity. Do you think the markings might vary between the right and left sides of the body? Why or why not?

    _____

    _____

5. Label these bony landmarks in the following illustration: carpals; metacarpals 1 to 5; proximal, middle, and distal phalanges. You may use colored pencils.

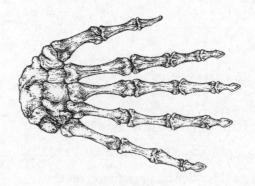

6. Label these bones and bony landmarks on the following illustration: radius, ulna, radial tuberosity, styloid process, olecranon notch.

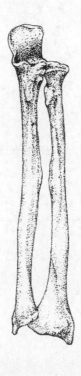

7. Label these bony landmarks on the following illustration: spine; acromion; vertebral, superior, and axillary borders; glenoid fossa.

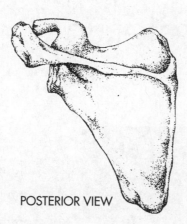

POSTERIOR VIEW

8. Label these bones and bony landmarks on the following illustration: tibia, fibula, tibial tuberosity, medial condyle, lateral condyle, medial malleolus, lateral malleolus.

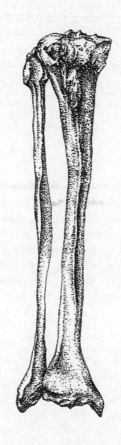

Chapter 8

The Axial Skeleton

Objectives

After completing this chapter you should be able to:

1. identify the major bones of the skull;

2. identify the major bones of the thorax and vertebral column;

3. identify the number and type of teeth in the adult mouth;

4. distinguish between cervical, thoracic, and lumbar vertebrae;

5. identify the major landmarks on the bony elements; and

6. understand the articulation of the bony elements.

Introduction

The **axial skeleton** can be divided into three parts: the skull, the thorax (chest), and the vertebral column. The axial skeleton functions to support and protect the brain; the spinal cord; and the thoracic organs, including the heart and lungs. This chapter will guide you to examine the bones of the axial skeleton and the landmarks or bony markings that your instructor identifies as the most important for your lab. The following sections present relevant features and views of these bones and landmarks. Use colored pencils to shade in the different features in the drawings provided; this will assist you when studying at home.

The Skull

The skull houses several of the sense organs and is an area of vital interest to biological anthropologists. The complex three-dimensional structure of the skull makes it a difficult area for some students to learn. However, examining the individual bones of the skull and how they come together to form the composite whole can be a fascinating area of study. Many of the individual bones are visible from different perspectives, so you should examine all views (anterior, inferior, lateral).

The skull is composed of the **cranium**, which encloses the brain (or brain-case) and includes the face and the **mandible**, or lower jawbone (Figure 8-1). All the bones of the skull articulate at nonmoving, fibrous joints called *sutures*, except for the mandible, which is attached to the cranium by a freely movable synovial joint. The cranial vault has two major areas: the *calvaria,* which forms the superior, lateral, and posterior walls of the braincase, and the *cranial base,* which forms the bottom of the skull. Internally, the base of the skull is divided into three regions that house the brain: the *anterior, middle,* and *posterior cranial fossae.* The bones of the braincase include the frontal, parietals, occipital, temporals, sphenoid, and ethmoid. The frontal, occipital, sphenoid, and ethmoid are all single bones found in the midline of the skull, while the temporals and parietals are paired (right and left) bones. The cranial vault or braincase may be differentiated from the face, which houses the eye orbits, nose, teeth, and muscles of facial expression. The face has 14 bones, 12 of which are paired (the maxilla, palatine, zygomatic, lacrimal, nasal, and inferior nasal concha) and 2 that are unpaired (the mandible and the vomer). Figures 8-1 through 8-10 depict the bones of the skull and their major landmarks.

The **frontal** bone forms the forehead and superior portion of the eye orbits. Several distinct landmarks are found on the frontal bone, including the *supraorbital foramen* (*notch*), an opening just above each orbit through which blood vessels and nerves pass; the *glabella,* the slightly raised area between the eyes; the *supraorbital margin,* which is the superior edge of the eye orbits; and the *superciliary arch,* which is the protruding ridge of bone above the eye orbits, also referred to as the *brow ridge.*

The **parietal** bone forms the top and sides of the cranium.

The **occipital** bone forms the posterior wall and the base of the skull. Four distinct landmarks are important to know on this bone. The *foramen magnum* is the large opening at the base of the skull, through which the spinal cord passes to connect to the brain; the *occipital condyles* are small facets on either side of the foramen magnum that articulate with the first cervical vertebra. Nodding your head yes and no occurs at this joint. The *hypoglossal canal* is a small opening just superior to each occipital condyle through which the 12th cranial nerve (hypoglossal nerve) passes on its way to the tongue. On the external surface of the occipital bone are the *nuchal lines* (a bony horizontal ridge) and the *external occipital protuberance* (a bump in the midline). The nuchal lines and the protuberance are areas of muscle attachment for muscles of the neck and shoulders and may be helpful in determining whether a skull is from a male or a female.

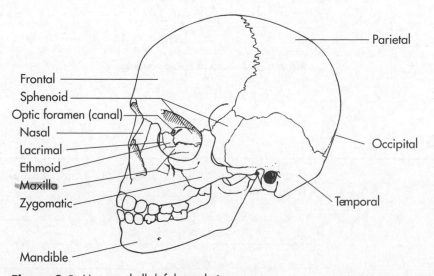

Figure 8-1 Human skull, left lateral view.

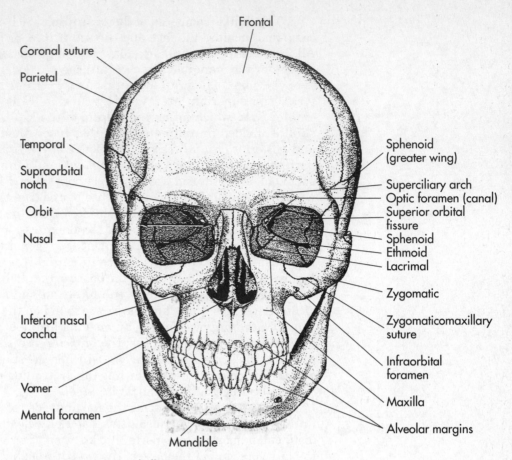

Figure 8-2 Human skull, anterior view.

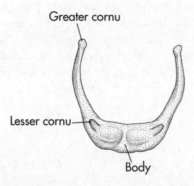

Figure 8-3 Human hyoid, anterior view.

EXERCISE 1

Why do you think the nuchal lines might be helpful for distinguishing males from females? _____

_____

_____

_____

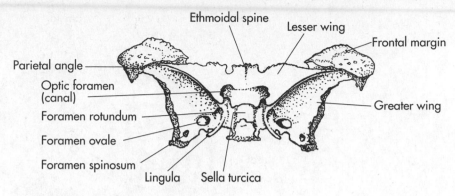

Figure 8-4 Human sphenoid, anterior view.

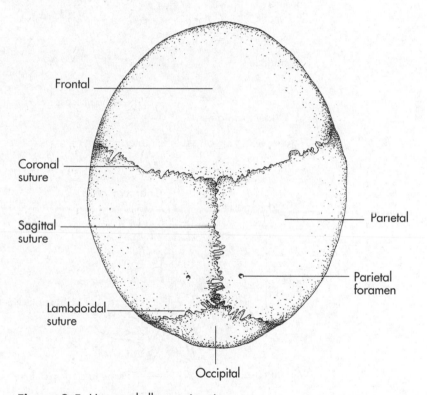

Figure 8-5 Human skull, superior view.

The **temporal** bone is found inferior to the parietal bone. It helps to make up the lateral wall of the braincase and houses our organs of hearing. Several important features are found on this bone. The smooth, flattened area just inferior to the parietal bone is the *squamous portion* of the temporal bone. The *zygomatic arch* juts anteriorly from the squamous portion to make up the cheekbone. The *mandibular fossa* is a small depression just inferior to the root of the zygomatic process, which is the point of articulation of the mandible to the cranium, the *temporomandibular joint,* or TMJ. The opening just posterior and inferior to the zygomatic root and the TMJ is the *external auditory (acoustic) meatus,* the ear canal. Inside lie the three tiny ossicles—the malleus, incus, and stapes—which are involved in hearing and balance. Posterior to the auditory meatus is the *mastoid process,* a somewhat large, rough projection of bone that drops inferiorly and is a point of muscle attachment for the neck muscles. The mastoid process is also often used to assist in sex determination from cranial remains. Looking inferiorly or internally at the inner portions of the

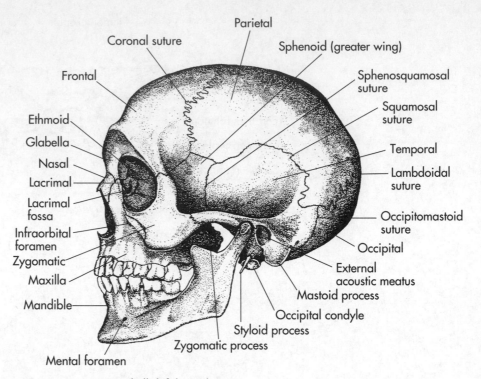

Figure 8-6 Human skull, left lateral view.

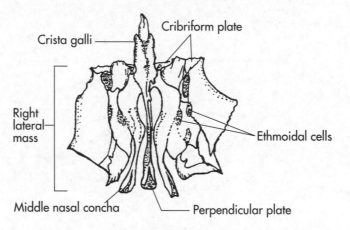

Figure 8-7 Human ethmoid, anterior view.

temporal bone, you will find the *petrous portion,* a thick, blocky region that houses the ear canal and several small foramina through which cranial nerves and blood vessels pass.

The **sphenoid** is a butterfly-shaped bone that is the cornerstone of the skull, connecting the cranial base to the face, and the face to the braincase. You may view sections of it from several angles: looking inside the eye orbits, laterally deep to the zygomatic arch, internally between the frontal and the occipital, and inferiorly anterior to the occipital. Numerous openings in the sphenoid exist to pass important cranial nerves and blood vessels to serve the face. The *greater wings* are viewed internally and externally anterior to the temporal bone, deep to the zygomatic arch. You may also view the greater wings by looking inside the eye orbits. The *superior orbital fissure* is a long, jagged opening in the eye orbit through which nerves and blood vessels pass on their way to the eye. The small round opening adjacent to the superior orbital fissure is the *optic foramen,* which allows the passage of the optic nerve from the brain to the eye. The *lesser wings* are best viewed internally, where they provide an

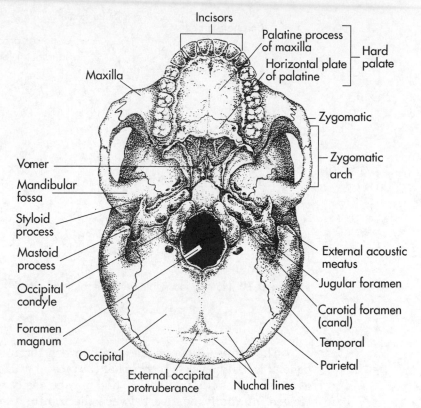

Figure 8-8 Human skull, inferior view.

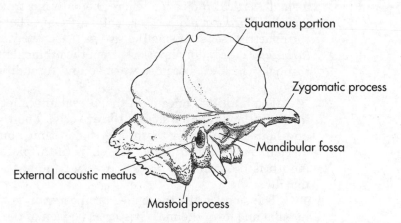

Figure 8-9 Human temporal, right lateral view.

anchoring site for the *meninges* (coverings) of the brain. The *sella turcica* (Turkish saddle) is viewed internally and is a small saddle-shaped region posterior to the greater and lesser wings that houses the pituitary gland.

EXERCISE 2

Examine the sphenoid bone. Looking at various angles, list at least four other bones that articulate with the sphenoid. _____

_____

_____

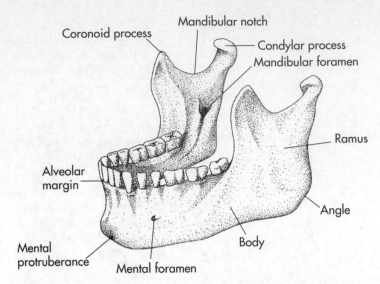

Figure 8-10 Human mandible, left anterolateral view.

The **ethmoid** bone is located between the frontal bone and the sphenoid bone. It is best viewed by looking at the medial wall of the eye orbits, or if the top of the skull has been autopsied, and may be easily removed, the ethmoid can be viewed internally, nestled between the frontal and the sphenoid. Besides the medial wall of the eye orbits, the ethmoid also forms the roof of the nasal cavity and the superior portion of the nasal septum. In particular, note the *crista galli,* a small vertical projection where the outermost meninges of the brain attach, and the *cribriform plate,* a horizontal area on either side of the crista galli where the olfactory (sense of smell) nerve passes on its way to the nose. Spiral-shaped *turbinates* descending inferiorly from the ethmoid make up the *ethmoid sinuses,* through which air becomes warmed and humidified before it passes into the lungs.

The **maxilla** bones form the lateral and inferior portions of the nose, the innermost and inferior edge of the eye orbit, and the anterior base of the cheek and houses the upper teeth; the region that houses the teeth is called the *alveolar margin* or *alveolus.* The horizontal plate that forms the roof of the mouth is the *palatine process.* Every bone of the face articulates with the maxilla.

The small **palatine** bones are posterior to the palatine process of each maxilla and form the most posterior portion of the palate.

The **zygomatic** bones lie between each maxilla and the temporal bone, creating the anterior part of each zygomatic process or cheekbone, and the lateral section of each eye orbit.

The tiny **lacrimal** bones are found in the medial portion of each eye orbit between each maxilla and the ethmoid. A small opening in the lacrimal allows for the passage of tears.

The tiny **nasal** bones are inferior to the frontal bone and form the bridge of the nose.

The **vomer** is a thin sheet of bone that forms the inferior nasal septum.

The **inferior nasal conchae**, also called the *turbinate* bones, are found inside the nasal cavity.

The **mandible,** or the lower jawbone, is made up of a horizontal *body* and vertical *ramus* on each side, where the *mandibular condyle* articulates with the temporal bone at the TMJ. The region that houses the teeth is the *alveolar margin* or *alveolus,* as in the maxilla bones. The area that just forward in the midline is called the *mental eminence* or *protuberance.*

The horseshoe-shaped **hyoid bone** is not a bone of the skull; rather, it is located in the throat above the larynx. It does not articulate with any other bone but has important functions in speaking and swallowing. As you study the bones of the skull illustrated in this chapter and in your lab, note that important bony landmarks are listed under the bone upon which they appear.

EXERCISE 3

Identify all the bones of the skull and the main sutures shown in Figures 8-1 through 8-10 and any lab models that are available. Your instructor will inform you of the bony landmarks he or she feels are most important for you to find. Color the bones of the skull depicted in this guide to differentiate them from one another.

Sutures

As mentioned, the bones of the skull are connected at sutures. The *coronal (frontal) suture* separates the frontal bone from the parietal bones. The *sagittal suture* is found along the midline of the skull (in the sagittal plane) and separates the left and right parietals. The *lambdoidal suture* separates the occipital bone from the parietal bones. The *squamosal suture* separates the temporal bone from the parietal bone. Numerous other sutures in the cranium are named for the bones they separate: for example, *parietomastoid, frontonasal,* and *zygomaxillary.*

EXERCISE 4

Examine either a picture or a model from your lab of the human skull. List four bones that articulate with the frontal bone. List four bones that articulate with the occipital bone. _____

_____

_____

_____

The Human Dentition

Humans and other mammals have two sets of teeth: the **deciduous** (baby) **teeth**, which are shed during childhood, and the **permanent** (adult) **teeth** (Figure 8-11). There are 20 deciduous teeth and 32 permanent teeth. Each tooth has three regions: the **crown**, which is the visible section above the gumline that is covered by **enamel**, the **neck**, which is the constricted section at the gumline, and the **root**, which lies below the gumline and is firmly anchored in the alveolar region of the maxilla and mandible (Figure 8-12). Humans and other mammals are *heterodont,* which means that the types of teeth in the mouth are different from each other. The four tooth types of mammals have different shapes and functions: **incisors, canines, premolars**, and **molars**. A **dental formula** is a count of the number and types of teeth in each quadrant of the mouth. The mouth is divided into four quadrants: upper left, lower left, upper right, lower right. In each adult human quadrant are two

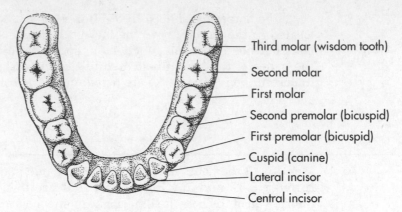

Third molar (wisdom tooth)

Second molar

First molar

Second premolar (bicuspid)

First premolar (bicuspid)

Cuspid (canine)

Lateral incisor

Central incisor

Figure 8-11 Permanent dentition of the adult human mandible.

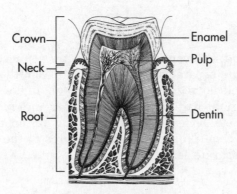

Crown

Neck

Root

Enamel

Pulp

Dentin

Figure 8-12 Human tooth structure, internal view.

incisors, one canine, two premolars, and three molars. Written in shorthand, this dental formula is: 2.1.2.3. Human children with all deciduous teeth erupted and present have the following dental formula: 2.1.0.2.

When referring to the mouth, different directional terminology is required:

- **Mesial/distal:** toward the midline (front) of the tooth row/toward the back of the tooth row

- **Buccal/lingual:** toward the cheek/toward the tongue

- **Incisal:** the biting edge of the anterior (incisors and canine) teeth

- **Occlusal:** the chewing surface of the premolar and molar teeth

The Vertebral Column

The vertebral column in the human surrounds and protects the spinal cord as it descends from the brainstem at the foramen magnum to the lower truck. Openings between each vertebra allow the spinal nerves to pass through. While the vertebral column provides the body's main axial support, it remains flexible. The vertebral column contains 24 individual bones, called *vertebrae*, and two fused bones, the *sacrum* and the *coccyx*. The first 7 vertebrae located in the neck are *cervical vertebrae,* followed by 12 *thoracic vertebrae* that

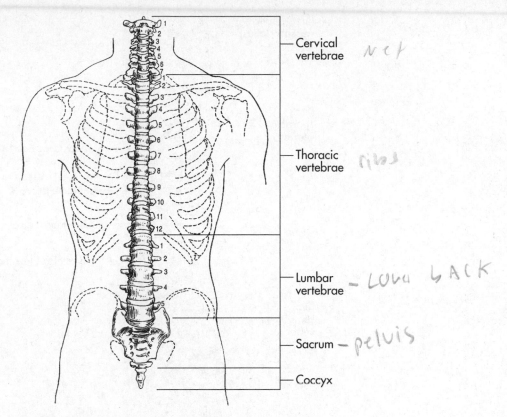

Figure 8-13 Human vertebral column, posterior view.

connect to the rib cage, and 5 *lumbar vertebrae* that comprise the lower back (Figure 8-13). Each of the vertebrae are separated by fibrocartilage pads, *intervertebral discs,* which act to cushion the vertebrae and absorb shock. A ruptured disc occurs when an intervertebral disc becomes thinner and compressed, causing a herniation of the disc's contents and pressure on the spinal nerves. Two prominent curves form in the vertebral column with age. The *cervical curve* is the first to form when the infant begins to hold up its head, and the concave *lumbar curve* forms when a young child begins to walk. This maintains balance and support for individuals who walk on two legs.

Due to their location and function in the vertebral column, the cervical, thoracic, and lumbar vertebrae differ in appearance. However, all the **typical vertebrae** share several features in common. Each vertebra has a *body (centrum),* the rounded portion in the center that faces anteriorly; a *vertebral arch* that extends posteriorly from the body and surrounds the spinal cord; *transverse processes,* which are the bilateral projections from the vertebral arch; and a *spinous process,* which is the posterior projection from the arch that extends out in the midline of the body (Figure 8-14).

The **cervical vertebrae** are numbered C1 through C7, and the first two (C1 and C2) are the smallest and lightest vertebrae and have specific functions and appearance. C1, the **atlas**, does not have a body and resembles a ringlike structure with concave depressions on each transverse process where the occipital condyles articulate (Figure 8-15). C2, the **axis**, has a vertical prominence called the **odontoid process** or **dens** on its body (Figure 8-16). The dens acts as a pivot, allowing rotation at the C1/C2 joint, which occurs when you turn your head side to side to say "no." C3 through C7 are more typical vertebrae, but you may use some features to distinguish them from thoracic or lumbar vertebrae. The spinous process is often short and *bifurcated*

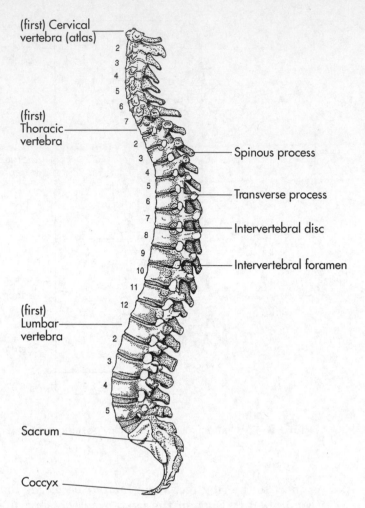

(first) Cervical vertebra (atlas)

(first) Thoracic vertebra

Spinous process

Transverse process

Intervertebral disc

Intervertebral foramen

(first) Lumbar vertebra

Sacrum

Coccyx

Figure 8-14 Human vertebral column, left lateral view.

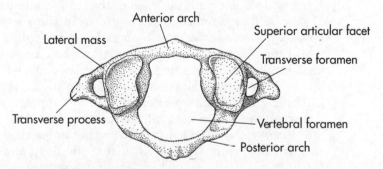

Anterior arch

Lateral mass

Superior articular facet

Transverse foramen

Transverse process

Vertebral foramen

Posterior arch

Figure 8-15 Atlas, superior view.

(divided into two branches), and each transverse process has a hole in it (*transverse foramen*), which allows the passage of the vertebral arteries to the brain (Figure 8-17).

The **thoracic vertebrae** are numbered T1 through T12. They are somewhat larger than the cervical vertebrae, and their spinous processes tend to be long, sharp, and pointed inferiorly. The lower thoracic vertebrae have shorter spinous processes that resemble lumbar vertebrae. One prominent difference is that each thoracic vertebra has one or two small facets on each side of the body, which are called *costal demifacets,* or *rib facets,* each of which articulates with a rib (Figure 8-18).

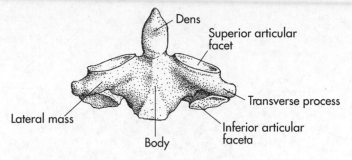

Figure 8-16 Axis, anterior view.

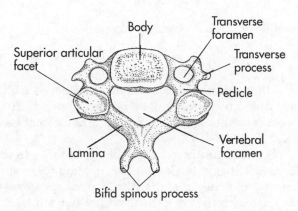

Figure 8-17 Typical cervical vertebrae, superior view.

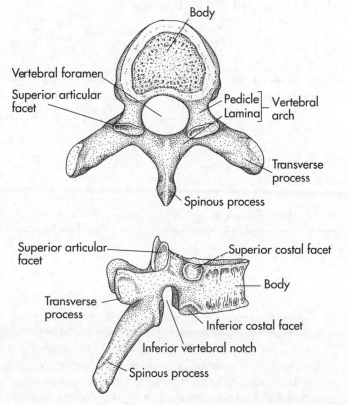

Figure 8-18 Thoracic vertebrae, superior (*top*) and right lateral (*bottom*) view.

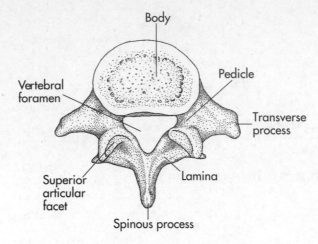

Figure 8-19 Lumbar vertebrae, superior view.

The **lumbar vertebrae** are numbered L1 to L5, are the largest vertebrae, and carry the weight of the upper half of the body. Their spinous processes are short and square, and they do not have transverse foramen or rib facets (Figure 8-19).

The **sacrum** is composed of 5 vertebrae that have fused together during adulthood. It is a large, somewhat triangular-shaped bone. The sides of the sacrum are made up of fused transverse processes and are called *alae,* which articulate with the pelvis at the sacroiliac joints. Blood vessels and nerves pass through the sacrum's many holes, the *sacral foramina,* on their way to the pelvis and lower limbs. The spinous processes are fused at the *median sacral crest* (Figure 8-20).

Between four and six tiny, irregularly shaped vertebrae fuse together to form the **coccyx**, or tailbone.

EXERCISE 5

Examine the vertebrae. How would you distinguish the cervical, thoracic, and lumbar vertebrae? _____

_____

_____

_____

_____

The Thorax

The thorax is composed of the ribs, sternum, and thoracic vertebrae. It surrounds and protects the heart, lungs, and other organs located in the chest cavity. The **sternum** is composed of three bones that have fused together and attach to 7 pairs of ribs. From superior to inferior, these are the somewhat triangular-shaped **manubrium**, the rectangular **sternal body**, and the **xiphoid process** (Figure 8-21). The manubrium also articulates with the medial ends of the clavicles and has a central depression, the *jugular notch,* which is easily palpable on your own body at the base of the throat.

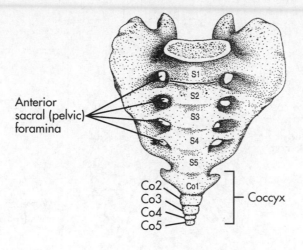

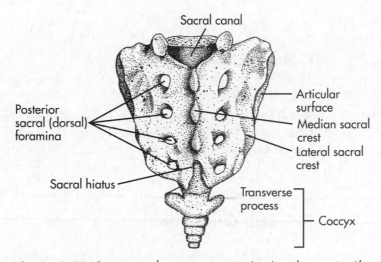

Anterior sacral (pelvic) foramina

Coccyx

Sacral canal

Posterior sacral (dorsal) foramina

Articular surface

Median sacral crest

Lateral sacral crest

Sacral hiatus

Transverse process

Coccyx

Figure 8-20 Sacrum and coccyx, anterior (*top*) and posterior (*bottom*) views.

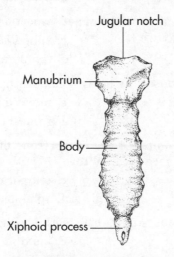

Jugular notch

Manubrium

Body

Xiphoid process

Figure 8-21 Sternum, anterior view.

The Ribs

There are 12 pairs of ribs. All the ribs articulate posteriorly with the thoracic vertebrae and curve downward and anteriorly to end in cartilage. The first 7 pairs are called *true ribs* and articulate directly with the sternum through

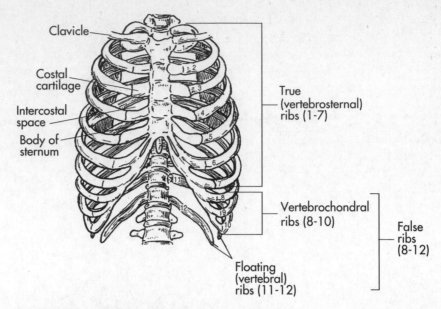

Figure 8-22 Thorax, anterior view.

costal cartilages. The next 3 pairs are called *false ribs* because their costal cartilages fuse together and connect indirectly to the sternum. The final two pairs are called *floating ribs* and do not attach to the sternum (Figure 8-22).

Pre-Lab Questions

1. Which of the following is not a function of the axial skeleton?
    a. protects the brain
    b. protects the spinal cord
    c. protects the reproductive organs
    d. protects the heart and lungs

2. The bone that makes up the superior portion of the eye orbits is the:
    a. frontal bone
    b. parietal bone
    c. sphenoid bone
    d. temporal bone

3. The bone that houses the hearing apparatus is the:
    a. temporal bone
    b. occipital bone
    c. maxilla bone
    d. frontal bone

4. The bone that composes the cornerstone of the skull and connects the braincase to the face is called the:
    a. occipital
    b. ethmoid
    c. temporal
    d. sphenoid

5. The bone that houses the upper teeth is called the:
    a. mandible
    b. sphenoid
    c. maxilla
    d. hyoid

6. How many cervical vertebrae are there?
    a. 5
    b. 12
    c. 7
    d. 8

7. The most inferior portion of the sternum is the:
    a. sternal body
    b. xiphoid process
    c. manubrium
    d. false ribs

8. How many pairs of true ribs are there?
   a. 7
   c. 2
   b. 3
   d. 5

9. **True or False:** The cervical curve forms when a child begins to walk on two legs.

10. **True or False:** Human teeth are homodont, meaning we have one set of teeth in our lifetime.

Post-Lab Questions

1. Fill in the blank with the correct word to complete the sentence.

   a. The suture that separates the frontal bone from the parietal bones is the _____ suture.

   b. The suture that separates the temporal bone from the parietal bones is the _____ suture.

   c. The _____ bone makes up the lower rim of the eye orbit and the side and bottom of the nose.

   d. The _____ bone houses the lower dentition.

   e. The ear canal is called the _____ and is found on the _____ bone.

   f. Another term for the brow ridge is the _____.

   g. The large opening at the base of the skull is called the _____.

   h. Another term for the cheekbone is the _____.

   i. The _____ are horizontal ridges across the occipital bone that are areas of muscle attachment.

   j. The only joint in the skull that is not a suture is the _____.

2. Match the distinguishing feature on the right to the vertebra on the left.

   a. _____ typical cervical   1. rib facets

   b. _____ axis   2. odontoid process (dens)

   c. _____ atlas   3. transverse foramen

   d. _____ thoracic   4. square spinous process

   e. _____ lumbar   5. facets for occipital condyles

3. Describe the differences among the true ribs, false ribs, and floating ribs. _____

   _____

   _____

   _____

   _____

4. Label these 10 bones in the following illustration and color them with different colored pencils: frontal, parietal, temporal, maxilla, mandible, sphenoid, nasal, lacrimal, ethmoid, mandible.

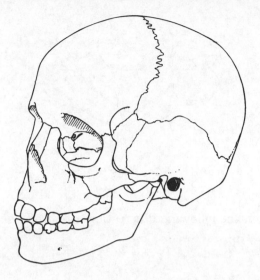

5. Label these bony landmarks on the following illustration: squamous portion, zygomatic arch, mastoid process, mandibular fossa (TMJ), external auditory meatus.

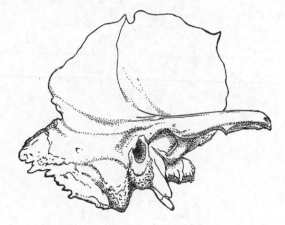

6. Label these teeth on the following illustration and color each of the four tooth types in a different shade with colored pencils: incisors, canine, premolars, molars.

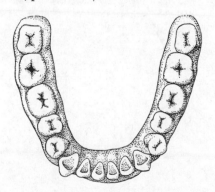

7. Label these bony landmarks on the following illustration: body, transverse foramen, spinous process. What type of vertebrae is this?

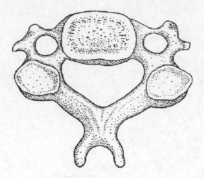

8. Label these bony landmarks on the following illustration: rib facet, spinous process, transverse process, body. What type of vertebrae is this?

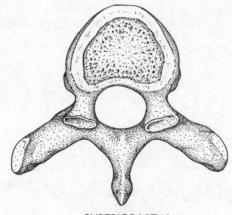

SUPERIOR VIEW

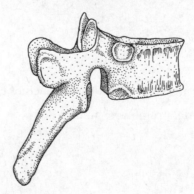

Chapter 9

Human Variation and Forensic Anthropology

Objectives	After completing this chapter you should be able to:
	1. use calipers and osteometric boards to measure human bones;
	2. calculate basic indices, including stature, from the measurements you took;
	3. use calipers to take basic measurements of students in your class;
	4. describe the differences between male and female skulls and os coxae;
	5. identify some of the basic features that distinguish ethnic affiliation; and
	6. describe the methods used to determine age at death of an individual.

Human Variation

The first practitioners of biological anthropology were interested in human variation. The early explorers of the eighteenth and nineteenth centuries brought back stories of exotic peoples and places, which the anthropologist was seldom able to see for himself. Sometimes, these explorers returned with skeletal remains that were later housed in museums for study. The mid-1800s witnessed the development of basic evolutionary theory and the discovery of early human fossils, the Neanderthals. The biological anthropologists became interested in humanity's place in the world, our relationship to previous ancestors, and the similarities and differences among living groups. The unification of the natural sciences with modern genetics allowed the creation of a comprehensive evolutionary theory based on the forces of evolution discussed in Chapter 5.

This emphasis on evolutionary process and advances in genetic technology changed the way human variation is studied. Today, human variation covers a wide range of themes usually based on populations rather than individuals. Topics include how humans adapt to environmental stress, the evolutionary history of human populations, and describing the similarities and differences within and between human groups, both skeletally and genetically. Biological anthropologists have found that humans differ far more within groups than between groups; that is, human populations show significant variation, and more variation may occur within a human population, such as the Chinese, than between groups, such as between the Chinese and the Europeans. Anthropologists have traditionally taken measurement of living humans and skeletal remains in an attempt to identify and classify individuals and groups.

Osteometry—Post-Cranial Measurements

Osteometry is the measurement of skeletal remains. These measurements assist in determining sex, age, ethnic affiliation, stature, nutritional status, and health from the remains. Generally, several types of laboratory equipment are used to measure skeletal elements, including the osteometric board, flexible tapes, and spreading and sliding calipers.

The *osteometric board* is used to measure the **maximum lengths** of all major long bones. For the femur, fibula, humerus, radius, and ulna, the bone is laid on the osteometric board with the distal end placed firmly at the stationary upright and held in place with the left hand. The right hand slides the movable upright to touch the proximal end of the bone. To obtain maximum length, one should move the proximal end of the bone back and forth, allowing the movable upright to register the maximum measurement. The measurement should be recorded in either centimeters or millimeters. Measuring the **maximum length of the tibia** is slightly tricky and requires recording of the diagonal measurement from the lateral condyle to the medial malleolus. The lateral condyle is placed along the stationary upright and held in place, while the medial malleolus rests against the movable upright. The distal end of the bone must be wiggled to obtain the maximum length, and the intercondylar eminences should not be included. Another common long bone measurement is the **bicondylar length of the femur**. In this case, both condyles of the femur are situated firmly against the stationary upright and held in place, while the proximal end rests against the movable upright. No wiggling is necessary here.

EXERCISE 1

Take the following measurements from the skeleton assigned to you in lab and record them in centimeters (cm). If you work in pairs or groups, be sure to take your own measurements.

Maximum length of the humerus _____

Maximum length of the radius _____

Maximum length of the ulna _____

Maximum length of the femur _____

Maximum length of the tibia _____

Maximum length of the fibula _____

Bicondylar length of the femur _____

Table 9-1 Stature formulae from the long limb bones grouped by sex and race

Formula	SE	Formula	SE
White Males		**White Females**	
3.08 × Hum + 70.45	4.05	3.36 × Hum + 57.97	4.45
3.78 × Rad + 79.01	4.32	4.74 × Rad + 54.93	4.24
3.70 × Uln + 74.05	4.32	4.27 × Uln + 57.76	4.30
2.38 × Fem + 61.41	3.27	2.47 × Fem + 54.74	3.72
2.52 × Tib + 78.62	3.37	2.90 × Tib + 59.24	3.66
2.68 × Fib + 71.78	3.29	2.93 × Fib + 59.61	3.57
Black Males		**Black Females**	
3.26 × Hum + 62.10	4.43	3.08 × Hum + 64.67	4.25
3.42 × Rad + 81.56	4.30	2.75 × Rad + 94.51	5.05
3.26 × Uln + 79.29	4.42	3.31 × Uln + 75.38	4.83
2.11 × Fem + 70.35	3.94	2.28 × Fem + 59.76	3.41
2.19 × Tib + 86.02	3.78	2.45 × Tib + 72.65	3.70
2.19 × Fib + 85.65	4.08	2.49 × Fib + 70.90	3.80

Stature Estimation

The long bone measurements described in the preceding section are useful for determining **stature** (i.e., height) of an individual. The first researchers to estimate stature from skeletal remains were Trotter and Gleser (1952, 1958) who determined that the maximum length of the long bones was correlated with a person's height. The formulae for determining stature are dependent on an individual's sex and ethnic affiliation. Table 9-1 shows the stature formulae for American Whites and Blacks of European and African descent, respectively (Trotter, 1970; Jantz, 1992). All formulae are followed by the abbreviation for standard error (SE), which provides an idea of how much variation or error is in the estimate. A low standard error indicates a better estimate. Because measurements are taken using the metric system, statures are reported in centimeters. To obtain values in the English system (U.S. customary units, English units), divide your stature estimate by 2.54 to get inches. That value may then be divided by 12 to get feet and inches.

EXERCISE 2

The unidentified skeleton of an individual has been determined to be a White female. The maximum length of her femur is 39.6 cm, and the maximum length of her humerus is 28.4 cm.

a. Calculate the estimated stature in feet and inches for this individual from each long bone, using Table 9-1.

b. Does the humerus or the femur provide a better estimate of stature? Why? _____

_____

_____

_____

c. Calculate the values assuming the individual was a Black female.

_____

_____

_____

_____

Osteometry—Cranial Measurements

Numerous measurements of the cranium are taken with the *spreading or sliding calipers*. Measurements of the skull are helpful for determining ethnic affiliation, sex, and population affinity. To measure the skull, some **cranial landmarks** must first be identified. Table 9-2 lists the common cranial landmarks you will need to complete the exercises in this chapter. Figure 9-1 provides an illustration of some of these landmarks. Table 9-3 lists 12 common cranial measurements and their definitions (Bass, 1995).

Table 9-2 Eleven common cranial landmarks

Landmark	Abbreviation	Definition
Alveolare	Al	The lowest possible point on septum between upper central incisors
Basion	Ba	Midpoint of inner border of anterior margin of foramen magnum
Bregma	Br	Intersection of coronal and sagittal sutures
Glabella	Gl	Most forwardly projecting point in midline of frontal bone, above nasal bones
Gnathion	Gn	Lowest midline point on inferior margin of the mandible
Nasion	Na	Intersection of nasal bones and frontal bone at the nasofrontal suture and internasal suture
Nasospinale	Ns	Midpoint of a line that connects the lower margins of the left and right nasal apertures
Orale	Or	Midpoint of palate on a line drawn tangent to the curves in the alveolar margin, just posterior to central incisors
Opisthocranion	Op	Most posterior point on braincase in the midline
Prosthion	Pr	Most anterior midline point in upper alveolar process between the central incisors
Staphylion	St	Midline point on posterior border of the hard palate, where a line drawn tangent to the curves of the posterior margin intersects the midline

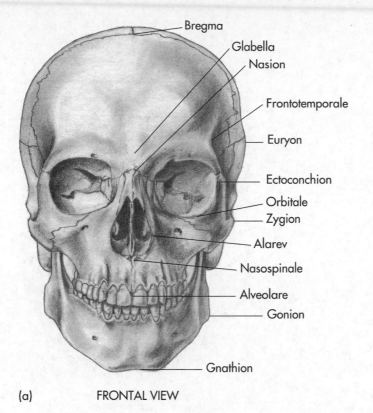

(a)   FRONTAL VIEW

Bregma
Glabella
Nasion
Frontotemporale
Euryon
Ectoconchion
Orbitale
Zygion
Alarev
Nasospinale
Alveolare
Gonion
Gnathion

(b)   LEFT LATERAL VIEW

Bregma
Apex
Pterion
Frontotemporale
Glabella
Nasion
Ectoconchion
Lambda
Opisthocranion
Alare
Nasospinale
Prosthion
Alveolare
Incision
Infradentale
Ectomolare
Gonion

Figure 9-1 Common cranial landmarks.

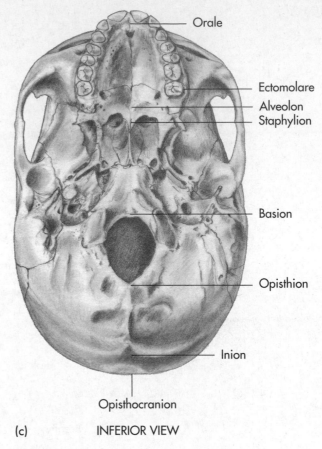

Orale

Ectomolare
Alveolon
Staphylion

Basion

Opisthion

Inion

Opisthocranion

(c)   INFERIOR VIEW

Figure 9-1 (*continued*)

Table 9-3 Common cranial measurements

Measurement	Calipers	Description
Maximum cranial length	Spreading	From glabella to opisthocranion
Maximum cranial breadth	Spreading	Maximum width of skull perpendicular to midsagittal plane, above the roots of the zygomatic arches
Maximum cranial height	Spreading	From basion to bregma
Bizygomatic breadth	Spreading	Maximum measurement on widest portion of zygomatic arches
Total face height	Sliding	From nasion to gnathion
Upper face height	Sliding	From nasion to alveolare
Nasal height	Sliding	From nasion to nasospinale
Nasal breadth	Sliding	Maximum breadth of the bony aperture
Palate length	Sliding	From orale to staphylion
Palate breadth	Sliding	Maximum breadth across alveolar process between inner borders of maxilla at the second molars
Cranial base length	Spreading	From basion to prosthion

EXERCISE 3

Using the skull provided to you in class, record the following measurements in centimeters. You may work in pairs or teams, but make sure you take your own measurements.

Maximum cranial length _____

Maximum cranial breadth _____

Maximum cranial height _____

Bizygomatic breadth _____

Total face height _____

Upper face height _____

Nasal height _____

Nasal breadth _____

Palate length _____

Palate breadth _____

Cranial base length _____

Indices

After cranial and postcranial measurements are taken, the recorded values are used to calculate indices. An **index** is the ratio of one value to another, shown as a percentage. Indices are useful for describing general cranial shape, limb proportions, and inferring population variation and history. The following are three common postcranial indices (Bass, 1995); all measurements are maximum length

- **Brachial Index:** Compares relative lengths of arm and forearm (radius length/humerus length) $\times$ 100

- **Crural Index:** Compares relative lengths of thigh and lower leg (tibia length/bicondylar femur length) $\times$ 100

- **Intermembral Index:** Compares relative lengths of upper limb and lower limb [(humerus length + radius length)/(bicondylar femur length + tibia length)] $\times$ 100

Several indices may also be calculated from cranial measurements (Bass, 1995). The final value may be compared to standards to describe basic head shape:

- **Cranial Index:** provides an idea of cranial shape (maximum cranial breadth/maximum cranial length) $\times$ 100

Narrow/long-headed	up to 74.9
Average/medium-headed	75.0–79.9
Broad/round-headed	80.0–84.9
Very round-headed	85.0 and higher

■ **Cranial Length/Height Index:** provides a ratio of height to length (maximum cranial height/maximum cranial length) × 100

Low skull	up to 69.9
Average/medium	70.0–74.9
High skull	75.0 and higher

■ **Cranial Breadth/Height Index:** provides a ratio of breadth to length (maximum cranial height/maximum cranial breadth) × 100

Low skull	up to 91.9
Average/medium	92.0–97.9
High skull	98.0 and higher

■ **Total Facial Index:** provides a ratio of height of face to breadth of face (total face height/bizygomatic breadth) × 100

Very broad face	up to 79.9
Broad face	80.0–84.9
Average/medium	85.0–89.9
Narrow face	90.0–94.9
Very narrow face	95.0 and higher

■ **Nasal Index:** provides a ratio of nasal breadth to nasal height (nasal breadth/nasal height) × 100

Narrow nasal aperture	up to 47.9
Average/medium	48.0–52.9
Broad/wide nasal aperture	53.0 and higher

■ **Palatal Index:** provides a ratio of internal measurements of palate (maximum palate breadth/maximum palate length) × 100

Narrow palate	up to 79.9
Average/medium	80.0–84.9
Broad/wide palate	85.0 and higher

EXERCISE 4

The unidentified skeleton of an individual has the following postcranial measurements: Hum = 28.7, Rad = 22.95, Bicondylar Fem = 39.60, Tibia = 34.20. Calculate the following indices for this individual:

a. Brachial Index

b. Crural Index

c. Intermembral Index

EXERCISE 5

Using the following measurements from a human cranium, calculate the indices that follow:

Max. cranial length	16.6
Max. cranial breadth	13.2
Max. cranial height	12.6
Bizygomatic breadth	11.9
Total face height	10.9
Nasal height	4.64
Nasal breadth	2.35

a. Cranial Index

b. Cranial Length/Height Index

c. Cranial Breadth/Height Index

d. Total Facial Index

e. Nasal Index

Anthropometry

The previous section introduced you to modern skeletal variation and descriptions of basic cranial shape and limb proportions. **Anthropometry** is the measurement of living peoples. Many anthropologists are employed by geneticists, health agencies, the military, and manufacturers of clothing and shoes to examine the health, growth, and overall condition of living humans. This is the way world health and growth norms—such as the standards used to compare the weight and development of an infant or a toddler to a larger population—are established.

Spreading and sliding calipers, scales, flexible tapes, anthropometer rods, and skin fold calipers are commonly used for measurement of living individuals. The following list describes some of the more common measurements taken on humans.

Measurements of the Head

- **Maximum Head Length:** Taken in midline of body at maximum points corresponding to glabella (between eyes) and opisthocranion (in occipital region). *Spreading calipers.*

- **Maximum Head Width:** The widest point of head, taken in a coronal plane above ears. *Spreading calipers.*

- **Nasal Width:** Maximum width across nostril region, taken on outside of nose; be careful not to distort nasal opening. *Spreading calipers.*

- **Nasal Length:** Taken from a point corresponding to nasion (root of nose) to tip of nose. *Sliding calipers*—be careful not to use pointed ends.

- **Minimum Frontal:** A minimum measurement along base of temporal lines, just lateral and superior to eye orbits. *Spreading calipers.*

- **Total Face Height:** Taken between points corresponding to nasion (root of nose) and gnathion (bottom of chin) in the midline. *Sliding calipers*—be careful not to use pointed ends.

- **Head Circumference:** The maximum circumference of head as measured above superciliary arches (brow ridges). *Flexible tape.*

Measurements of the Post-Cranium

- **Middle Finger Length:** Taken from center of metacarpal/proximal phalanx joint to tip of finger, combining all phalanges. *Sliding calipers*—be careful not to use pointed ends.

- **Upper Arm Circumference:** Taken at widest point of arm with elbow bent slightly and muscles relaxed. *Flexible tape.*

- **Standing Height:** Taken without shoes on, maximum height of individual from top of head. *Anthropometer rod.*

- **Sitting Height:** Taken from surface of table or chair to top of head. *Anthropometer rod.*

- **Arm Length:** Taken from acromion process of scapula to styloid process of ulna. Anthropometer rod.

EXERCISE 6

Measure at least five individuals in your class and fill in the following chart:

	Student 1	Student 2	Student 3	Student 4	Student 5
Head length					
Head width					
Nasal width					
Nasal length					
Minimum frontal					
Total face height					
Head circumference					
Middle finger length					
Upper arm circumference					
Standing height					
Sitting height					
Arm length					

Forensic Anthropology

Forensic anthropology is a subfield of biological anthropology that uses biological anthropological methods to analyze human remains from a medico-legal context. *Forensic archaeology* is involved in the recovery of those remains. Generally, the human remains are partially or completely skeletonized, making an autopsy impossible. It is the job of the forensic anthropologist to describe characteristics of the skeleton (e.g., sex, age at death) that may assist in identifying the individual(s). Forensic anthropologists are trained in general anthropology and specialize in the study of the human skeleton. They may work on occasional forensic cases that come to the attention of local law enforcement (e.g., a body is found in a field) or in human rights missions (e.g., identifying individuals from mass disasters or victims of ethnic cleansing). Most forensic anthropologists have a Ph.D. in anthropology, some training in the hard sciences, which may include biology and chemistry, and work in universities as professors.

The measurements you took for the first half of this chapter are often used for metric identification of individuals. However, multiple visual indicators are found on the skeleton that assist us in identifying individuals.

Sex Determination

In humans, males are usually bigger than females. Modern humans exhibit moderate **sexual dimorphism**, which is a term that describes form differences due to sex (e.g., the mane of male lions, the tail feathers of male peacocks, and the overall robusticity of human male skeletons when compared to female skeletons). Sexual dimorphism in humans is **population specific**, meaning that levels of difference will vary depending on the population under study. Some populations, such as Native American Indians, are highly *robust* in shape due in part to a rigorous lifestyle. Other populations, such as some groups in Southeast Asia, are more *gracile* in shape or lightly built. If you compared an

Table 9-4 Sex differences in the human pelvis

Trait	Male	Female
Overall size	Large, rugged	Small, gracile
Iliac blade	High, vertical	Broad, flared
Pelvic inlet	Heart-shaped, narrow	Rounder, broad
Subpubic angle	Narrow, V-shaped	Wide, U-shaped
Greater sciatic notch	Narrow	Wide
Preauricular sulcus	Absent or straight	Straight or scalloped
Ventral arc	Absent	Present
Subpubic shape	Convex, straight	Concave
Partuition scars (pregnancy scars)	Absent	Present sometimes
Shape of sacrum	Narrow, curved	Wide, straight

Table 9-5 Sex differences in the human skull

Trait	Male	Female
Mastoid process	Large, projecting	Smaller, less projecting
Superciliary arch/glabella	Large, projecting	Smaller, smoother
Supraorbital margin	Smooth, rounded	Sharp
Nuchal lines	Rugged, hook	Smoother, no hook
Palate	Deep	Shallow
Chin	Square, broad	Narrow, pointed

American Indian female to a Southeast Asian male, the female may look larger than the male! So one must be careful not to compare males and females on size alone but to compare them on shape differences. Clearly, it helps to know from which population an individual comes.

It is quite common in society today to refer to one's *sex* as *gender*. These terms are not interchangeable. Sex refers to one's biological traits that are heritable, whether an individual is born as a male or a female. Gender refers to the behaviorally, culturally, and psychologically determined traits typically associated with one sex, which may take years to develop and relate to the attitudes, beliefs, and roles with which an individual determines his or her level of masculinity or femininity. An anthropologist analyzing skeletal remains cannot determine gender from a skeleton.

The best areas for estimation of sex are the skull and the pelvis. The pelvis can accurately determine sex 90% to 95% of the time, while the skull is accurate 80% to 90% of the time. Tables 9-4 and 9-5 describe the traits on the pelvis and skull that are most helpful for sex determination (Krogman, 1962; Phenice, 1969).

EXERCISE 7

Why do you think the pelvis provides higher accuracy in sex estimation?

_____

_____

_____

_____

EXERCISE 8

a. An unknown individual exhibits a rugged nuchal region with no hook, a broad square chin, smooth supraorbital margins, and a palate that is indeterminate. What is the sex of this individual? _____

_____

b. An unknown individual exhibits a ventral arc, wide subpubic concavity, and wide sciatic notch. What is the sex of this individual?_____

_____

c. An unknown individual exhibits a narrow sciatic notch, a scalloped preauricular sulcus, parity pits, a concave subpubic region, large mastoid processes, and a rugged nuchal area. What sex do you think this individual was? Why? _____

_____

_____

EXERCISE 9

Examine the casts or skeletons set up in your lab. What is the sex of each individual? List at least one feature that helped you make this determination.

Individual #1   _____

Individual #2   _____

Individual #3   _____

Individual #4   _____

Individual #5   _____

Population Affinity: Ancestry or Race

In assisting law enforcement to identify individuals, forensic anthropologists are responsible for estimating as much information from a skeleton as possible. One trait that helps law enforcement to identify missing persons is **race** (ethnicity or ancestry). *Race* is a complicated term in biological anthropology, fraught with controversy. Anthropologists distinguish between **biological race** and **social race**. Human populations are characterized by biological adaptations to local environments—cold, sunlight, altitude, and so on—that affect the way individuals in that environment appear, such as skin color or nose form. However, because these differences are due to adaptations to different and local environments, they do not follow simple continental boundaries. Anthropologists identify this type of variation as **clinal variation**. A **cline** is a gradient of genotypes over geographical space (think of a temperature map). Thus, from a *biological standpoint*, there is no justification for race because humans demonstrate gradations of variation (think of the darkest-skinned people in the world; many are from Sub-Saharan Africa, but many dark-skinned people are also found in southern India and Australia).

Socially, however, many people classify themselves into one group or another. Generally, these are broad groupings, such as White, Black, Asian, or Hispanic. However, Hispanics present an interesting example of a *social* race in the United States. People from Spain are considered White. However, determining race becomes much more complicated when considering Latin Americans. The Caribbean shows a large African influence from the slave trade, Mexico shows a large influence of indigenous (American Indian) peoples, and other

Table 9-6 Common traits for determining ancestry

Feature	Whites	Blacks	Asians
Nasal root/bridge	High, narrow	Low, rounded	Low, ridged
Nasal width	Narrow	Wide	Medium
Nasal border	Sharp sill	Guttered	Flat, sharp
Nasal spine	Large	Small	Small
Facial profile	Straight	Projecting	Intermediate
Facial shape	Narrow	Narrow	Wide
Zygomatic bone	Receding	Receding	Projecting
Brow ridges	Heavy	Small	Small
Cranial muscle markings	Rugged	Smooth	Smooth
Upper incisors	Spatulate	Spatulate	Shoveled

areas of Central America and South America show a mix of people, with a lot of admixture from Europe. However, most people from Latin America consider themselves Hispanic, even though their genetic backgrounds may be quite different. Anthropologists attempt to determine biological race to assist in identifying unknown skeletal remains. Table 9-6 describes some of the basic traits that are helpful in determining one's ancestry in broad groups (Gill & Rhine, 1990; Krogman, 1962).

EXERCISE 10

a. An unknown individual exhibits a guttered nasal border, a wide nasal width, and smooth cranial muscle markings. What is the likely ancestry of this individual? _____

_____

b. An unknown individual exhibits a projecting zygomatic bone and shoveled upper incisors. What is the likely ancestry of this individual?

_____

c. An unknown individual exhibits small brow ridges and smooth cranial muscle markings. Can you determine the ancestry of this individual? Why or why not? _____

_____

_____

_____

EXERCISE 11

Examine the casts or skeletons set up in your lab. What is the race of each individual? List at least one feature that helped you make this determination.

Individual #1   _____

Individual #2   _____

Individual #3   _____

Individual #4   _____

Individual #5   _____

Table 9-7 Epiphyseal fusion rates for males (Buikstra & Ubelaker, 1994)

Bone	Segment	Age
Clavicle	Sternal end	19–30
Humerus	Head	14–23
	Distal end	11–16
	Medial epicondyle	11–16
Radius	Proximal end	14–18
	Distal end	17–22
Scapula	Acromion	14–22
Femur	Head	15–19
	Greater trochanter	16–20
	Lesser trochanter	15–19
	Distal end	14–21
Tibia	Proximal end	15–22
	Distal end	15–19
Fibula	Proximal end	14–21
	Distal end	15–21
Sacrum	Begins caudally	17–25
Os coxae	Ilium/ischium/pubis	13–15
	Iliac crest	14–22

Age at Death Estimation: Juvenile

It is much easier to determine the age of juveniles than adults. Juvenile age determination is based on the fusion of the cranial elements (primary centers of ossification), fusion of the long bones (epiphyses) and dental development and eruption. The primary centers of ossification in the infant cranium fuse at known rates. The bones of the skull are separated by gaps, called **fontanelles**, which allow room for brain growth prior to complete fusion of the cranial bones. The *anterior fontanelle* fuses during the second year of life; the *posterior fontanelle* fuses during the first year of life. The *mandible* halves fuse during the second year, while the *frontal bone* fuses in the midline also during the second year. The *occipital bone* begins as four separate parts: the *squamous* portion fuses to the condylar regions during the fifth year of life, and the *condylar* regions fuse to the basilar part during the sixth year of life (Stewart, 1979).

Recall from Chapter 6 that the shaft of the long bone (diaphysis) and the epiphyses are separated at birth. These segments fuse at known rates and are reported in Table 9-7 for males. Females generally mature more quickly than males, and one to two years may be subtracted from the ranges for female skeletons. However, due to the difficulty of determining sex from juvenile remains, one may not know the sex *a priori*. Dental formation and eruption are generally more reliable than fusion for determining age because fusion may be influenced by nutritional deficiencies or disease.

EXERCISE 12

What is the age of a skull demonstrating complete fusion of fontanelles, mandible, and frontal bone with an unfused occipital bone? _____

EXERCISE 13

Examine the information in Table 9-7. What is the age of an individual who exhibits complete fusion of the three portions of the os coxae, and the distal humerus, but whose humeral head is completely unfused? _____

_____

EXERCISE 14

Examine the casts and/or skeletal material set up for you in lab. What is the approximate age of each individual?

Individual #1   _____

Individual #2   _____

Individual #3   _____

Individual #4   _____

Individual #5   _____

Age at Death Estimation: Adult

Adult age determination is more difficult because growth has ceased and all teeth are erupted. Most methods for age determination in the adult skeleton are based on degenerative changes. The pubic symphysis and auricular surface undergo changes due to advancing age. Cranial suture fusion offers another option, although the sutures exhibit a wide amount of variation in their fusion rates and are not considered as helpful in determining age.

The changes to the pubic symphyseal face were first described by Todd in 1920. The method was revised by subsequent researchers, and today the most common method for age determination from the **pubic symphysis** is that of Brooks and Suchey (1990). When young, the symphyseal face demonstrates horizontal ridges and furrows (billowing) that extend throughout the entire surface. At this time, the superior and inferior extremities are not delimited. With advancing age, these ridges and furrows fill in, beginning on the dorsal surface of the symphyseal face and proceeding anteriorly. By middle age, the pubic face is flattened and has a fine-grained texture. In old age, the texture becomes pitted and eroded. As the billows are filling in, the dorsal margin of the symphyseal face forms a plateau or rim, which extends over the posterior surface of the pubic bone. The ventral (anterior) margin of the symphyseal face undergoes a slightly more complicated formation, beginning with the development of a ventral rampart (rim) that first begins inferiorly and proceeds upward, followed by a superior rampart that proceeds downward until the two portions of the rampart fuse in the middle. The ventral rampart is actively forming in middle age and completed by advanced middle age. The formation of the dorsal plateau and the ventral rampart create an oval rim around the pubic symphyseal face by middle age. With old age, the rim begins to break down and the margins may curl outward, which is known as *lipping*.

Age estimation from changes on the **auricular surface** of the ilium was described by Lovejoy et al. (1985) and Meindl et al. (1985). The region may be divided into three regions: *apex* (anterior–superior edge), *auricular surface,* and *retroauricular area* (region behind the auricular surface). In young individuals, the auricular surface is characterized by transverse organization. This transverse organization begins as gentle billows, followed by more pronounced striae, or lines, that are eventually lost with age. The texture transforms from a fine grain to a coarse grain with age, which will give way to dense bone. Young individuals will exhibit little if any porosity; however, microporosity increases with age, so eventually individuals will exhibit larger macroporosity. The apex breaks down with age, losing its definition. The retroauricular area may be flat or wavy during young adulthood; however, with age this region becomes rough and coarse with bony outgrowths, called *osteophytes,* with age.

EXERCISE 15

Determine whether the following descriptions refer to a young adult, middle-aged adult, or old adult.

Pubic symphysis: Oval outline complete _____

Pubic symphysis: Prominent billowing _____

Pubic symphysis: Flattened face with fine-grained texture _____

Auricular surface: Rough retroauricular area with osteophytes _____

Auricular surface: Fine-grained texture _____

Auricular surface: Gentle billowing _____

EXERCISE 16

Examine the casts and/or skeletal material set up for you in lab. What is the approximate age of each individual?

Individual #1 _____

Individual #2 _____

Individual #3 _____

Individual #4 _____

Individual #5 _____

Pre-Lab Questions

1. The measurement of skeletal remains assists in the determination of:
   a. sex
   b. nutritional status
   c. stature
   d. all of the above

2. The osteometric board is used to measure:
   a. long bone length
   b. cranial breadth
   c. cranial height
   d. palate length

3. Stature was first determined in the 1950s by:
   a. Jantz
   b. Trotter and Gleser
   c. Darwin
   d. Watson and Crick

4. The cranial landmark located at the intersection of the coronal and sagittal sutures is:

   a. basion   c. glabella

   b. bregma   d. gnathion

5. The index that compares the relative lengths of the upper and lower limb is the:

   a. intermembral index   c. brachial index

   b. crural index   d. cranial index

6. The field of study that uses the methods of biological anthropology to assist in identifying individuals from a medico-legal context is:

   a. osteometry   c. anthropometry

   b. forensic archaeology   d. forensic anthropology

7. A ventral arc is found in:

   a. males   c. both sexes

   b. females   d. neither sex

8. Age determination from the pubic symphysis was first described in 1920 by:

   a. Brooks and Suchey   c. Lovejoy et al.

   b. Todd   d. Trotter and Gleser

9. **True or False:** The way people classify themselves into an ethnic group when they are alive is their social race.

10. **True or False:** The fontanelles fuse immediately after birth because most brain growth is finished by that time.

Post-Lab Questions

1. Which bone most commonly provides the best estimate of stature? How do the standard errors of the upper limb compare to the standard errors of the lower limb? Why do you think there is a difference?

_____

_____

_____

_____

_____

2. An unknown skeleton has been identified as a Black male. Answer the following questions with these maximum lengths for the long bones: Hum = 31.05, Rad = 23.75, Uln = 25.80, Fem = 41.65, Tib = 36.05, Fib = 34.95.

   a. Calculate the stature of this individual in feet and inches using the appropriate equations from Table 9-1.

   _____

   _____

   _____

   _____

   b. An error was made in sex determination and the individual was later identified as a Black female. Calculate stature using the preceding measurements and this new information. _____

   _____

   _____

   _____

   c. Which bone(s) provide(s) the best estimate of stature? Does this differ depending on the sex of the individual? _____

   _____

   _____

   _____

   _____

3. Using the postcranial measurements you took in class for Exercise 1, assume that the individual you measured was a White male.

   a. Using the equations provided in Table 9-1, calculate the stature of this individual from each of the long bones. _____

   _____

   _____

   _____

b. Now determine the stature of this individual assuming the person was a Black male. _____

_____

_____

_____

c. How do the estimates differ? _____

_____

_____

_____

d. Which bone(s) provide(s) the best estimate? Does this differ depending on whether the individual was of White or Black ancestry? _____

_____

_____

_____

_____

4. Maximum lengths of the long bones are recorded as follows: Hum = 31.05, Rad = 23.75, Tib = 36.05, Bicondylar Fem = 41.50. Calculate the following indices using these measurements.

a. brachial index _____

_____

_____

_____

b. crural index _____

_____

_____

_____

c. intermembral index _____

_____

_____

_____

5. Using the postcranial measurements you took in class for Exercise 1, calculate the following indices for the individual.

a. brachial index _____

_____

_____

_____

b. crural index _____

_____

_____

c. intermembral index _____

_____

_____

6. Using these measurements from a human cranium, calculate the following indices:

Max. cranial length   18.3

Max. cranial breadth   13.3

Max. cranial height   13.7

Bizygomatic breadth   13.1

Total face height   13.1

Nasal height   5.48

Nasal breadth   2.33

a. Cranial Index _____

_____

_____

_____

b. Cranial Length/Height Index _____

_____

_____

c. Cranial Breadth/Height Index _____

_____

_____

d. Total Facial Index _____

_____

_____

e. Nasal Index _____

_____

_____

7. Using the cranial measurements you took in class for Exercise 3, calculate the following indices for the individual.

a. Cranial Index _____

_____

_____

_____

b. Cranial Length/Height Index _____

_____

_____

_____

c. Cranial Breadth/Height Index _____

_____

_____

_____

d. Total Facial Index _____

_____

_____

_____

e. Nasal Index _____

_____

_____

_____

8. Using the anthropometric measurements you took in class for Exercise 6, was there a difference between the male and female students you measured? Why or why not? _____

_____

_____

_____

9. Would you expect a difference between left and right arm circumference? Why or why not?

_____

_____

_____

_____

10. Can you think of any variables that might affect an individual's height? _____

_____

_____

_____

11. An unknown individual exhibits a narrow sciatic notch, a lack of a ventral arc, and a narrow subpubic concavity. What sex is this individual? Would your determination of sex differ if this individual also had small mastoid processes, a smooth nuchal region, and a smooth brow? Why or why not?

_____

_____

_____

_____

_____

12. A fragmented cranium is found washed up from a local cemetery after a flood. You are able to determine that it has a sharp supraorbital margin, small mastoid processes, and a sharp nasal sill with a prominent nasal spine. What was the likely sex and ancestry of this individual? _____

_____

_____

_____

13. How would you expect the bones of two children to compare: one from a middle-class U.S. family and the second from a rural Central American village that suffered periodic malnutrition? Do you think they would have the same stature? How might any differences in their skeletons affect age estimation form the long bones and dentition? _____

_____

_____

_____

14. How might the os coxae of a 40-year-old woman who has had six children compare to the os coxae of a 40-year-old woman who has never had any children? How might any differences in their pelves affect age estimation? _____

_____

_____

_____

Primate Classification

After completing this chapter you should be able to:

1. explain the difference between common names and scientific names;

2. define *Linnaeus, binomial nomenclature, taxonomy, phylogeny, homology, analogy, cladistics, evolutionary taxonomy, species;*

3. identify the traits that link the mammals together when compared to other classes;

4. identify and describe the traits that link the primates as a taxon within the Mammalia;

5. describe the differences between the two schools of classification of the primate order; and

6. identify and describe the differences between a prosimian and an anthropoid; a New World monkey and an Old World monkey; a monkey and an ape.

Introduction

Every day, we classify the objects and organisms around us. You may recognize a dog or a cat on the street, in the park, or in your home. However, there are several different kinds of dogs—poodles, collies, greyhounds, pit bulls, among others—so it helps to refine our classification by mentioning the breed of dog, which provides more information. These familiar terms are **common names**. Scientists from around the world do not speak the same language. The common name *border collie* would likely be unfamiliar to a Russian or Chinese biologist. Sometimes the same organism even goes by a different name within our own language and culture, such as a *woodchuck* or a *groundhog*. The same common name might even refer to many different organisms, such as the more than 200 different flowers called *irises* and several different species of fish called *snapper*. Due to these various inconsistencies and language differences, scientists throughout the world use **scientific names** that are unique to each organism.

In biology, the system of classification that we use today was developed by the Swedish naturalist Carolus **Linnaeus** (1707–1778). Using the Latin language, Linnaeus named and classified all plants and animals by means of a two-part naming system called **binomial nomenclature**. The binomial consists of the *genus* name (plural: *genera*) and the *species* name. For example, humans are classified as *Homo sapiens,* lions are classified as *Pantera leo,* and wolves are classified as *Canis lupus.* For proper notation, the genus name is always capitalized, the species name is not. Both terms should be italicized or underlined. The scientific name includes both the genus and the species names for an organism. Linnaeus also established a hierarchical system of classification above the genus and species levels. Groups at any level may be referred to as a **taxon** (plural: *taxa*). Using humans as an example, this system includes the following:

Kingdom	Animalia
Phylum	Chordata
Class	Mammalia
Order	Primates
Family	Hominidae
Genus	*Homo*
Species	*sapiens*

These levels are further divided into other categories, such as suborders, superfamilies, and subfamilies. At each level, organisms are grouped by traits they have in common with each other due to shared ancestry. The more closely related two organisms are to each other, the more categories they will share.

EXERCISE 1

Use a binomial system to classify the immediate members of your family (mother, father, siblings). Write their names in the spaces provided so that your system reflects the system used to designate species (e.g., the author of this book would be *Hens samantha*, her brother would be *Hens joseph*).

_____

_____

_____

_____

_____

_____

EXERCISE 2

If someone owns a large music collection composed of different styles of music, how might they classify and group their collection? _____

_____

_____

Taxonomy and Phylogeny

Taxonomy is the science of classification and nomenclature, or categorizing and naming, respectively. Biologists and biological anthropologists prefer to use a system that groups organisms together on the basis of shared descent. Classification schemes that utilize **phylogeny**, a system that indicates the evolutionary relationships among the organisms under consideration, is considered superior to just grouping organisms because they look similar to one another. Some organisms may resemble one another because they share a common adaptation, such as sharks and dolphins, which share a streamlined body useful for maneuvering through the water, although they are not closely related (sharks are fish, and dolphins are mammals, separated by millions of years of evolution), or birds and butterflies, which both have wings used for adaptation to flying through the air (birds are vertebrates, butterflies are invertebrates). In these examples, the body shape of the sharks and dolphins and the wings of butterflies and birds are **analogous characters**, or analogous traits, that are shared among organisms because they have a common adaptation but not a recent common ancestor and arise as a result of *convergent evolution*. Thus, these organisms may look similar, but they are not closely related. Analogous traits should be avoided when classifying organisms in a scientific context. Traits that should be used to classify organisms under a phylogenetic scheme are **homologous characters**, or traits that are shared by organisms because they have a recent common ancestor—that is, they inherited the traits from their ancestors.

Scientists regularly argue over which traits or characters are the most important for classification. This has led to two schools of classification (Mayr, 1981):

1. **Cladistics:** Cladists base their classifications on evolutionary lineages. All groups that are descended from the same common ancestor should be grouped together. Cladistic classifications are based heavily on *shared, derived characters,* which are evolved from *primitive characters* seen in ancient ancestors. Cladists discount change along a lineage and are interested primarily in branching events, or *cladogenesis.*

2. **Evolutionary taxonomy:** This school of thought considers the evolutionary lineage of an organism but also places importance on change that may occur along a lineage—*anagenetic* evolution—over time.

Primate Taxonomy

All primates are mammals. Numerous features link mammals as a class and separate them from other classes, such as the amphibians and reptiles. All mammals have numerous traits in common:

- Hair
- Homeothemy (warm-blooded)

- Lactation (breast feeding)
- Defined or distinct epiphyses (allow a range of motion at the joint)
- One lower jawbone on either side of the midline
- **Diphyodont** dentition (two sets of teeth: deciduous and permanent)
- Four-chambered heart with separation of oxygenated and deoxygenated blood

A **species** has been defined by biologist Ernst Mayr (1942, 1963) as a group of potentially interbreeding organisms in nature that are capable of having fertile offspring. About 250 species of primate are currently recognized. The smallest primate is the mouse lemur, weighing in at 2 ounces (40 g), while the largest primate is the adult male gorilla, which weighs approximately 450 pounds (200 kg). The primates display an enormous range of diversity, not only in body size but also in diet, locomotion, coat color, habitat, and group social structure. However, all primates have grasping hands, large brains, and an emphasis on learned behavior. Primates may be separated from the other mammals by a suite of traits that they share in common. The traits may be grouped into two clusters: anatomical traits and behavioral or life-history traits.

The *anatomical traits* shared by primates emphasize the importance of vision rather than the sense of smell, along with the excellent grasping ability seen in the hands and feet, which are traits that are essential for **arboreality** or tree-living, and include the following:

- Five digits on the hands and feet
- **Prehensility** (grasping ability) of the hands and feet with **opposability** (having a thumb or big toe that can touch the other four digits in the hand or foot, respectively)
- Nails, instead of claws
- Clavicles
- Emphasis on vision, including forward-facing eyes with *binocular* (overlapping) and *stereoscopic* (depth perception) vision
- Generalized dental pattern, including incisors, canines, premolars, and molars
- Reduction of the snout and sense of smell
- Enclosed eye orbits, which may be complete or partial (a **postorbital bar**)

Primates mature and reproduce slowly, live long lives, and are strongly reliant on learned behavior rather than instinct. The *behavioral traits,* or life-history traits, shared by the primates emphasize these characters and include the following:

- Single offspring for most
- Extended juvenile periods
- Large brains
- Dependence on learned behavior
- Mother–infant bond
- Adult males usually associated with the group

EXERCISE 3

Examine the casts in the laboratory comparing the anatomical traits of a non-primate mammal to a primate skeleton. Fill in the following chart.

	Nonprimate Skeleton	**Primate Skeleton**
Grasping hands/feet?		
Opposable big toe/thumb?		
Nails or claws?		
Five digits?		
Clavicle?		
Orbital closure?		
Reduced snout?		

The primate order is divided into two suborders (Fleagle, 1998; Groves, 2001). Using a traditional scheme based on anatomy and evolutionary taxonomy, these suborders are the **Prosimii** (lemurs, lorises, and tarsiers) and the **Anthropoidea** (monkeys, apes, and humans). A more modern classification groups the taxa into the **Strepsirhini** (lemurs and lorises) and the **Haplorhini** (tarsiers, monkeys, apes, and humans). Figure 10-1 illustrates both taxonomic groupings.

At first glance, it may seem that the Prosimii (or prosimians, the "lower primates") are the same as the Strepsirhini, or the strepsirhine primates. However, the tarsier is not classified with the other strepsirhines under the recent scheme and are discussed here with the haplorhines (the "higher primates"). The **lemurs** are found only on the island of Madagascar off the eastern coast of Africa and include such groups as the true lemurs, the dwarf lemurs, the indri and sifaka, and the aye-aye. The lemurs display a wide variety of diversity in diet, locomotion patterns, and social systems. The **lorises** live in tropical Africa and Asia and include animals such as the slow loris, slender loris, potto, and bush baby (or galago). All lorises and galagos are nocturnal and most are solitary. Figures 10-2 through 10-4 depict common strepsirhine (prosimian) primates. All strepsirhines share the following features:

- Longer snout with whiskers and a wet nose (**rhinarium**), reliance on smell

- Triangular, high, and sharp-cusped molars

- Mandible that is unfused in the midline

- Large, mobile ears

- A **grooming claw** on the second digit of the foot in many taxa

- Scent glands

- Nocturnality common, with associated large eye orbits

- **Tooth comb** for grooming in some, formed by the lower incisors and canines jutting forward

- **Postorbital bar**, partial orbital closure

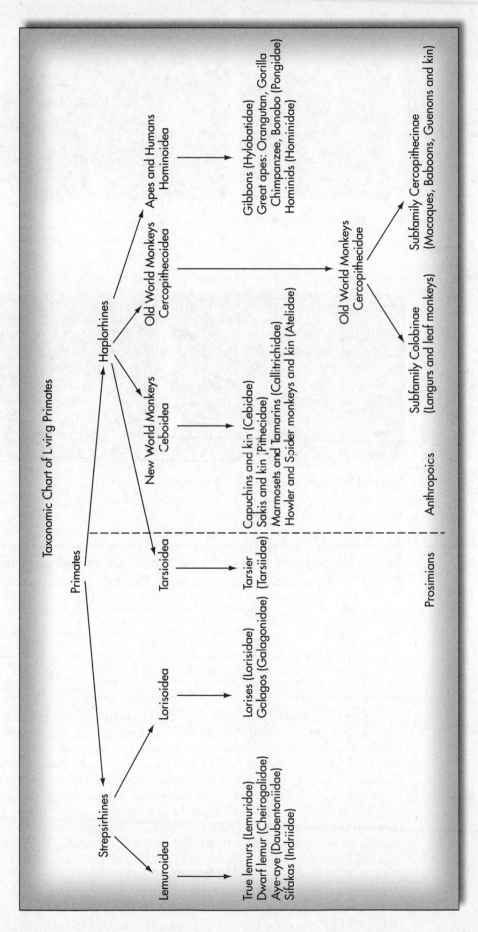

Figure 10-1 Taxonomic chart of the living primates.

Figure 10-2 *From left to right*: Ring-tailed lemur, red-bellied lemur, ruffed lemur.

Figure 10-3 A sifaka, the largest of the living lemurs.

Figure 10-4 *Left*: A loris. *Right*: A galago (bush baby).

EXERCISE 4

Examine Figures 10-2 through 10-4. Which two animals are nocturnal? How can you tell? _____

_____

_____

_____

_____

The Haplorhini are different from the Anthropoidea because of the inclusion of the tarsier in the former. The **tarsier** is a haplorhine but also a prosimian. It is closely related to the monkeys, apes, and humans and represents a link between the higher and lower primates. Tarsiers are small primates that live on the islands of Southeast Asia. They are nocturnal and have the largest eye orbits relative to head size of any living mammal. They are named for their elongated tarsal (ankle) bones, which allow them to leap through the canopy. They are insectivorous and carnivorous and eat a variety of small vertebrates, such as lizards and bird eggs. Despite their locomotion, diet, and nocturnality, which links them to the strepsirhines, tarsiers do not have many of the anatomical traits described for the lemurs and lorises, such as a rhinarium or a postorbital bar (instead they exhibit almost complete closure of the eye orbit), and they show differences in the placenta that are more similar to the higher primates, the anthropoids. Figure 10-5 illustrates the tarsier.

Figure 10-5 Tarsiers.

All Anthropoids (monkeys, apes, and humans) share the following traits:

- Generally larger body and brain size
- Reduced sense of smell, reduced snout, no rhinarium
- Diurnality, small eye orbits with complete orbital closure
- Square molar teeth with flatter cusps
- Fused mandible in the midline
- Small ears

EXERCISE 5

Examine the primate skeletons in the laboratory, comparing a prosimian/strepsirhine to an anthropoid/haplorhine. Fill in the following chart to describe the differences.

	Prosimian	Anthropoid
Prehensility?		
Opposability?		
Grooming claw?		
Five digits?		
Clavicles?		
Postorbital bar/complete closure?		
Size of orbits?		
Snout length?		
Tooth comb?		
Molar tooth cusps?		
Fused mandible?		

As illustrated in Figure 10-1, the Anthropoidea are divided into three superfamilies: the Ceboidea (New World monkeys), the Cercopithecoidea (Old World monkeys), and the Hominoidea (apes and humans). The **Ceboidea** include all the nonhuman primates in the Americas, all of which are monkeys. All ceboids are classified into the infraorder *Platyrrhini,* which indicates that their nose is broad and flat with widely spaced nostrils (platyrrhine nose).

Figure 10-6 *Clockwise from top left*: Golden lion tamarin, uakari, spider monkey.

They live in Mexico and South America. All **New World monkeys** are arboreal; all are diurnal, but one, the exception being the aptly named owl monkey. New World monkeys are small, ranging from approximately 1 pound (< 1 kg) to 25 pounds (12 kg). All New World monkeys have three premolars, giving them a 2.1.3.3. dental formula. While all New World monkeys have tails, some also have prehensile tails. Researchers have classified the Ceboidea into two to four taxonomic families, including the capuchins, the sakis, the howler and spider monkeys, and the marmosets and tamarins (Figure 10-6).

EXERCISE 6

Examine the illustrations of New World monkeys in Figure 10-6. Which monkey displays a prehensile tail? _____

How would you describe the shape of the nose visible in the uakari and the tamarin? _____
_____
_____
_____
_____

How do the noses in the New World monkeys above compare to the noses seen in Figures 10-2 through 10-4, which depict strepsirhines? _____

_____

_____

_____

_____

What do you notice about the location of each animal? Are they found in the trees or on the ground? _____

_____

_____

_____

The **Cercopithecoidea** includes all the **Old World monkeys**. All belong to the infraorder *catarrhini*, indicating that the nose is narrow, with nostrils close together and pointing downward. The Cercopithecoids live across the continents of Africa and Asia, in various habitats ranging from tropical forests and savannas, to snowy Japan. Some Old World monkeys spend considerable time on the ground, while others occupy arboreal habitats. All have two

Figure 10-7 Old World monkeys belonging to the subfamily Colobinae. *Clockwise from top left*: black and white colobus monkey, red colobus monkey, Hanuman langurs.

Figure 10-8 Common Old World monkeys belonging to the subfamily Cercopithecinae. *From left to right*: baboons, DeBrazza's monkey (a guenon), and the rare lion-tailed macaque.

premolars in each quadrant of the mouth, for a dental formula of 2.1.2.3. Their molars are called **bilophodont** because they have a unique design, where the cusps form two ridges for shearing leaves and other plant material. While the Old World monkeys have tails, their tails are never prehensile. They also exhibit **ischial callosities**, which are thickened calluses for sitting on the rump. Some species are **sexually dimorphic**, indicating that males are larger than females, especially in body size and canine size. The Old World monkeys are separated into two subfamilies, the *Cercopithecinae* and the *Colobinae*. The colobine monkeys have a sacculated stomach for breaking down the cellulose found in leaves. Colobine monkeys include the langurs and various groups called the leaf monkeys. The cercopithecine monkeys include the macaques, baboons, guenons, mangabeys, and patas monkeys. Figure 10-7 illustrates some of the common Old World monkeys belonging to the colobine subfamily. Figure 10-8 illustrates some of the cercopithecine monkeys.

EXERCISE 7

How do the Old World monkeys pictured in Figures 10-7 and 10-8 compare to the New World monkeys in terms of location? _____

_____

_____

_____

How would you describe the differences in the nose shape of the lion-tailed macaque and the golden lion tamarin? _____

Old = catrin nos

N.v. outward

Are any of the monkeys pictured above nocturnal? How can you tell?

_____

_____

_____

_____

EXERCISE 8

Examine the pictures and/or skeletons in the lab. Fill in the following chart to compare New World monkeys to Old World monkeys.

	New World Monkey	Old World Monkey
Nose shape/septum width		FAce doun
Prehensile tail?	X	
Dental formula	2.1.3 3	2.1.32
Arboreal/terrestrial?		
Diurnal/nocturnal?	DiurNAl	

The final superfamily within the Anthropoidea is the **Hominoidea**. The **apes** and **humans** have much in common with the Cercopithecoids, including a catarrhine nose, a 2.1.2.3 dental formula, and sexual dimorphism. However, numerous traits distinguish the apes from the monkeys. In apes, the thorax is broad from side to side, not deep anteriorly–posteriorly as it is in monkeys. Apes do not have a tail, most ape species have a larger body size, and apes have long arms and shorter legs, indicating that all generally use some sort of suspensory (arm-hanging) locomotion. This group includes two ape families, the **Hylobatidae** (gibbons and siamangs) and the **Pongidae** (orangutans, gorillas, chimpanzees, and bonobos), and one human family, the **Hominidae**. The apes eat a variety of fruits and leaves and have different social structures (see Chapter 12). The gibbons and siamangs live in the tropical forests of south and southeast Asia and are called the "lesser apes" due to their smaller body size. The "great apes," or Pongids, have a much larger body size. Orangutans are the other Asian apes and are found exclusively in the tropical forests of the Indonesian islands of Borneo and Sumatra. The African apes consist of the gorillas, common chimpanzees, and the bonobos, which are close cousins to the chimpanzees. The gorillas are confined to the forests of west and central Africa, the chimpanzees live in diverse habitats across equatorial Africa, and the bonobo is restricted to rain forests of the Congo. Figure 10-9 depicts four of the apes.

EXERCISE 9

How would you describe the shape of the nose in the pictures in Figure 10-9?

_____

_____

_____

_____

Describe the shape of the thorax of the langur in Figure 10-7 and the gibbon in Figure 10-9. _____

_____

_____

_____

Figure 10-9 Members of the Hominoidea. *Top row (left to right)*: white-faced gibbon, orangutan. *Middle row (left to right)*: gorilla, common chimpanzee. *Bottom row*: bonobo.

Are all the apes pictured in Figure 10-9 diurnal? How can you tell?

_____

_____

_____

_____

EXERCISE 10

Examine Figure 10-9 and the skeletons or photos in your lab. Fill in the following chart to compare the catarrhines: the Old World monkeys, the apes, and humans.

	Old World Monkey	Ape	Human
Lumbar region (long, medium, short)			
Shape of rib cage (narrow, broad)			
Forelimb length (long, short)			
Finger length (long, short)			
Tail? (yes, no)			
Molar crown shape			

Pre-Lab Questions

1. Classifying an animal as a "pit bull terrier" is an example of:
   a. a scientific name
   b. a common name
   c. a binomial
   d. phylogeny

2. Which early scientist(s) developed the system of classification that we use today?
   a. Darwin
   b. Mendel
   c. Linnaeus
   d. Watson and Crick

3. The scientific name for the orangutan is *Pongo pygmaeus*. *Pongo* is the:
   a. family name
   b. suborder name
   c. genus name
   d. species name

4. Which scientific name for the ring-tailed lemur is presented correctly?
   a. Lemur Catta
   b. Lemur catta
   c. *Lemur Catta*
   d. *Lemur catta*

5. The science of classifying and naming organisms is called:
   a. taxonomy
   b. phylogeny
   c. morphology
   d. binomial nomenclature

6. Traits that are similar to each other due to common adaptation, but not common descent, are called:
   a. binomial
   b. adaptive
   c. homologous
   d. analogous

7. Which of the following primates is more likely to be nocturnal?
   a. howler monkey
   b. loris
   c. baboon
   d. gorilla

8. Which of the following primates has a platyrrhine nose?
   a. New World monkey
   b. Old World monkey
   c. prosimian
   d. tarsier

9. **True or False:** Old World monkeys sometimes have a prehensile tail.

10. **True or False:** All New World monkeys are arboreal, but Old World monkeys show a combination of arboreality and terrestriality.

Post-Lab Questions

1. Review the organisms classified below. Which two organisms are the most closely related? Why?

	Organism 1	**Organism 2**	**Organism 3**	**Organism 4**
Order	Primates	Primates	Primates	Primates
Suborder	Haplorhini	Strepsirhini	Haplorhini	Haplorhini
Superfamily	Hominoidea	Lemuroidea	Hominoidea	Cercopithecoidea
Family	Pongidae	Lemuridae	Pongidae	Cercopithecidae
Genus	*Pongo*	*Lemur*	*Pan*	*Papio*
Species	*pygmaeus*	*catta*	*troglodytes*	*anubis*

_____

_____

_____

2. Review the organisms classified below. Which two organisms are the most closely related? Why?

	Organism 1	**Organism 2**	**Organism 3**	**Organism 4**
Order	Primates	Primates	Primates	Primates
Suborder	Haplorhini	Strepsirhini	Haplorhini	Haplorhini
Superfamily	Cercopithecoidea	Lemuroidea	Hominoidea	Cercopithecoidea
Family	Cercopithecidae	Lemuridae	Pongidae	Cercopithecidae
Genus	*Papio*	*Lemur*	*Pan*	*Papio*
Species	*cynocephalus*	*catta*	*troglodytes*	*anubis*

_____

_____

_____

3. Examine the primate photo shown here and answer the following questions.

a. Is this primate a prosimian or an anthropoid? How can you tell? Can you determine any further information about this animal? _____

_____

_____

_____

b. Is this primate diurnal or nocturnal? How can you tell? _____

_____

_____

_____

_____

4. Examine the following primate photo and answer the following questions.

a. Describe the nose shape of this primate. Based on this information, is this animal a platyrhine or a catarrhine? _____

_____

_____

_____

_____

b. Describe the shape of the thorax of this primate. Based on this information, what type primate is this?

_____

_____

_____

_____

5. Examine the following primate photo and answer the following questions.

a. Is this animal diurnal or nocturnal? How can you tell? _____

_____

_____

_____

b. Describe the type of nose seen in this animal. Based on this information, can you determine what type of primate this is? _____

_____

_____

_____

_____

c. List two visible features that illustrate the differences between a nonprimate mammal and a primate.

_____

_____

_____

_____

6. What features link the tarsier to the lemurs and lorises, supporting the view that they should be grouped together as prosimians? _____

_____

_____

_____

_____

7. Compare and contrast the following terms:

a. homology/analogy _____

_____

_____

_____

b. cladistics/evolutionary taxonomy _____

_____

_____

_____

_____

8. Match the traits on the left with their group, nonprimate mammal or primate, on the right.

_____ Claws   a. Nonprimate mammal trait

_____ Five digits   b. Primate trait

_____ Lack of opposability

__A__ Excellent sense of smell

__B__ Emphasis on vision

__B__ Diphyodont dentition

__B__ Clavicles

__B__ Enclosed eye socket

9. Match the traits on the left to the group of primates that exhibit them on the right.

_____ Tooth comb   a. Prosimian

_____ Broad thorax   b. New World Monkey

_____ Broad nose   c. Old World Monkey

__A__ Rhinarium   d. Ape

__A__ Nocturnality common

__D__ Lack of a tail

__B__ Prehensile tail

__C__ Bilophodont molars

10. Can you think of any traits that humans have that are not shared by the apes? _____

_____

_____

_____

_____

Chapter | 11

Comparative Primate Anatomy

Objectives

After completing this chapter you should be able to:

1. describe the four main types of locomotion and their subcategories;

2. identify the type of locomotion shown with articulated primate skeletons;

3. calculate approximate intermembral indices for different primates and identify the type of locomotion from these measurements;

4. identify the sexually dimorphic traits seen in different primate specimens;

5. describe the dental specializations seen in the primates and relate them to diet; and

6. identify the social structure of a primate based on their dentition.

Introduction

Chapter 10 explained that primates are linked together as a taxon because of the many traits they share in common, such as forward-facing eyes, nails, grasping hands and feet, reduced snout, clavicles, and enclosed eye orbits. Primates may be differentiated from other mammals based on these traits, and different primate groups may be identified because of details in their anatomy, such as size of the eye orbits and the dental formula. All these traits are observable in the primate skeleton, and many soft-tissue traits, such as coat color and nose shape, are also valuable for identifying primates. In this lab, you will examine the skeletal traits that assist us in determining the locomotor pattern, diet, and social structure of the primates. These analyses are essential for understanding how extinct primates, including early humans, once lived and assist us in interpreting the fossil record.

Locomotion

Primate use four major locomotor patterns. Each type of locomotion will demonstrate recognizable morphological differences in many regions of the skeleton.

1. **Quadrupedalism:** This type of locomotion involves using four limbs to support the body above the ground or a tree limb. Thus, quadrupedalism may be either arboreal (branch runner) or terrestrial. The hands may be held in numerous positions, which are often group specific: on the palm (*palmigrade*), on the fingers (*digitigrade*), on the fist, or on the middle phalanges (**knuckle-walking**). Quadrupedalism is common in many prosimian and monkey species, while knuckle-walking is specifically used by the African apes when they are on the ground. Figure 11-1 illustrates each of the types of quadrupedalism. Specific quadrupedal morphology for the prosimians and monkeys includes the following:
   - Arms and legs approximately the same length
   - Long, flexible lumbar spine
   - Usually have a tail for balance and communication
   - Deep, not broad, thorax
   - Scapula located laterally
   - Foramen magnum placed posteriorly, near rear of cranium

2. **VCL:** This type of locomotion is referred to as vertical clinging and leaping. The body is held in an upright position while the animal grasps onto the vertical trunks of the tree. The animal moves about by using its long, powerful hind limbs for jumping to another location. This locomotor pattern is common in the prosimians, such as the galago and the tarsier. A leaper is shown in Figure 11-2. Specific morphology to examine includes the following:
   - Long legs
   - Vertical body posture
   - Small to medium body size

3. **Suspension:** This type of locomotion involves supporting the body using the forelimbs to hang beneath a tree branch. Thus the body is supported under the arms. The animal moves about by a hand-over-hand grip, or "arm swinging." Suspension can divided into three types: (a) **true**

Figure 11-1 Quadrupedalism. *From left to right*: terrestrial quadrupedalism in the baboon, arboreal quadrupedalism in the lemur, hand position for knuckle-walking in the chimpanzee.

Figure 11-2 The sifaka, famous for acrobatic vertical clinging and leaping.

brachiation, exhibited only by the Hylobatidae, refers to traditional arm swinging and is very fast; (b) **semi-brachiation**, seen in both New World and Old World monkeys, is a combination of arm swinging and leaping (some New World monkeys have a prehensile tail to assist); and (c) **slow-climbing**, witnessed in the great apes, involves a slower form of locomotion wherein a combination of climbing and swinging is utilized. The orangutan is famous for **quadrumanual** locomotion or "four-handed locomotion," in which the feet are nearly indistinguishable from the hands and are used extensively. Some examples of suspension are shown in Figure 11-3. Specific morphology includes the following:

- Long upper limbs, including the fingers
- Short thumbs in the hylobatids for a hooklike hand grip
- Short, stable lumbar spine
- No tail
- Large body size, especially the slow climbers
- Broad thorax, not deep
- Scapula on dorsum of body
- Foramen magnum in intermediate location

4. **Bipedality:** Bipedality involves standing and moving on the two hind limbs. The weight of the body is supported on the hind limbs at all times and is above a firm terrestrial support, the ground. One primate uses bipedal locomotion regularly: *Homo sapiens*. Bipedality is discussed in detail in Chapter 13. For now, note the following morphology that is specific to human bipeds:

- Longer legs
- Cranium balanced on erect trunk
- Broad thorax
- Scapula on dorsum of body
- Foramen magnum centrally located under cranium
- Big toe in line with other toes (nondivergent)

hAng

——>

A. true BrAchAtion

B. semi

C. slow climing

Figure 11-3 Suspension. *Left*: chimpanzee in typical suspensory posture. *Right*: white-faced gibbon, a "true brachiator."

EXERCISE 1

a. Can you think of any reason the great apes use slow climbing as opposed to another form of suspension? _____

_____

_____

b. Can you think of any other animals that move bipedally? _____

_____

c. If you find a primate skeleton that had long hind limbs, how might you tell whether it was a VCL or a biped? _____

_____

_____

_____

EXERCISE 2

Examine the following illustration and answer the following questions:

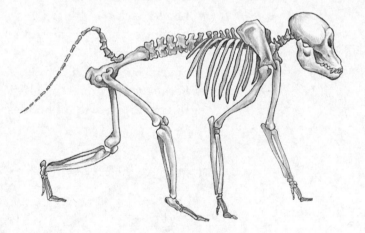

a. What is the locomotor pattern of this primate? _____

_____

b. How would you describe the hand position of this animal? _____

_____

_____

_____

c. Describe the ratio of arm to leg length in this primate. _____

_____

_____

_____

d. Give one example of a primate with this locomotor pattern. _____

_____

EXERCISE 3

Examine the following illustration and answer the following questions:

a. What is the locomotor pattern of this primate? _____

_____

b. Describe the ratio of arm to leg length in this primate. _____

_____

_____

_____

c. Give one example of a primate with this locomotor pattern. _____

_____

The **intermembral index** (IM index) is used to help determine the locomotor pattern of a primate from its skeleton. Recall the following (from Chapter 9):

$$\text{intermembral index} = \frac{\text{humerus length} + \text{radius length}}{\text{femur length} + \text{tibia length}} \times 100$$

After the IM index is calculated, the value can be compared to the following chart to determine the locomotor pattern:

IM Index	Locomotor Pattern
50–80	Bipedal or VCL
80–100	Quadrupedal
100–150	Brachiation

If the IM index identifies the animal as a quadruped, a comparison of the length of the trunk relative to the length of the limbs will indicate if the animal is primarily arboreal or terrestrial.

short limbs/long trunk = arboreal

long limbs/short trunk = terrestrial

EXERCISE 4

Using the illustration in Exercise 2, use sliding calipers to approximately measure the long bone lengths.

a. Calculate the IM index for this animal.

b. If quadrupedal, determine whether the animal is terrestrial or arboreal.

_____

_____

c. Does your answer agree with your visual inspection in Exercise 2?

_____

_____

_____

_____

EXERCISE 5

Using the illustration in Exercise 3, use sliding calipers to approximately measure the long bone lengths.

a. Calculate the IM index for this animal.

b. If quadrupedal, determine whether the animal is terrestrial or arboreal.

_____

_____

c. Does your answer agree with your visual inspection in Exercise 3?

_____

_____

_____

_____

EXERCISE 6

Using the preceding information, fill in the following table after you approximately measure the five skeletons in your lab, calculate their IM indices, and determine the locomotor pattern of each.

Primate	Humerus Length	Radius Length	Femur Length	Tibia Length	IM Index	Locomotor Pattern
Gibbon						
Squirrel monkey						
Baboon						
Tarsier						
Human						

Sexual Dimorphism

Sexual dimorphism indicates a difference between males and females. Some species may exhibit differences in overall body size, tooth size, feather color, tail length, and so on. Differences may be slight or substantial. In sexually dimorphic primates, males tend to be larger in overall body size than females, have larger canine teeth, and sometimes have a prominent sagittal crest. Figure 11-4 shows the highly dimorphic orangutan; note the huge male on the right and the smaller female on the left.

Figure 11-4 Substantial sexual dimorphism in the orangutan.

EXERCISE 7

Can you think of any animals that are sexually dimorphic outside of the primate order? _____

_____

_____

_____

_____

EXERCISE 8

Examine the following photo. Are these primates sexually dimorphic?

_____

_____

_____

_____

EXERCISE 9

Using the preceding information, compare the male and female crania of the following species for the traits listed. Indicate whether the traits in question show large, medium, or slight differences between the sexes.

	Gibbon	Orangutan	Gorilla	Chimp	Human
Canine size					
Overall size					
Sagittal crest					
Dimorphic? (large, medium, slight)					

Primate Dentition and Diet

The teeth are genetically determined and are considered strongly **genetically conservative**—that is, they do not evolve easily over time but tend to maintain their structure. The tooth surface can be altered in life by breakage, dental caries (i.e., cavities), or by dental wear, which wears away the enamel and/or dentin. The dentition provides the critical first step in ingesting and digesting food. The teeth provide insight into the type of diet an animal had during life.

Recall from previous chapters that there are four tooth types: incisors, canines, premolars, and molars. Figure 11-5 shows the number and types of teeth in a typical catarrhine primate maxilla. The number of teeth in the jaws is described by the dental formula (Stanford et al., 2006).

■ Humans are 2.1.2.3.

■ Apes are 2.1.2.3.

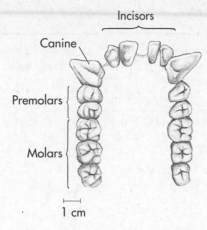

Figure 11-5 A typical catarrhine primate maxilla.

- Old World monkeys are 2.1.2.3.
- New World monkeys are 2.1.3.3.
- Prosimians are variable.

Some primate species show distinctive tooth shapes, which assist in determining diet:

- High, sharp cusps with pointed incisors indicate an insectivorous diet.
- Low, rounded cusps with broad, flat incisors indicate a fruit-eating diet (**frugivore**).
- Molar teeth with ridges (crests) for shearing, indicate a leaf-eating diet (**folivore**).
- Teeth with molar crests are called **bilophodont molars** and are common in many Old World monkeys.
- Prosimians often show a **tooth comb**—that is, lower incisors and canines jut forward, forming a single structural complex.

EXERCISE 10

What is the dental formula of the primate shown in the following illustration?

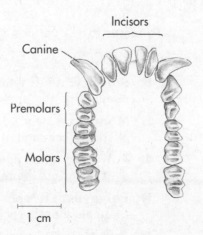

EXERCISE 11

Examine the dental arcade of the primates set out by your instructor, count the tooth types, and fill in the dental formulae in the following table for these or similar primates.

Animal	Dental Formula
Lemur	
Squirrel monkey	
Rhesus monkey	
Baboon	
Gorilla	
Orangutan	
Cat	

EXERCISE 12

Examine the primate teeth or teeth of similar primates set out by your instructor, and indicate the cusp shape and probable diet in the following table.

Primate	Cusp Shape	Diet
Tarsier		
Stump-tailed macaque		
Chimpanzee		
Marmoset		
Human		

Social Structure

Primates live in various social groups including the following (Stanford et al., 2006):

- **Solitary:** Adult females will also have their dependent offspring, common among the prosimians.
- **Monogamy:** One adult male and one adult female with their dependent offspring, common in gibbons.
- **Polyandry:** One adult female and two or three adult males with dependent offspring, common in marmosets and tamarins.
- **Polygyny:** Multiple adult males and females with dependent offspring, common in anthropoids, especially baboons and chimpanzees.
- **One Male Polygyny** (*sometimes* **Two Male Polygny**): A harem structure with one or two adult breeding males with several adult females and dependent offspring, common in gorillas and Hanuman langurs.

One can also sometimes determine social structure from the teeth, in particular the canine. Large, projecting canines are indicative of polygynous groups in which males compete for females. This is common in one or two male polygynous groups and polygynous multi-male/multi-female groups. Small canines that do not project are indicative of groups with little or no male–male competition. These groups are often monogamous (or sometimes multi-male/multi-female). It is important to compare the canines of both sexes to determine social structure, as both sexes may have large canines!

EXERCISE 13

Examine the dental arcades of *both sexes* of these primates and report their canine size and probable social structure in the following table.

Primate	Male Canine	Female Canine	Probable Social Group
Gorilla			
Gibbon			
Chimpanzee			
Baboon			

Pre-Lab Questions

1. Using all four limbs to support the body over a horizontal support is called:
   a. suspension
   b. true brachiation
   c. quadrupedalism
   d. VCL

2. Which of the following is not a type of suspension?
   a. true brachiation
   b. semi-brachiation
   c. leaping
   d. slow-climbing

3. Primates known to knuckle-walk when on the ground include the:
   a. African apes
   b. gibbons
   c. New World monkeys
   d. galago

4. Which primate has a reduced thumb for a hook-like hand grip while brachiating?
   a. chimpanzee
   b. orangutan
   c. sifaka
   d. gibbon

5. The intermembral index is useful for determining:
   a. diet
   b. locomotion
   c. sexual dimorphism
   d. social structure

6. Bilophodont molars are used for shearing:
   a. fruit
   b. meat
   c. insects
   d. leaves

7. Low, rounded cusps indicate a diet of:
   a. fruit
   b. leaves
   c. insects
   d. meat

8. Large sexually dimorphic canines indicate a social structure that is:

   a. polyandrous

   c. monogamous

   b. polygynous

   d. multi-male bachelor groups

9. **True or False:** All New World monkeys have the dental formula 2.1.2.3.

10. **True or False:** Animals that are sexually dimorphic may exhibit differences in canine size between males and females.

Post-Lab Questions

1. Examine the following illustration and answer these questions:

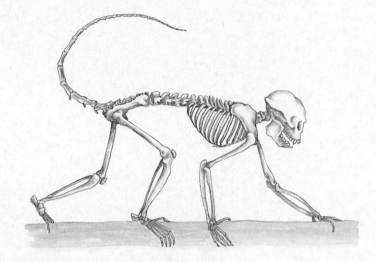

a. What is the locomotor pattern of this primate? _____
_____

b. Describe the ratio of arm to leg length in this primate. _____
_____
_____
_____

c. Give one example of a primate with this locomotor pattern. _____
_____

d. Using a simple ruler for measurements, calculate the IM index for this animal. _____
_____
_____
_____

e. If quadrupedal, determine whether the animal is terrestrial or arboreal. _____
_____

f. Does your answer agree with your visual inspection? _____
_____
_____
_____

2. Examine the following illustration and answer these questions:

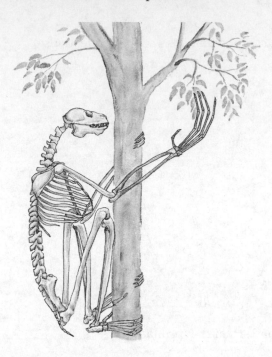

a. What is the locomotor pattern of this primate? _____
_____

b. Describe the ratio of arm to leg length in this primate. _____
_____
_____
_____

c. Give one example of a primate with this locomotor pattern. _____
_____

d. Using a simple ruler for measurements, calculate the IM index for this animal. _____
_____
_____
_____
_____

e. If quadrupedal, determine whether the animal is terrestrial or arboreal. _____
_____

f. Does your answer agree with your visual inspection? _____
_____
_____
_____

3. What form of locomotion is being used by the animal shown in the following illustration? Write your answer under the photo.

_____

4. Are the following primates exhibiting sexual dimorphism? Why or why not?

_____

_____

_____

_____

5. Match the tooth shape/cusp pattern on the left with the diet on the right.

_____ Low, rounded cusps   a. Leaves

_____ High, sharp cusps   b. Fruit

_____ Bilophodont molars   c. Insects

6. Explain why large canines may indicate a polygynous social structure. _____

_____

_____

_____

Primate Behavior

After completing this chapter you should be able to:

1. contrast r-selection and k-selection;

2. understand how the field of sociobiology is used in primatology to explain social structure;

3. describe the differences in male and female reproductive strategies and how their reproductive success is limited;

4. distinguish between aggressive behavior, threat displays, and affiliative behaviors;

5. name some ecological factors that also influence primate society;

6. discuss the ability of primates to demonstrate culture and tool use;

7. discuss the variables involved in observing primates in a free-ranging versus a captive environment; and

8. complete a primate observation study of your own at a local zoo.

Primate Sociality

Recall from Chapter 10 that the primate order exhibits many behavioral traits related to life history that link different species together as a group. Primates mature and reproduce slowly, usually with single births, and infants are cared for closely by the mother and carried everywhere, creating a strong mother–infant bond. The extended juvenile period allows a prominent emphasis on learning rather than instinct. Primates are **k-selected**, meaning that they have few offspring and spend a substantial amount of time caring for their young. Many other animals are **r-selected**, indicating that they have many offspring and invest little time in the care or raising of their young—for example, snakes, insects, and fish. **Sociobiology** is a field of research that studies the impact of natural selection on behavior. The logic is that if morphology is under selection, why not behavior? All behaviors have a genetic and an environmental component, and an individual with successful behavioral adaptations should survive longer and produce more young, increasing reproductive fitness (Williams, 1966; Wilson, 1975).

Primatologists interested in a sociobiological approach to primate behavior and group structure examine the differences between male and female **reproductive strategies**. A female primate is limited in her reproductive success by access to food. She requires nourishing food not only for herself but also to maintain a healthy pregnancy, nurse her newborn infants, and assist her weaned offspring in finding food. Thus, the more food she obtains, the more likely she is to have larger, healthier offspring. On the other hand, males are not limited in their reproductive success by access to food sources. A male need only obtain enough food for himself. Males thus expend their energy in competition for mates. This explains the **evolution of sexual dimorphism**. Many male primates have larger canines and body size than the females of their species. Males compete for access to females during a female's **estrus**, or peak fertility time. In some species, selection favors males that are larger and/or stronger than other males, who can succeed in an aggressive encounter.

The most common primate community has a core of related females who bond together along family lines to defend food sources, such as fruit trees. The savanna baboons of East Africa provide an excellent example. These primates have large multi-male/multi-female groups with a stable core of related females (*matrilines*) at their center. Upon maturity, a female attains the rank immediately below her mother, while male offspring move to another group in which they may attain rank through competition with other males. High-ranking individuals of both sexes may displace lower-ranking individuals from food resources. Higher-ranking males get more mating at peak estrus than lower-ranking males, suggesting that high-ranking males have higher fitness. Figure 12-1 depicts two male baboons in competition.

The savanna baboons also demonstrate the **dominance hierarchies** witnessed in some primate groups. Dominant individuals, both male and female, have priority access to food resources and regularly establish order within the group. Increasing dominance, especially in males, may lead to **aggressive behavior** but oftentimes actually decreases the amount of violence in the group through a series of **threat displays**. Often, only a threat gesture, including gestures such as blinking, yawning, or showing the genitals, is enough to exert control and decrease tension in the group! Gorilla males often threaten

Figure 12-1 Male–male competition among baboons.

others by slapping their chests and tearing up vegetation, while chimpanzee males regularly exhibit hair bristling, screaming, and running around in an effort to intimidate other males. **Affiliative behavior** promotes group cohesion and individual submission, and the most important probably is **grooming**. Grooming is common to most primate groups and involves combing through an individual's hair with the fingers and picking out parasites. Grooming is performed by almost all individuals within the group. Dominant individuals groom subordinates, and vice versa; adults may groom juveniles, and juveniles groom adults; males and females groom each other. This behavior promotes comfort and calm in the group and seems to be enjoyed by everyone.

While reproductive strategies clearly affect social structure, primate societies are also influenced by an animal's body size, the distribution of food resources, diet, and predation. Viewing primates within their natural habitat is possible through **ecology**, which studies the interconnectedness of animals with their physical environment. None of the apes have related females at the core of their society, thus different ecological factors centering on diet and predation are likely working in these groups. In Exercise 1, the ecology and environment of four ape species are described. The gibbons live in monogamous families; orangutans are semi-solitary; gorillas generally live in harem groups with one or two males leading several unrelated females; and chimpanzees exist in multi-male/multi-female groups characterized as fission–fusion societies, in which group members may forage on their own for a few days before rejoining the main group.

EXERCISE 1

Given the following information, answer the questions about great ape societies:

a. Gibbons live in ecological niches in which the food is evenly distributed in patches. Males do not compete with each other, but males and females bond together to defend a patch of forest; they are highly territorial. Would you expect gibbons to be sexually dimorphic? Why or why not?

_____

_____

_____

_____

b. Orangutans are semi-solitary and prefer a diet of fruit. They have been heavily hunted by humans for several decades and are near extinction. Orangutans are also very large, with males weighing 300 pounds or more at adulthood. Can you think of two reasons why would it be advantageous for orangutans *not* to form large social groups? _____

_____

_____

_____

_____

c. Orangutans are highly dimorphic, with males being twice the size of females. What does this mean for male–male competition? _____

_____

_____

_____

d. Chimpanzees have a unique social structure described as a fission–fusion society, in which males and females may wander off in search of food by themselves or in small groups, rejoining the main group at a later time. Chimpanzees are only slightly dimorphic. What do you think this means for mating patterns in chimpanzee society? _____

_____

_____

_____

_____

Primate Intelligence

Culture may be defined as the learned rules of a society that govern the behavior of the individuals of that society. Culture has both functional (obtaining food, rearing offspring) and symbolic (language, ritual behavior) elements. Many anthropologists believe that nonhumans do not exhibit culture but rather learned behaviors. However, many others who study the evolution of culture in humans, look to our primate relatives for the behavioral patterns that may lead to the rise of culture. Japanese macaques on Koshima Island demonstrated cultural behavior to researchers in the 1950s. The macaques were provisioned with sweet potatoes, and about a year later one young female, Imo, began to wash her sweet potatoes in the ocean. Eventually, the behavior spread throughout the group, with all but a few elderly members washing their sweet potatoes prior to ingesting them. This is an example of a learned behavioral variation that is passed through the group and demonstrates the ability of some primates to display incipient culture. Orangutans are known to use leaves as napkins and sticks to scratch their backs, revealing basic **tool use**. Numerous studies of chimpanzees show their great capacity for cultural behavior and tool use. Chimpanzees are known to use twigs to "fish" termites out of termite mounds; while this seems a very simple behavior, chimpanzees are very selective about the size and weight of their sticks, demonstrating an understanding of what tool type will accomplish the task at hand. Chimps also use leaves as sponges and use rocks to break open nuts. More important, primatologists have examined numerous instances of regional variation in tool use, indicating that these local traditions are learned and not instinctual. Figure 12-2 shows a chimpanzee practicing termiting.

Figure 12-2 Chimpanzee termiting.

EXERCISE 2

Do you think these behaviors reflect true culture or just behavioral variation? Why or why not? _____

_____

_____

_____

_____

Observing Living Primates

Historically, primates were studied in the wild for a few days or weeks, providing the researcher a brief glimpse of primate behavior and social structure. A more modern approach to studying **extant** (living) primates involves spending anywhere from several months to two years in the field with the animals while incorporating extensive information about the environment in which the primates live for an ecological approach. This type of field study may be quite difficult for many reasons: some primates are nocturnal, some live quite high in the canopy and are difficult to see, some may be quite small and hard to find, while others may live in harsh desert or swamp conditions through which the scientist must maneuver. It is very difficult to control the variables in this type of study. Some primates are also studied in captive (e.g., zoo) or *semi–free-ranging* environments (e.g., game parks) where more variables may be controlled.

Primate behavior may be observed in several ways, including the following:

1. **Scan Sampling:** An individual or the entire group is observed at regular time intervals (e.g., every 30 seconds or every minute), and all behaviors are recorded for all individuals in the population.

2. **Focal Sampling:** One animal is chosen and followed, and all behaviors are recorded throughout the time interval chosen.

3. **Ad-Lib Sampling:** This is similar to keeping a diary and involves a lot of writing. One individual or multiple animals are watched and behaviors are recorded.

EXERCISE 3

a. Describe some of the variables that cannot be controlled in a study of free-ranging primates. _____

_____

_____

_____

b. How might these change in a study of captive primates? _____

_____

_____

_____

_____

c. What are some disadvantages of studying primates in a captive environment? _____

_____

_____

_____

_____

EXERCISE 4

In class you will watch a movie depicting primates. While gaining some practice at basic primate observation, answer the following questions, and any others your instructor may assign.

a. What primate group are you viewing? Can you give its scientific name and its common name? _____

_____

_____

b. Describe the environment in which the primates live. _____

_____

_____

_____

_____

c. How many animals are in the group? _____

_____

d. Can you distinguish the males form the females? If so, how; if not, why not? _____

_____

_____

_____

_____

e. How many females have infants or other dependent offspring? _____

_____

f. How do the animals move around? Are they in the trees or on the ground?

_____

_____

_____

g. Are there any affiliative behaviors, such as grooming? If so, which animals are involved?

_____

_____

h. Can you identify the dominant individual(s)? How can you tell he or she is dominant? _____

_____

_____

_____

i. Has any other behavior occurred that you would like to discuss? _____

_____

_____

_____

_____

Pre-Lab Questions

1. An animal that has numerous offspring for whom it provides very little care is said to be:
   a. k-selected
   b. r-selected
   c. dominant
   d. displaying culture

2. When a female is ready to mate and is at her peak fertility time, she is said to be:
   a. dominant
   b. subordinate
   c. in estrus
   d. k-selected

3. Dominant individuals within a primate group experience:
   a. fewer opportunities to mate
   b. more cultural behavior
   c. smaller body size
   d. more access to resources

4. The evolution of sexual dimorphism may be explained through:
   a. male–male competition
   b. male–female competition
   c. adult–juvenile competition
   d. access to fruit trees

5. Males are limited in their reproductive success by:
   a. access to food
   b. access to grooming
   c. access to mates
   d. all of the above

6. Considering the environment in which the primates live and how it affects social structure is using what kind of approach?
   a. ecological
   b. behavioral
   c. ad-lib sampling
   d. evolutionary

7. The observation technique in which one animal is chosen and followed and all behaviors are recorded is called:
   a. scan sampling
   b. focal sampling
   c. ad-lib sampling
   d. captive observation

8. **True or False:** Extant primates are living primates.

9. **True or False:** Grooming is an example of an aggressive behavior.

10. **True or False:** In some primate groups, blinking or yawning may be threat gestures.

Post-Lab Questions

1. In this lab we reviewed a few examples of tool use in nonhuman primates. Using the library or the Internet, describe any other examples of tool use by animals that you have found. _____

   _____

   _____

   _____

   _____

2. If a male chimpanzee signals his desire to mate to a female chimpanzee by shredding leaves, would you call this an example of the functional aspects or symbolic aspects of culture? Explain your answer.

   _____

   _____

   _____

   _____

3. Using the library or the Internet, identify five primate species that are endangered. Where do these primates live? Why are they near extinction? Is anything being done to help them survive? _____

   _____

   _____

   _____

   _____

   _____

Supplemental Post-Lab Exercise

Primate Observations at the Zoo

You will be responsible for visiting the local zoo in your town and reporting on the nonhuman primates housed there. You instructor will inform you how many groups you should visit and the length of time you are required to observe the animals. On the following pages you will find copies of scan sampling and focal sampling worksheets. Make extra copies if you will be viewing more than one group. After the worksheets, you will find a classification chart that you should fill in for each group you observe.

     If your local city or town does not have a zoo available, it is still possible to perform the following observations on other subjects, such as squirrels or even humans. Check with your instructor to see if this is an option for you. If choosing humans, select a group in a public place, watch them, and record your observations.

Scan Sampling Technique: Focal Animal or Group

Start time: _____   End time: _____

Describe weather conditions.

_____

_____

_____

_____

Time intervals (circle one): 30 seconds, 1 minute, 2 minutes, 5 minutes

Focal Animal or Group Scan (circle one)

Describe focal animal (adult/juvenile, male/female) or indicate number of individuals in the group, including number of adult males, adult females, and juveniles.

_____

_____

_____

_____

Observations at each time interval.

_____

_____

_____

_____

_____

_____

Supplemental Post-Lab Exercise

Primate Observations at the Zoo

Focal Animal Technique

Start time: _____   End time: _____

Describe weather conditions.

_____

_____

_____

_____

Time intervals (circle one): 30 seconds, 1 minute, 2 minutes, 5 minutes

Describe focal animal (adult/juvenile, male/female).

_____

_____

_____

_____

In the following table, place a checkmark in the appropriate box if the animal is exhibiting that behavior during the time interval.

Behavior	Time Intervals																			
	1	2	3	4	5	6	7	8	9	10	11	12	13	14	15	16	17	18	19	20
Sitting																				
Standing																				
Sleeping																				
Resting																				
Traveling																				
Eating																				
Drinking																				
Scratching																				
Vocalizing																				
Grooming																				
Aggression																				
Submission																				
Playing																				
Copulation																				
Present																				
Other																				

Supplemental Post-Lab Exercise

Primate Observations at the Zoo

Fill out the following classification chart for each primate or primate group observed.

Common Name: _____

Scientific Name: _____

Suborder (traditional scheme/modern scheme): _____

Superfamily: _____

Genus: _____

Species: _____

Additional taxonomic information: _____

Number of primates in enclosure: _____

Number of adult males: _____

Number of adult females: _____

Number of juveniles: _____

Sexual dimorphism? _____

Diet (if observable)? _____

Arboreal or terrestrial? _____

Nocturnal or diurnal? _____

Locomotion: _____

Where are these primates found in the wild? _____

Are they endangered? _____

Chapter 13

The Bipedal Adaptation and Our Earliest Ancestors

Objectives

After completing this chapter you should be able to:

1. recognize and describe the six hallmark traits that we use to identify the members of the Hominidae;

2. identify and describe the skeletal modifications necessary for bipedal locomotion;

3. identify and describe the anatomical characteristics of the earliest hominids and the gracile and robust australopithecines;

4. define Rift Valley, "Lucy," Laetoli footprints, Taung child, the Black Skull;

5. be able to compare and contrast the anatomical differences between an australopithecine and a modern human or a chimp;

6. be able to compare and contrast the anatomical differences between a gracile and a robust australopithecine; and

7. recognize illustrations, photos, and casts (if available) of the different major hominid groups.

Recognizing the Hominidae

At the end of the Miocene, between 5 and 7 million years ago (mya), a new family arose within the primate order, the **Hominidae**. This family includes modern humans and our extinct ancestors since the divergence from the last common ancestor with chimpanzees. (Some researchers base their classifications on the molecular evidence and call this group *Hominins*.) DNA evidence and protein studies indicate that the last common ancestor to the chimpanzee and human lineages evolved at this time (Goodman, 1999; Goodman et al., 1998; Ruvolo, 1997; Sarich & Wilson, 1967). However, the biochemical evidence does not tell us about what these early ancestors looked like. The anatomical evidence gleaned from the study of fossil remains allows us to interpret our morphological evolution. When this anatomical evidence is added to the behavioral evidence we have from living primates, we can begin to put the pieces of the puzzle together, developing a more complete picture of our ancestors. The hominids may be divided into three broad groups based on the order of their appearance: (1) the earliest possible hominids (before the genus *Australopithecus*), (2) the australopithecines, and (3) early *Homo*. The first two of these groups are discussed in more detail in the following pages. The earliest members of the genus *Homo* are discussed in Chapter 14.

Modern humans differ from the apes in several obvious behavioral ways: speech and the highly advanced use of symbolic language, complex material culture, relaxation of the estrous cycle and concealed ovulation, and advanced cognition. However, not all our fossil ancestors will exhibit these traits, which evolved more recently in the hominid lineage; and many of these behavioral traits are difficult to distinguish in fossil remains, so we must look to the anatomical evidence to recognize members of our evolving lineage. **Hominids**, members of the taxonomic family Hominindae, may be distinguished from the apes by the following anatomical traits:

- Larger brain size
- Bipedal locomotion, with a striding gait
- Parabolic dental arch
- Reduced prognathism (facial projection)
- No C/P3 hone
- Thick molar enamel

It is important to realize that many of these traits evolved in a *mosaic* fashion. Many of the earliest hominids, discussed in this chapter, will show not all of these traits but a subset of them. This can cause controversy in classification, as different researchers may emphasize the importance of certain traits over others.

The **cranial capacity** of modern humans is estimated to be between 1,300 and 1,400 cubic centimeters (cc), with an average of about 1,350 cc. The common chimpanzee's cranial capacity is approximately 350 to 400 cc. Thus, if the chimpanzee's brain size reflects the primitive condition, we can expect to see an increase in brain size over time along the hominid lineage. Over time in this lineage, the brain of humans is positioned higher on the cranium, creating a high, rounded, globular cranium, eventually creating a forehead, while the snout retreats and the face does not project forward as far as in the apes. This **reduced prognathism**, or less facial projection, characterizes the hominids.

Numerous dental characteristics differ between apes and humans (Stanford et al., 2006). Due to their diet consisting of softer fruits and tender

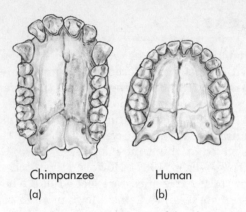

Chimpanzee   Human
(a)   (b)

Figure 13-1 Comparison of the chimpanzee and human dental arch shape.

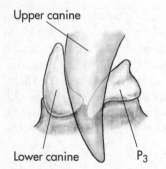

Upper canine

Lower canine   P₃

Figure 13-2 C/P3 hone, or honing complex, in the chimpanzee.

leaves and shoots, the African apes have thin molar enamel on their teeth. However, hominids evolved on a coarser diet, including tough roots and tubers from dry savanna environments, and they have **thick enamel** on their molar teeth as an adaptation to the tougher diet. In both humans and apes, the *muscles of mastication* are used for chewing, especially the *masseter* and *temporalis muscles*. Because apes slice their food while chewing, the emphasis is on the back of the muscles, while humans crush and grind the food, emphasizing the front of the muscles. Humans also have a **parabolic dental arch**, as opposed to the parallel tooth rows found in the chimpanzee (Figure 13-1). An ape has a large, projecting canine, which fits into a space (**diastema**) behind the lower first premolar. Each time the mouth is closed, the back edge of the canine hones on the front of the premolar, maintaining a sharp edge on each tooth that is helpful for slicing fruits and leaves. The premolar is called a *sectorial premolar* and the dental complex is called a **honing complex**, or a **C/P3 hone** (Figure 13-2). Hominids have reduced canines that are in line with the incisors and do not have the honing complex or sectorial premolar.

In addition, the landmark adaptation found in the hominids is the adoption of **bipedality** as the primary mode of locomotion. Many organisms move bipedally (e.g., birds, dinosaurs, kangaroos), with their body weight over their hind limbs, but the *bipedal stride* is unique to the hominids. Studies of extant (living) apes suggest that hominids may have first utilized bipedal locomotion as a feeding behavior while in the trees. As the climate cooled and dried at the end of the Miocene, organisms were under considerable pressure to adapt to changing environments, which included decreasing forests, expanding savannas, and changing food sources. Bipedalism provided several advantages for living on the savannah: the ability to spot predators and an efficient (i.e., biomechanical and thermoregulatory) means of locomotion, which allowed travel between distant clumps of trees.

EXERCISE 1

Compare the skulls of the ape and the human in the lab. Which of the characteristics described in the preceding section can you identify on the skulls?

_____

_____

_____

_____

EXERCISE 2

Examine the following photo. Is this the palate of a human or an ape? How can you tell?

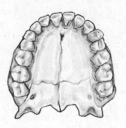

_____

_____

_____

_____

Bipedal Morphology

The evolution of the unique bipedal striding gait led to several skeletal modifications. As you might expect, changes occur throughout the entire lower limb, including the hip, knee, and foot. However, changes have also occurred in the vertebral column and in the base of the skull. You may be able to anticipate some of these changes after having studied primate locomotion in Chapter 11. At the base of the skull, the head rests on the occipital condyles, which are laterally located to the foramen magnum. In bipeds, the **foramen magnum** is anteriorly placed so that the head is balanced in a vertical orientation appropriate for upright posture and movement. In the apes, the foramen magnum is more posteriorly located and better situated for quadrupedalism (Figure 13-3).

The human **vertebral column** is S-shaped, with two spinal curves: the cervical curve and the lumbar curve. The two spinal curves in the biped allow the weight of the body to be carried directly over the knees and feet in the midline. In apes, the vertebral column is straighter, causing the weight to be thrust forward when standing erect (Figure 13-4).

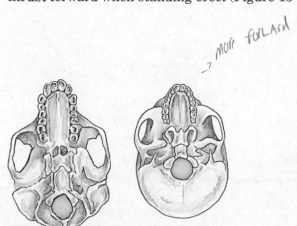

→ more forLard

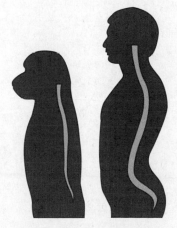

Figure 13-3 Note placement of the foramen magnum in the chimpanzee (*left*) and the modern human (*right*).

Figure 13-4 Vertebral column in chimpanzee (*left*) and modern human (*right*).

EXERCISE 3

The cervical and lumbar curves in the human vertebral column are not present at birth. The cervical curve forms within the first few months after birth while the lumbar curve forms around the first year or so. Can you think of why these characteristics might develop? _____

_____

_____

_____

_____

The **pelvic girdle** is short and broad in bipedal individuals, allowing the center of gravity to be located in the pelvic basin. The iliac blades are curved around in an anterior–posterior orientation, creating a pelvic "bowl" (Figure 13-5). The gluteal muscles attach on the posterior surface of the ilia and act to stabilize the hip when one foot is off the ground, as when striding. Thus, when the right foot is lifted in stride, the gluteal muscles of the left hip act to maintain balance on the left foot. Apes demonstrate a very different pelvic girdle that is tall and narrow, with iliac blades that are located along the posterior surface of the truck and a center of gravity that is in front of the body (Figure 13-5). The gluteal muscles act as hip extensors in the ape and allow forward propulsion when walking quadrupedally. Apes cannot balance for long on one foot and will fall toward the unsupported side—that is, if the right foot is off the ground, the animal will fall toward the right.

In the human biped, the **femur** is also modified to bring the knees into the midline. Each femur is angled inward from the hip to the knee, where it articulates with the tibia to form the knee joint. As the femur meets the tibia at an angle, it creates the **valgus knee** seen in humans. In contrast, the ape femur drops straight down from the hip socket and articulates with the tibia to create a **verus knee** (Figure 13-6).

As you might expect, the **foot** exhibits multiple modifications in the bipedal human in order to bear the weight of the entire body when walking. The apes have long toes for grasping, and their **hallux** (big toe) is divergent, retaining its prehensility and opposability. The human foot has short toes, and

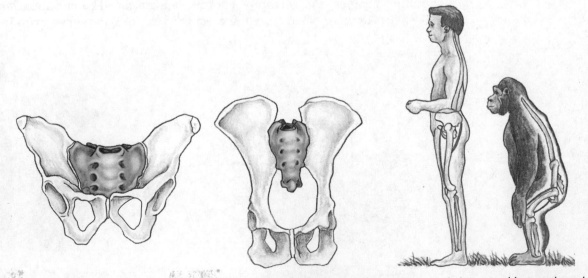

Figure 13-5 Human pelvis (*far left*) compared to chimpanzee pelvis (*center*) and chimp and human bipedal posture (*right*) demonstrating center of gravity due to vertebral column and pelvic girdle.

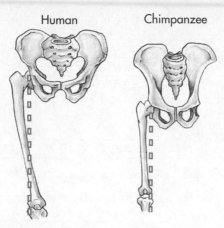

Figure 13-6 Femur and tibia of human (*left*) and ape (*right*), showing the angled femur in the human.

Long toes divergent

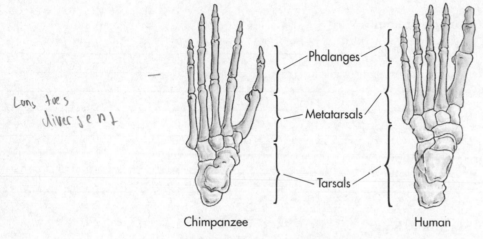

Figure 13-7 Ape foot (*left*) and human foot (*right*), showing the short toes and large, nondivergent hallux in the human.

the hallux is large, weight bearing, and not divergent (Figure 13-7). This position allows the hallux to act as a primary force for propulsion, moving the body forward off the hallux. All the weight of the human body is passed through the ball of the foot and the hallux during locomotion. The calf muscles provide strong propulsion. Humans and apes both have a **transverse arch** in the foot, running from medial to lateral, or from the inside of the foot to the outside of the foot. However, only humans have the **longitudinal arch**, running from heel to toes. The two arches in the human foot provide support and cushioning for shock absorption during locomotion.

EXERCISE 4

Examine the materials provided in your lab comparing human and ape skeletal anatomy. Describe the differences you see between elements at each station.

Station 1: Pelvis

- Chimpanzee _____

_____

_____

_____

- *Homo sapiens* _____
  _____
  _____
  _____

Station 2: Knee

- Chimpanzee _____
  _____
  _____
  _____

- *Homo sapiens* _____
  _____
  _____
  _____

Station 3: Femur

- Chimpanzee _____
  _____
  _____
  _____

- *Homo sapiens* _____
  _____
  _____
  _____

Station 4: Foot

- Chimpanzee _____
  _____
  _____
  _____

- *Homo sapiens* _____
  _____
  _____
  _____

Station 5: Foramen magnum

- Chimpanzee _____
  _____
  _____
  _____

- *Homo sapiens* _____
  _____
  _____
  _____

The Earliest Possible Hominids

[handwritten: evidence of bipedualism]

The earliest fossil remains that may belong to the hominid lineage date to the time period between approximately 7 and 4 million years ago. Most of these fossil remains have been discovered quite recently, within the last ten years or so. Each of the following genera exhibit a mosaic of characteristics linking them to both the chimpanzee and the human lineages. It is possible that these fossils belong in Hominidae, or they may be representatives of the Pongidae, ancestors to the chimpanzees or gorillas. They are important because they are evolving right at the ape–human divergence.

Sahelanthropus tchadensis: 7 to 6 Million Years Ago   *[handwritten: Central Africa]*

A complete skull was found in 2001 by researcher Michel Brunet and coworkers (Brunet et al., 2002) in the desert of Chad in Central Africa. The hominid-like characteristics exhibited by *Sahelanthropus* include a nonhoning chewing complex and a foramen magnum positioned at the base of the skull, indicating that it was bipedal. However, the cranial capacity is small and within the range of chimpanzees, the specimen has a huge brow ridge, and the enamel is thinner than found in other hominids.

Orrorin tugenensis: About 6 Million Years Ago   *[handwritten: East Africa]*

Brigitte Senut and Martin Pickford (Pickford & Senut, 2001) discovered the remains of at least five individuals on the western side of Lake Turkana in Kenya in the Rift Valley of eastern Africa in 2000. Both cranial and postcranial elements were identified. The researchers have suggested that *Orrorin* was bipedal and had nonhoning canine teeth and thick enamel on the molars. The upper canine of *Orrorin* is large and apelike, throwing a shred of doubt on its hominid status.

Ardipithecus ramidus: 5.8 to 4.4 Million Years Ago   *[handwritten: East Africa]*

[handwritten: mixing of climbing and bipedal adaptation]

The Awash River Valley in Ethiopia is the site where an international team of researchers discovered cranial and postcranial fossils belonging to *Ardipithecus* at the site of Aramis (White et al., 1994). The *Ardipithecus* fossils demonstrate bipedal adaptations linking them to the Hominidae. However, some dental traits, including thinner enamel, a large canine, and a possible C/P3 hone, suggest *Ardipithecus* may not belong on the hominid line but may be a sister taxon.

The Australopithecines

The **East Africa Rift Valley** is a massive 1,200-mile-long valley that cuts through three countries: Ethiopia, Kenya, and Tanzania (Figure 13-8). This region is geologically active and contains millions of years of exposed strata with excellent chronometric dates. Numerous sites containing a wealth of fossil hominid remains are located throughout the region, including the sites of

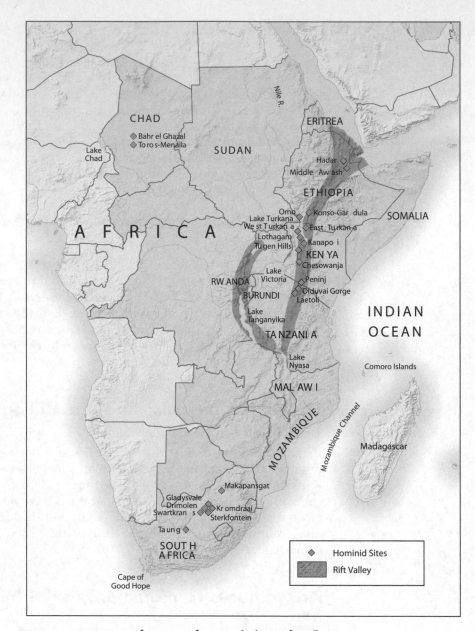

Figure 13-8 Map of sites in Africa, including Rift Valley.

Aramis and Lake Turkana. Fossil hominids from several genera have been found here, including some members of a group of hominids dating to approximately 4 to 1 million years ago and called the **australopithecines**. All the australopithecines have thick enamel and are bipedal, although many exhibit characteristics suggesting that they may have spent some time in the trees. Earlier specimens are more primitive, with small body sizes of around 4 feet in height (5 feet in males), while the later specimens are quite derived. Brain size increases only slightly over the time period from approximately 400 cc to 500 cc for the later groups. One interesting trend seen in this group is an increase in craniodental robusticity through time—that is, the later specimens have large cheek teeth (premolars and molars), sometimes called *post-canine megadontia,* and large faces with significant muscle markings on the skull, indicating a diet of heavy chewing.

EXERCISE 5

a. Considering the information provided, why might some of the australopithecines have spent time in the trees? _____

_____

_____

_____

b. The australopithecines exhibit a body size difference, where males are larger than females. What term is used to describe this? _____

_____

c. What kind of foods might the later australopithecines have been eating to cause adaptations related to heavy chewing? _____

_____

Australopithecus anamensis: Approximately 4 Million Years Ago

Remains of this species are known from two localities in Kenya: Allia Bay and Kanapoi. *A. anamensis* shows a mosaic of traits linking to the chimps and human lines (Leakey et al., 1995). In particular, they have parallel tooth rows and a C/P3 honing complex, although the canine is somewhat reduced. These specimens may demonstrate a link between the earlier *Ardipithecus* (previously described) and the later *A. afarensis* (described next).

Australopithecus afarensis: Approximately 4 to 3 Million Years Ago

The best known of all early hominids is *A. afarensis*, discovered in the 1970s at two sites: Hadar in Ethiopia and Laetoli in Tanzania. Johanson, Taieb, and White (Johansen & Taieb, 1976) described a fabulous find of a young adult female, approximately 40% complete, which they nicknamed **Lucy**. Dozens of fossils representing numerous individuals have been discovered since that time period, including a **footprint trail** left behind in volcanic ash at Laetoli. Lucy's remains indicate she was adept at bipedal locomotion, although her stride length was shorter than comparable humans of similar height. Also, her arms were quite long, with powerful muscle markings, and her digits were long and curved, suggesting she may have spent some time in the trees. The average brain size for *A. afarensis* individuals is about 400 cc, and they do exhibit sexual dimorphism. The canine is reduced, so there is no true C/P3

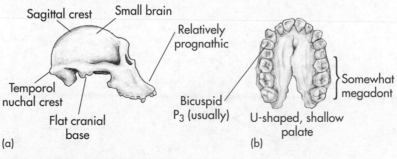

Figure 13-9 Morphology of *A. afarensis*.

hone. Members of this group had an emphasis on chewing, as demonstrated by the bony crests on the top of the skull (**sagittal crest**) and posterior of the skull (**compound temporonuchal crest**) that are attachment points for the temporalis and nuchal (neck) muscles (Figure 13-9).

EXERCISE 6

Examine the following illustration. Name one trait that is similar in the australopithecine pelvis and the modern human pelvis. Name one way in which these pelves differ. If casts of hominid pelves are available in your laboratory, examine them for similarities to modern human pelves.

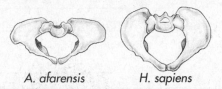

A. afarensis   H. sapiens

_____

_____

Australopithecus africanus: Approximately 3.5 to 2 Million Years Ago

The first australopithecine ever found was a child skull discovered at the South Africa site of **Taung** in 1924 and described by Raymond Dart in 1925. *A. africanus* specimens have since been discovered by Dart and his colleague Robert Broom at two other South Africa sites of Sterkfontein and Makapansgat. Most South Africa sites are cave sites where the fossils are embedded in limestone beds called *breccia* and are dated using relative dating techniques. Although *A. africanus* is considered a gracile form like *A. afarensis,* the *A. africanus* specimens also show derived characteristics, including a slightly larger braincase, a lack of crests on the cranium, and less prognathism, while the molars are larger (Figure 13-10).

Robust Australopithecines

The robust australopithecines exhibit an array of craniodental characteristics that are highly derived relative to their earlier, gracile counterparts. The robust forms include three species: *A. robustus* from South Africa and *A. boisei* and *A. aethiopicus* from East Africa. Due to their distinctive cranial adaptations, they are sometimes categorized into a different genus, *Paranthropus.*

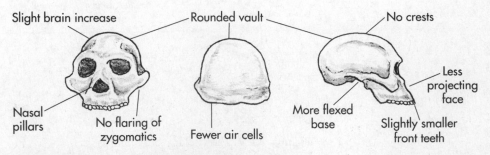

Figure 13-10 Morphology of A. *africanus.*

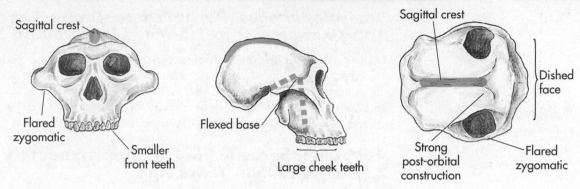

Figure 13-11 Anatomical adaptations of the robust australopithecines.

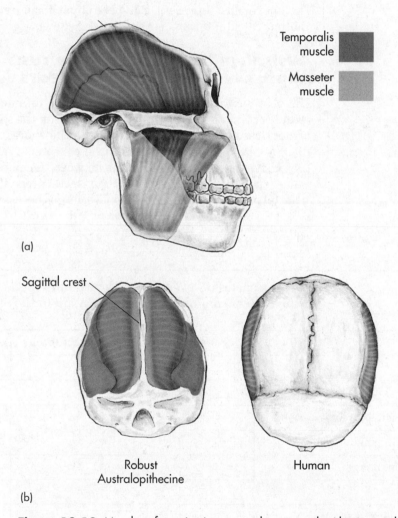

Figure 13-12 Muscles of mastication on a robust australopithecine and a modern human.

Regional variations between the South Africa and East Africa forms confound easy classification. The robust forms display several anatomical traits related to heavy chewing, or **hard object feeding** (e.g., hard-shelled nuts and/or fibrous vegetation), including a sagittal crest and postorbital constriction for the insertion of the **temporalis** muscle; nuchal crest for insertion of the nuchal musculature; postcanine megadontia; small anterior teeth (incisors and canines); and a large, robust mandible with widely flaring zygomatics and dished face for the attachment of the **masseter** muscle (Figures 13-11 and 13-12). The "robusts" represent a specialized lineage that eventually went extinct.

Australopithecus (Paranthropus) robustus: Approximately 2 to 1.5 Million Years Ago

This species is the South Africa representative for the robust australopithecines and demonstrates the suite of craniodental traits that characterize the robust forms. Two of the better known South Africa sites are Kromdraii and Swartkrans, which were originally excavated by Robert Broom, who discovered the first fossils there in 1938 (Broom, 1947).

Australopithecus (P.) boisei: Approximately 2.5 to 1.0 Million Years Ago

A. boisei was first discovered by Mary Leakey, the wife of the famous paleoanthropologist Louis Leakey, in the Olduvai Gorge in Tanzania (Leakey, 1959). Sites across Kenya, Tanzania, and Ethiopia have yielded *A. boisei* remains. The specimens represent a hyper-robust form, with even more exaggerated anatomical adaptations for specialized chewing.

Australopithecus (P.) aethiopicus: Approximately 2.6 Million Years Ago

The best known of these individuals is the infamous **Black Skull**, so named because it is stained black from the minerals in the sediment. The Black Skull and related fossil remains were found along the shores of Lake Turkana, Kenya, in 1985 by Alan Walker and Richard Leakey (son of Louis and Mary) (Walker et al., 1986). The species represents a link between the more primitive *A. afarensis* specimens (small brain size, larger anterior teeth, prognathism) and the later *A. boisei* (sagittal and nuchal crests, dished face, large cheek teeth) found in the region.

EXERCISE 7

Casts or photos of several australopithecine species are available in your laboratory. After examining them carefully, fill in the following chart.

Traits	*afarensis*	*africanus*	*aethiopicus*	*robustus*	*boisei*	*chimp*
Dates						
Sites						
Size of incisors (small/large)						
Size of cheek teeth (small/large)						
Size of canine (small/large)						
Diastema (yes/no)						
Molarized premolars (yes/no)						
Cranial capacity						
Projecting face (yes/no)						
Compound temporonuchal crest (yes/no)						
Nuchal crest (yes/no)						
Sagittal crest (yes/no)						
Flaring zygomatics (yes/no)						
Dished face (yes/no)						

Pre-Lab Questions

1. Which of the following traits characterizes the early hominids?
   - a. C/P3 hone
   - b. parabolic dental arch
   - c. thin enamel
   - d. sectorial premolar

2. A femur that drops down on an angle to bring the knees together in the midline of the body is called a:
   - a. valgus knee
   - b. verus knee
   - c. hip stabilizer
   - d. divergent hallux

3. Which of the following traits characterizes the bipedal human?
   - a. verus knee
   - b. divergent hallux
   - c. long toes for grasping
   - d. gluteal muscles acting as hip stabilizers

4. Which of the following traits characterizes the quadrupedal ape?
   - a. valgus knee
   - b. divergent hallux
   - c. S-shaped vertebral column
   - d. two arches in foot

5. Which of the following genera is not one of the earliest hominids dating from 4 to 7 million years ago?
   - a. *Ardipithecus*
   - b. *Sahelanthropus*
   - c. *Australopithecus*
   - d. *Orrorin*

6. Which australopithecine species was the very first ever discovered?
   - a. *A. afarensis*
   - b. *A. africanus*
   - c. *A. robustus*
   - d. *A. boisei*

7. Elements of Lucy's anatomy that suggest she may have spent some time in the trees include:
   - a. short legs
   - b. broad pelvis
   - c. long arms
   - d. short, straight digits

8. Which of the following traits does not represent the robust australopithecines?
   - a. sagittal crest
   - b. nuchal crest
   - c. dished face
   - d. small molar teeth

9. **True or False:** A C/P3 hone involves the upper canine sliding across the lower first premolar.

10. **True or False:** *Australopithecus robustus* and *A. boisei* are considered "robust" because they have a much larger body size and brain size than the gracile specimens.

Post-Lab Questions

1. What is the purpose of a diastema? _____

   _____

   _____

   _____

2. Why did the early hominids have thick enamel? What kind of foods might they have been eating?

   _____

   _____

   _____

   _____

3. Examine the following illustration. Does this foot belong to a human or an ape? Name three characteristics that helped you decide.

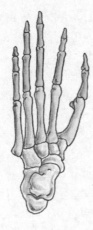

   _____

   _____

   _____

   _____

4. Examine the following illustration. Does this pelvis belong to a human or an ape? Name two features that helped you decide.

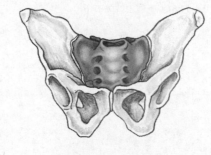

   _____

   _____

   _____

5. How did the adoption of bipedalism affect estrus in females? _____
_____
_____

6. What are some disadvantages to bipedalism? _____
_____
_____

7. Why do you think bipedalism might be an advantage for the early hominids? In other words, how might
being bipedal have helped them survive? _____
_____
_____
_____

8. Examine the following photo. Is this the palate of a human or an ape? How can you tell?

_____
_____
_____
_____

9. Fill in the following chart with information comparing apes to humans.

Trait	Ape	Human
Sectorial premolar (yes/no)		
Diastema for canine (yes/no)		
C/P3 hone (yes/no)		
Molar enamel (yes/no)		
Tooth rows/Dental arcade (yes/no)		
Brain size		
Foramen magnum location		
Vertebral column		
Pelvic girdle		
Femur/Knee		
Foot, arches		
Foot, hallux		
Foot, toe length		
Gluteal muscles		
Calf muscles		

10. Based on the comparison you made in lab (Exercise 6), do you think the australopithecines had a loco-motor pattern more like chimpanzees or like humans? Explain. _____

_____

_____

_____

_____

11. Examine the following photo. Describe the similarities and differences between the australopithecine morphology of the pelvic girdle, femur, and knee when compared to the morphology of the human and chimpanzee.

Chimpanzee   *Australopithecus*   Human

_____

_____

_____

_____

12. Examine the fossil cranium depicted here. Is this individual a gracile or a robust australopithecine? Name three features that helped you decide.

_____

_____

_____

_____

13. Examine the fossil cranium depicted here. Is this individual a gracile or a robust australopithecine? Name three features that helped you decide.

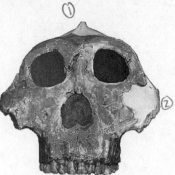

   - SAgittAl crest

    - FlAred zygomatic

14. The individual hominid skull found at Taung in South Africa is a child with fully erupted deciduous dentition and erupted permanent first molars. The first molar erupts at age six in modern humans and at age three in chimpanzees. How old do you think the Taung child was at death? Do you think she or he aged like an ape or a human or perhaps something in between? _____

_____

_____

_____

15. Review the information that you recorded in class for Exercise 7 and answer the following questions.

a. Name at least two features in the australopithecines that are still ape-like. _____

_____

b. Name three features of the skull (not teeth) used to distinguish the robusts from the graciles.

_____

_____

c. Name three dental features that distinguish the robusts from the graciles. _____

_____

d. Does brain size increase much in the australopithecines through time? _____

_____

e. What were the robusts using those huge teeth for anyway? _____

_____

The Rise of the Genus *Homo*

Objectives

After completing this chapter you should be able to:

1. define adaptive strategy;

2. describe the morphological differences between the australopithecines and early *Homo*;

3. discuss the debate surrounding *Homo habilis*;

4. identify some of the main sites where *Homo erectus* is found; and

5. identify the parts of the cranial buttressing system and distinguish *Homo erectus* from *Homo habilis* and later *Homo sapiens*.

The Earliest Members of Our Genus

By 1 million years ago, the robust australopithecines went extinct. Several scenarios have been proposed for this event, but most likely it was due to their specialized diet and narrow environmental niche. Prior to this time, at about 2 million years ago, at the Plio-Pleistocene boundary, the lineage leading to *Homo* evolved in Africa, most likely from a gracile australopithecine ancestor. This lineage demonstrates a broader environmental adaptation with increased dietary flexibility, in other words, a change in **adaptive strategy**. The first discoveries of early *Homo* were made by Louis Leakey in the 1960s in East Africa's Olduvai Gorge (Leakey et al., 1964). At that time the species was said to exhibit a larger brain size, more modern body proportions, and the use of stone tools. However, numerous discoveries since then suggest that some members of early *Homo* were almost as primitive as the australopithecines, and the australopithecines may have been making and using stone tools themselves. We distinguish the earliest members of the *Homo* lineage by their larger brain size (over 600 cc), a rounder skull, smaller faces and posterior teeth, with less prognathism and no "dishing," a parabolic dental arcade, and a lack of cranial crests that characterized the later australopithecines.

Homo habilis: Approximately 2.4 to 1.6 Million Years Ago

The earliest members of the genus *Homo* belong to this enigmatic group known from sites across Ethiopia, Kenya, Tanzania, and South Africa. *Homo habilis* ("Handy Man") is a taxon fraught with controversy because it contains specimens that challenge our understanding of species variability. Two specimens in particular demonstrate the difficulty in assigning both fossils into one group (Figures 14-1 and 14-2).

- **KNM-ER 1470:** This relatively complete cranium found at Lake Turkana has a larger brain size (775 cc) but also a relatively larger face and larger teeth.

- **KNM-ER 1813:** This cranium is also from Lake Turkana, but this specimen has a much smaller brain size (510 cc) with a smaller face and smaller teeth.

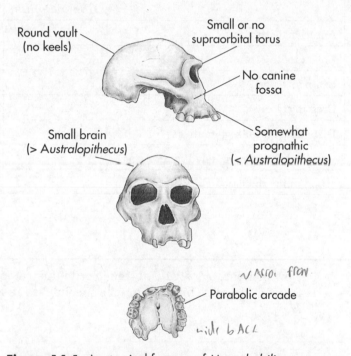

Figure 14-1 Anatomical features of *Homo habilis*.

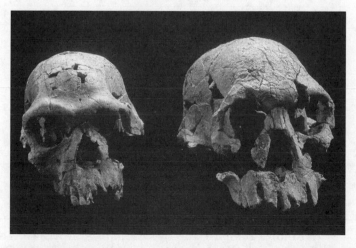

Figure 14-2 Comparison of the *H. habilis* crania: KNM-ER 1813 (*left*) and KNM-ER 1470 (*right*).

In addition, some representatives from Olduvai Gorge have quite primitive limb proportions, within the range seen for the australopithecines. Some scientists believe that 1470 is a male and 1813 is a female and that *H. habilis* is a highly dimorphic species. However, others question the amount of variability in the group and believe that more than one species is represented here. Scholars with this understanding place 1470 and similar specimens into a separate species: *Homo rudolfensis*. Either way, early *Homo* is evolving alongside the later australopithecines in East Africa.

EXERCISE 1

Casts or photos of a robust australopithecine and *H. habilis* are available in your laboratory. After examining them carefully, fill in the following chart.

	Homo habilis	Robust Australopithecine
Anterior tooth size		
Cheek tooth size		
Brain size		
Cresting?		
Dished face/wide zygomatics?		
Occipital contour (rounded/compressed)		
Mandibular robusticity		

EXERCISE 2

Now compare *H. habilis* to the gracile australopithecines for the same set of features. Do you think the gracile specimens are a reasonable ancestor to early *Homo*?

	Homo habilis	Gracile Australopithecine
Anterior tooth size		
Cheek tooth size		
Brain size		
Cresting?		
Dished face/wide zygomatics?		
Occipital contour (rounded/compressed)		
Mandibular robusticity		

EXERCISE 3

Finally, compare the two *H. habilis* skulls, side by side. If casts are available in your laboratory, examine them carefully. Otherwise, you may examine Figure 14-2. Do you think these two fossils might be from the same species and sexually dimorphic? Or do you think they are from two different species? Defend your answer.

_____

_____

_____

_____

_____

Homo erectus: Out of Africa

The earliest representatives of *Homo erectus* appeared in East Africa about 1.8 million years ago and quickly moved out to explore other regions of the Old World. Specimens from this taxon were first discovered in Indonesia during the 1890s by **Eugene Dubois**, a Dutch physician. Since then *Homo erectus* fossils have been discovered at many sites across Africa (Lake Turkana), Western Asia (Dmanisi), East Asia (Zhoukoudian), and Southeast Asia (Trinil, Sangiran) dating from 1.8 million to 300,000 years ago. Some of the more famous representatives of the group are **KNM-ER 3733** and **KNM-ER 3883**, two skulls from East Africa that are some of the earliest in time; **WT 15000**, also known as the **Nariokotome Boy**, or **Turkana Boy**, a skeleton of a young boy of about 11 years of age that is about 80% complete; **Peking Man**, several crania discovered in China but lost in World War II; and **Java Man**, several crania discovered on the island of Java and recently re-dated to almost 1.7 million years ago (Larick et al., 2001; Swisher et al., 1994).

Homo erectus is characterized by modern body proportions and modern height, a larger brain size (averaging about 900 cc, increasing over time), thickened cortical bones in the limbs, a long and low cranium with a sloping frontal bone, and a series of thickened regions on the cranium referred to as a **cranial buttressing system**. This cranial buttressing system includes a series of thickened ridges (*tori*; singular = *torus*) that give each *H. erectus* skull a distinctive appearance. The buttresses serve as a biomechanical adaptation for absorbing stress on the cranium, probably *H. erectus* were using their teeth as tools. It is important to realize that these thickenings are very different from the cranial crests we saw in the robust australopithecines, which are due to increased muscle development for chewing. The **supraorbital torus** is a prominent brow ridge above the eye orbits; the **sagittal keel** is a raised portion along the sagittal suture; the **nuchal (occipital) torus** is a thickened ridge of bone running horizontally across the occipital bone; the **angular torus** runs horizontally along the posterior–inferior portion of the parietal (Figures 14-3 and 14-4). Not all *H. erectus* specimens display the complete suite of cranial characteristics to the same degree, but rather they display regional variation. The African forms seldom show a sagittal keel, which is common of the Asian forms. The angular torus is best viewed in the Javan specimens, while the Chinese specimens also have **shovel-shaped incisors**, where the lingual side of the tooth has ridges along the edges, creating a "shovel." Due to the differences in morphology between sites, some researchers separate the early African specimens into *Homo erectus* and *Homo ergaster.*

LATERAL VIEW

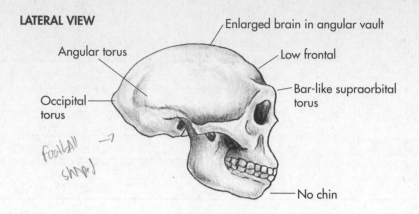

Enlarged brain in angular vault

Angular torus

Low frontal

Bar-like supraorbital torus

Occipital torus

football shape →

No chin

FRONTAL VIEW

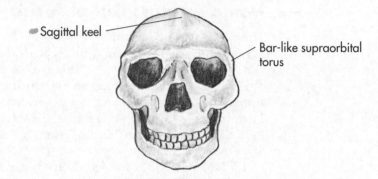

Sagittal keel

Bar-like supraorbital torus

PENTAGONAL REAR VIEW

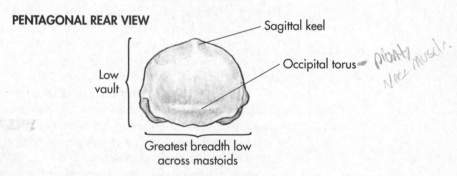

Sagittal keel

Occipital torus — *plants Neck muscle*

Low vault

Greatest breadth low across mastoids

Figure 14-3 Anatomical features of *Homo erectus*.

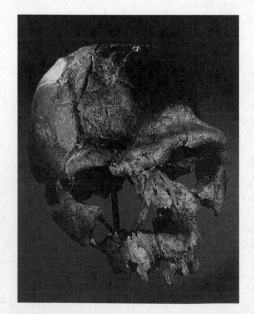

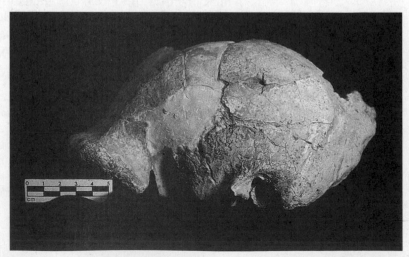

Figure 14-4 KNM-ER 3733 (*left*) and OH9 (*right*), two examples of *Homo erectus*.

EXERCISE 4

What cultural adaptations do you think may have allowed *H. erectus* to migrate into temperate zones?

_____

_____

_____

_____

EXERCISE 5

Casts or photos of *H. erectus* specimens are available in your laboratory. Examine them carefully and locate the parts of the cranial buttressing system, including supraorbital torus, sagittal keel, nuchal torus, and angular torus. Can you distinguish between the African and Asian forms? If so, how?

_____

_____

_____

_____

EXERCISE 6

Compare the femora of *H. habilis* and *H. erectus* and note the following:

- Size _____

- Cortical thickness _____

What might explain the differences you see here? _____

_____

_____

_____

_____

Stone Tools

Debate continues as to who were the first toolmakers. Australopithecines and *H. habilis* fossils have been found in association with stone tools at the Plio-Pleistocene boundary (1.8 million years ago). The first stone tools are a part of the **Oldowan stone tool complex** and are composed predominantly of *cores*, which are lumps of stone that have been slightly modified by removing small pieces, or *flakes*, to create a sharp edge (Schick & Toth, 1993) (Figure 14-5). These flakes are very sharp and useful for butchering animal carcasses. *Hammerstones* were also used to crack open the bones to extract the nutrient-rich marrow. These crude, simple choppers and cutting tools are simplistic in design, yet they allowed early hominids to exploit a new niche: animal resources and meat eating.

The **Acheulean stone tool industry** used by *H. erectus* displays an advance over the earlier Oldowan tools. The Acheulean tools appear in the

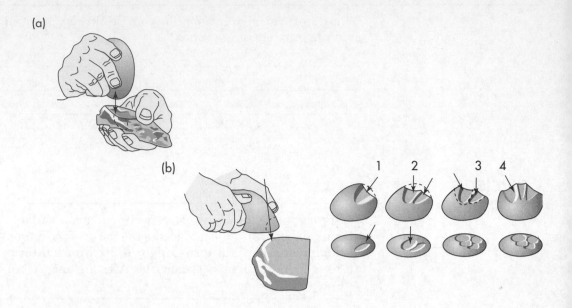

Figure 14-5 Oldowan tool manufacture.

Figure 14-6 Acheulean hand axes.

fossil record about 1.4 million years ago in Africa. The Acheulean tools are *bifacially* worked, meaning that they have flakes removed from two opposing sides to create a sharp edge (Figure 14-6). These tools are made with a mental template, with a preconceived idea in mind; they are not simplistic in the same way as the Oldowan tools. The Acheulean toolkit is composed primarily of the hand axe, a teardrop-shaped tool, along with assorted cleavers.

EXERCISE 7

Examine the examples of Oldowan and Acheulean stone tools available in your laboratory. Note the improved technology and style in the Acheulean tools.

_____

_____

Pre-Lab Questions

1. *Homo habilis* was first discovered in East Africa by:
   a. Charles Darwin
   b. Raymond Dart
   c. Eugene Dubois
   d. Louis Leakey

2. The genus *Homo* is characterized by:
   a. larger brain size
   b. large cheek teeth
   c. parallel tooth rows
   d. a large brow ridge

3. The parts of the cranial buttressing system seen in *Homo erectus* include the:
   a. supraorbital torus
   b. sagittal crest
   c. nuchal crest
   d. smaller cheek teeth

4. Which of the following traits represents *Homo erectus*?
   a. small brain size
   b. thin cortical bone
   c. modern limb proportions
   d. cranial crests

5. The earliest representatives of *Homo erectus* are from _____, but the first fossils were discovered in _____.
   a. Indonesia, East Africa
   b. East Africa, Indonesia
   c. East Africa, China
   d. Western Asia, Indonesia

6. Shovel-shaped incisors are found in which *H. erectus* specimens?
   a. Indonesia
   b. East Africa
   c. China
   d. Western Asia

7. The stone tool industry associated with the hand axe is the:
   a. Acheulean
   b. chopper tool
   c. Olduwan
   d. flake tool

8. **True or False:** Scientists agree that the *Homo habilis* taxon is sexually dimorphic, represented by large males and small females.

9. **True or False:** The earliest members of the genus *Homo* represent a shift in adaptive strategy from the robust australopithecines.

10. **True or False:** *Homo erectus* is the first fossil hominid to move out of Africa and live in other areas of the Old World.

Post-Lab Questions

1. Considering that *Australopithecus boisei* and *Homo habilis* were evolving alongside one another in East Africa, discuss how their adaptive strategies may have been different and how their morphology reflects this.

   _____

   _____

   _____

   _____

   _____

2. Using the information your recorded in the chart for Exercise 1, what evidence is there that *H. habilis* may have had a different diet than *A. boisei*? _____

   _____

   _____

   _____

3. Name three sites where we find *Homo erectus*. _____

   _____

   _____

   _____

4. Name the parts that make up the cranial buttressing system. Do you see this system in *H. habilis*? Can you think of any reason why *H. erectus* may have needed this cranial support (i.e., in what activities may they have been engaged)? _____

   _____

   _____

   _____

   _____

5. How do you think they were able to determine the age of the Nariokotome skeleton so precisely? His limbs suggest he was five feet, six inches at the time of his death and would have reached six feet if he would have survived into adulthood. With this information, do you think it is fair to say that he aged like a human rather than like a chimpanzee? Why or why not? _____

   _____

   _____

   _____

   _____

6. The brain size of *Homo erectus* is significantly larger than any preceding hominids. Discuss some reasons why *Homo erectus* would need such a large brain and increased intelligence. _____

_____

_____

_____

_____

_____

_____

7. If the Olduwan stone tools were made only by early *Homo,* how might this indicate a change in behavior from the australopithecines? _____

_____

_____

_____

_____

_____

8. Examine the following photo. Label the supraorbital torus and the sagittal keel. Which hominid group does this represent?

_____

_____

_____

_____

9. Examine the following photo. Does this cranium belong to *Homo habilis* or *Homo erectus*? Name two features that helped you decide.

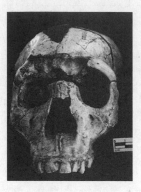

_____

_____

10. Examine the following photo. Does this cranium belong to *Homo habilis* or *Homo erectus*? Name two features that helped you decide.

_____

_____

Chapter | 15

Later *Homo* and Modern Human Origins

Objectives

After completing this chapter you should be able to:

1. identify the suite of characteristics that characterize anatomically modern humans;

2. recognize the traits that characterize the archaic *Homo sapiens,* as well as identify those that are shared with *Homo erectus* and those that are classified as modern;

3. understand the debate surrounding the Neanderthals and their relationship to modern humans;

4. identify the Neanderthal traits that are associated with cold adaptations and the traits that are unique to the Neanderthals; and

5. compare and contrast the Replacement and Multiregional Models for the origin of modern humans.

Anatomical Moderns

Modern humans belong to the taxonomic group *Homo sapiens sapiens.* A suite of characteristics defines human morphology as **anatomically modern**, as compared to the archaic *Homo* discussed in the following section (Clark, 1975). Anatomically modern *Homo sapiens* have a large brain size (~1350 cc on average); a high, rounded, globular cranium; a vertical forehead; an *orthognathic* face (tucked under the cranium, leaving a flatter facial profile); a prominent chin; small jaws and teeth; a lack of prominent crests or tori on the cranium;

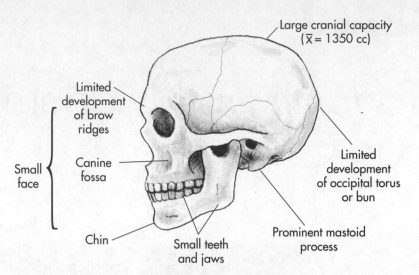

Anatomically modern *Homo sapiens*

Large cranial capacity
($\bar{x}$ = 1350 cc)

Limited
development
of brow
ridges

Canine
fossa

Small
face

Chin

Small teeth
and jaws

Limited
development
of occipital torus
or bun

Prominent mastoid
process

Figure 15-1 Anatomical features defining modern *Homo sapiens*.

and a slim, gracile skeleton (Figure 15-1). Fossil hominids with this suite of characters are considered modern humans.

Archaic *Homo sapiens*

Fossil hominids from approximately 400,000 years ago have a more transitional appearance, retaining *Homo erectus*-like characteristics while also resembling anatomically modern *Homo sapiens*. These transitional hominids are recognizable throughout the Middle Pleistocene, until about 125,000 years ago, throughout Europe, Africa, and Asia and are commonly referred to as "archaic *Homo sapiens*." Similar to *H. erectus*, the archaic hominids retain a large brow ridge, nuchal torus, and long, low cranium (Figure 15-2). However, tooth size is similar

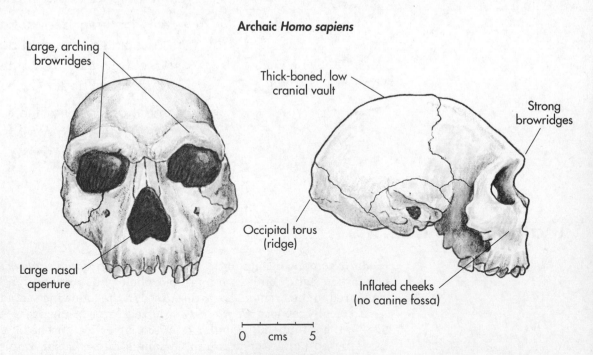

Archaic *Homo sapiens*

Large, arching
browridges

Thick-boned, low
cranial vault

Strong
browridges

Large nasal
aperture

Occipital torus
(ridge)

Inflated cheeks
(no canine fossa)

0   cms   5

Figure 15-2 Anatomical features for archaic *Homo sapiens*.

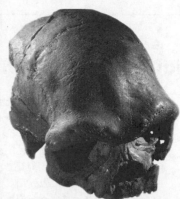

Figure 15-3 The Kabwe, Zambia (*left*), and Dali, China (*right*), archaic *Homo* crania.

to that of modern humans, and brain size increases in the archaic hominids to an average of 1200 cc, close to the range of anatomical moderns. Regional variation between the geographic areas causes some scientists to categorize this group into different species based on locality (e.g., *Homo heidelbergensis* in Europe).

Archaic fossils are best known from sites in Europe and Africa. European sites dating to just under 400,000 years ago with well-preserved fossil specimens include **Petralona**, Greece; **Steinheim**, Germany; **Arago**, France; and the **Sima de los Huesos** ("pit of bones") site, Sierra de Atapuerca region of Spain (Arsuaga et al., 1997). An earlier site from the Atapuerca region, known as **Gran Dolina**, dates to 800,000 years ago and contains the remains of the earliest fossil hominids in Europe, which are likely precursors to the archaic group (Arsuaga et al., 1999). Two of the best-known sites in Africa are **Bodo**, Ethiopia, and **Kabwe**, Zambia (Figure 15-3). Younger specimens are found in both China and India.

EXERCISE 1

Examine the following photo of the Petralona cranium. List at least three traits that this cranium has in common with *Homo erectus*.

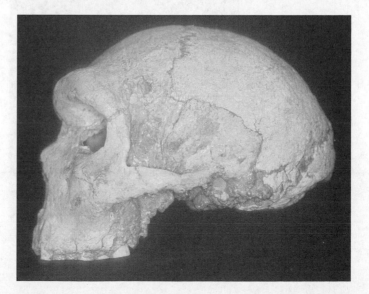

_____

_____

_____

_____

Late Archaic *Homo sapiens*: The Neanderthals

The **Neanderthals** are a Late Pleistocene group of specialized hominids who lived in Europe, Western Asia, and the Middle East approximately 130,000 to 25,000 years ago. Some researchers refer to them as *specialized archaics*. Sites yielding Neanderthal remains are numerous and found throughout the region. Some of the more famous sites are from Western Europe and represent the *Classic Neanderthals*, including **Saint Cesaire**, **La Ferrassie**, and **La Chapelle** in France. They extended east into Western Asia and the Middle East at such famous sites as **Shanidar**, Iraq; **Teshik Tash**, Uzbekistan; and **Kebara**, **Amud**, and **Tabun**, Israel (Figure 15-4). In 1856 in the Neander Valley of Germany, the Neanderthals became the first fossil hominids ever discovered. Shortly after, the fossils were misinterpreted by some researchers as pathological modern humans who were in no way ancestral to modern humans, an idea that remains ingrained in some today.

Considerable controversy continues among researchers as to whether or not the Neanderthals were ancestral, in whole or in part, to modern humans. Those who do not believe the Neanderthals were ancestral, essentially resulting in an evolutionary dead end, refer to the Neanderthals with a separate species designation: *Homo neanderthalensis*. However, many others believe that the Neanderthals were at least partially ancestral to modern humans and separate them only by the subspecies designation: *Homo sapiens neanderthalensis*. Recent studies of ancient DNA (aDNA) recovered from eight Neanderthal specimens demonstrate that Neanderthals were outside the range of variation seen in modern humans. In addition to these findings, aDNA from the Neanderthals also falls outside the range of variation seen in early modern humans (Krings et al., 1999; Schmitz et al., 2002). Whether

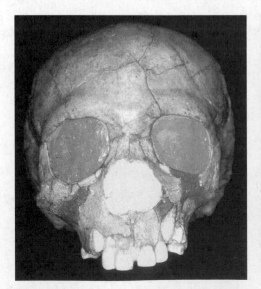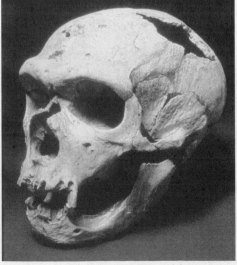

Figure 15-4 Neanderthal crania: Teshik-Tash (*left*) and La Chapelle (*right*).

NEANDERTHAL

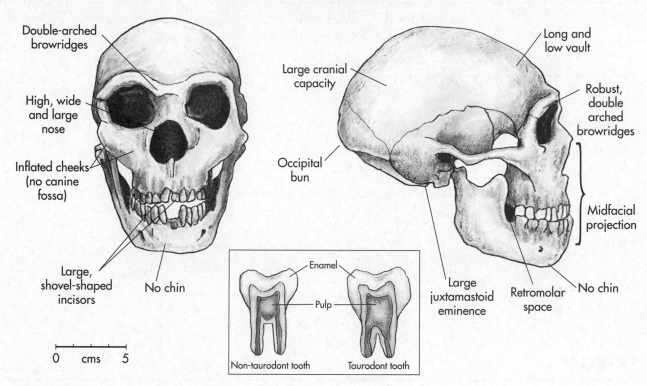

Figure 15-5 Anatomical features of the Neanderthals.

this indicates a Neanderthal extinction or leaves the door open for a Neanderthal–human admixture remains hotly debated.

Neanderthal morphology is quite distinctive. Neanderthals had a large brain (1500 cc average) but retained the long, low cranium, receding forehead, and supraorbital torus of the archaics preceding them. However, it is important to recognize that Neanderthals lived in glacial climates and demonstrate **cold adaptations** in their morphology. The shorter distal limb segments (forearm and lower leg) and barrel chest decreased the surface area to volume ratio of the body in order to retain body heat (Holliday, 1995). Some researchers have argued that the large nose with midfacial prognathism provided an extended distance for air to travel before reaching the lungs, warming and humidifying the cold dry air, although this idea is not widely accepted. Neanderthals also exhibit some **unique features**, including an occipital bun (raised bulge on the occipital bone), a retromolar space (between the third molar and the ascending ramus of the mandible), and very large incisors with extreme dental wear (Figure 15-5).

EXERCISE 2

Why do you think the Neanderthals have such large incisors and heavy dental wear on their teeth? _____

_____

_____

_____

EXERCISE 3

Compare the femora of the Neanderthal and an anatomically modern human and fill in the following information.

	Neanderthal	Modern Human
Length		
Joint size		
Thickness		

What might explain the differences you see here? _____

_____

_____

_____

_____

EXERCISE 4

Examine the following illustrations of the Neanderthal and modern human crania. Describe three differences that you observe between the Neanderthal and the modern human crania.

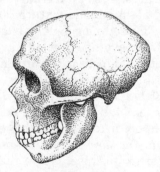 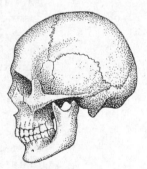

Neanderthal   Anatomically modern
                               Homo sapiens

_____

_____

_____

_____

EXERCISE 5

Casts or photos of the skulls of several species from the genus *Homo* are displayed in the laboratory. After careful examination, fill in the following chart:

Traits	*Homo erectus*	Archaics	Neanderthal	Modern Human
Time period				
Geographic range				
Average brain size (in cc)				
Supraorbital torus (large, medium, small)				
Contour of occipital (high/low, rounded/flat)				
Cresting (sagittal/nuchal)				
Chin (yes, no)				
Forehead (sloping, vertical)				
Any unique features				

The Rise of Modern Humans

Figure 15-6 Anatomically modern human cranium from Cro-Magnon, France.

The archaic forms evolved into modern *Homo sapiens* possibly as early as 100,000 to 200,000 years ago in Africa, and in occupied Europe as late as about 30,000 years ago. Moderns were everywhere by around 25,000 to 30,000 years ago and are represented by numerous well-known fossils. A few key sites include **Cro-Magnon**, France; **Skhul** and **Qafzeh**, Israel; **Klasies River Mouth** and **Border Cave** in South Africa; and the **Upper Cave** of Zhoukoudian in China (Figure 15-6). All these specimens, along with many others not listed here, are defined on the basis of derived features linking them to modern humans (refer to the traits listed at the beginning of this chapter).

Two main arguments address the emergence of modern humans: the *Replacement Model* and the *Multiregional Model.* The **Replacement Model** suggests that modern humans arose in Africa, from a cladogenetic speciation event, and then migrated out into the rest of the Old World where they completely replaced all other archaic species of humans they encountered with no interbreeding. The **Multiregional Model** for the origin of modern humans states that moderns arose in different places and at different times throughout the Old World and were interconnected at all times through gene flow. The Replacement Model is strongly supported by genetic evidence from both nuclear DNA and mitochondrial DNA. The genetic evidence shows that the most variation in DNA exists in Africa, indicating that African genes are the oldest on earth and suggests that moderns arose between 100,000 and 200,000 years ago in East Africa. However, the Multiregional Model is well-supported by the fossil evidence, which shows continuity between fossil species, indicating that local, in-situ evolution occurred and that Neanderthals were able to interbreed with modern humans migrating to their region. Although the debate has raged fiercely for over two decades, it is likely that some **assimilation** occurred between moderns and other archaic groups, possibly including the Neanderthals, and that the archaics were at least partly ancestral to moderns, although their genetic contribution may have been small.

Stone Tools and Cultural Behavior

The stone tool technology presented in Chapter 14 was still present in the Middle Pleistocene with the archaic *Homo sapiens.* Acheulean tools continued to be produced, although we do see some refinement in technique. In particular, the toolmakers used a *prepared core,* indicating that the core was modified in such a way as to remove flakes of a specific size and shape. One technique is known as

THE LEVALLOIS TECHNIQUE

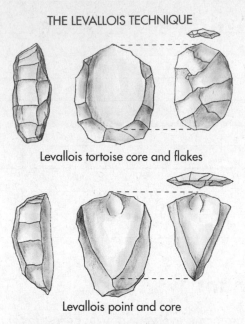

Levallois tortoise core and flakes

Levallois point and core

Figure 15-7 The Levallois technique for preparing a core.

Figure 15-8 A beautiful point from the Upper Paleolithic.

the **Levallois technique** (Figure 15-7). The discovery of well-crafted, wooden spears in Schoningen, Germany, in 1997 provided the first direct evidence of nonstone tools. The association of stone tools with faunal remains indicates that these hominids were hunting large game. The **Mousterian stone tool culture** characterizes Neanderthal tools, and the tools of some early modern humans, and represents additional small modifications of Middle Pleistocene tools and prepared cores. As the Upper Paleolithic commences and the modern humans become widespread across the Old World, numerous modifications of stone tools are seen and stone tools manufacture becomes regionally specialized. One common development is the use of *blade tools* (Figure 15-8): long flakes that were used for the production of a variety of flake tools and *microliths*, which are small tools meant to be attached to a handle.

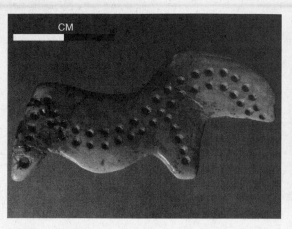

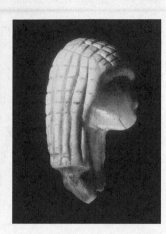

Figure 15-9 Examples of portable art from the Upper Paleolithic.

The Upper Paleolithic is also characterized by an explosion of art and ritual. Cave art, personal ornamentation (i.e., "jewelry"), and portable art—small figures that may be carried by an individual, become commonplace (Figure 15-9).

Pre-Lab Questions

1. Features such as a prominent chin and a vertical forehead are indicative of:
   a. Neanderthals
   b. archaic *Homo sapiens*
   c. anatomical modern humans
   d. *Homo erectus*

2. Which of the following is an archaic *Homo sapiens* site?
   a. Sima de los Huesos
   b. Teshik Tash
   c. La Chapelle
   d. Shanidar

3. Which of the following is a Neanderthal site?
   a. Sima de los Huesos
   b. Petralona
   c. La Chapelle
   d. Steinheim

4. Neanderthals exhibit adaptations to a cold glacial climate including:
   a. an occipital bun
   b. heavy dental wear
   c. large incisors
   d. large nose

5. Large incisor teeth, heavy dental wear, and an occipital bun are all traits that characterize:
   a. archaic *Homo sapiens*
   b. Neanderthals
   c. *Homo erectus*
   d. anatomical modern humans

6. The idea that modern humans arose in Africa over 100,000 years ago and did not interbreed with other archaics represents the:
   a. Multiregional Model
   b. Replacement Model
   c. Assimilation Model
   d. fossil evidence

7. Anatomically modern humans are found worldwide by:
   a. 25,000 years ago
   b. 125,000 years ago
   c. 400,000 years ago
   d. 1 million years ago

8. **True or False:** The archaic *Homo sapiens* share some traits in common with *Homo erectus*, including a large brow ridge.

9. **True or False:** The first hominids ever discovered were archaic *Homo sapiens* from Petralona cave in 1856.

10. **True or False:** The replacement model for the origin of modern humans is well supported by the fossil evidence.

Post-Lab Questions

1. Compare and contrast the three main groups of hominids described in this chapter as belonging to late *Homo*. Include in your answer a discussion of morphological differences between the groups.

   _____
   _____
   _____
   _____
   _____

2. In Exercise 5 in this chapter, what trends do you see in brain size? How is this shown in the bone?

   _____
   _____
   _____
   _____

3. Examine the following photo. How would you classify this cranium? List three features that helped you decide.

   _____
   _____
   _____
   _____

4. Examine the following photos. The Neanderthal is on the left with an anatomically modern human on the right. Compare and contrast at least three features you see here that differentiate the individuals.

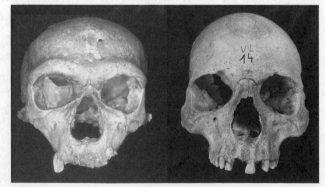

   - occipital bun
   - double arched brow

   _____
   _____

5. Match the hominid remains on the right to the site where they were found on the left.

_____ Steinheim, Germany   a. Archaic *Homo sapiens*

_____ Shanidar, Iraq   b. Neanderthal

_____ Arago, France   c. anatomical modern human

_____ Krapina, Croatia

_____ Bodo, Ethiopia

_____ Cro-Magnon, France

_____ La Chapelle, France

6. List three features that are linked to cold adaptation and three features that are unique to the Neanderthals. _____

_____

_____

_____

7. Examine the following photo comparing the body builds of a Neanderthal (*left*) and an anatomically modern human (*right*). List two features that distinguish these individuals postcranially.

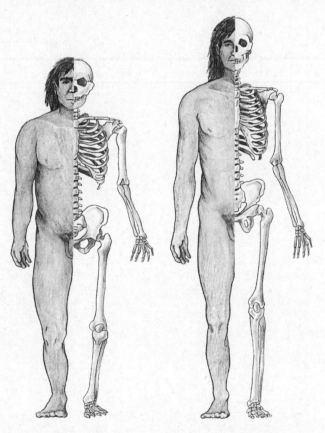

_____

_____

_____

_____

8. What do you think about the rise of modern humans? Do you support the Replacement or the Multiregional model, or some level of assimilation? Defend your answer.

_____

_____

_____

_____

_____

_____

abduction   Movement away from the midline of the body.

Acheulean stone tool industry   Group of tools which are bifacially worked and comprised primarily of the hand-axe and assorted cleavers; used by *Homo erectus*.

adaptive strategy   Adjustable approach of an organism toward interacting with its environment.

adduction   Movement toward the midline of the body.

affiliative behavior   Submissive personal action used to promote group solidarity and individual submission.

agglutination   The clotting of red blood cells.

aggressive behavior   Personal actions which are perceived as threatening to another individual; may arise from increasing dominance within a group.

alleles   Alternate forms of a gene.

amino acids   Building blocks of proteins, coded for by DNA.

analogous characters   Traits shared by organisms because they share a similar adaptation due to convergent evolution, not because of a recent common ancestor.

anatomical position   Universally accepted standard position for the human body.

anatomically modern   Possessing the suite of characteristics that defines the morphology of *Homo sapiens sapiens*.

angular torus   Horizontally placed ridge of bone along the posterior-inferior portion of the parietal.

anterior   In humans, directional term referring to placement along the frontal or coronal plane of the body; used to indicate that an anatomical feature is more toward the front than another anatomical feature.

Anthropoidea   Suborder of the primate order based on a traditional scheme that includes monkeys, apes, and humans.

anthropometry   The measurement of living peoples.

antigens   Proteins on the surface of red blood cells.

apes   Group of primates that includes two families, Hylobatidae (includes gibbons and siamangs) and Pongidae (includes orangutans, gorillas, chimpanzees and bonobos).

appendicular skeleton   Region of the skeleton comprised of the bones of the pectoral (shoulder) girdle, upper limb, pelvic girdle and lower limb.

arboreality   The ability to live in the trees.

assimilation   Genetic incorporation of one group of early humans with another.

atlas   First cervical vertebra (C1); has no body and resembles a ring-like structure; articulates with the occipital bone and allows the head to move in a nodding motion.

auricular surface   Area of articulation between the sacrum and the iliac portion of the os coxae; can be used for age estimation.

australopithecines   Group of fossil hominids that lived in Africa ~4 to 1 ma.

axial skeleton   Region of the skeleton comprised of the bones of the skull, thorax (chest) and vertebral column.

axis   Second cervical vertebra (C2); has a vertical prominence on the body called the odontoid process or dens which acts as a pivot allowing the head to rotate side to side.

bipedal   Type of locomotor pattern that involves standing and moving on the two hindlimbs.

Bicondylar length of the femur   measurement of the femur during which both condyles of the femur are placed firmly against the stationary upright of the osteometric board.

bilophodont   Molars with two ridges of cusps specially designed for shearing leaves and other plant material.

Binomial nomenclature   Method of identifying organisms utilizing a two-part naming system.

biological race   An individual's genetic ancestry, separate from social identity.

"Black Skull"   Nickname of a fossilized skull of *Australopithecus aethiopicus* that is stained black from minerals in the sediment.

bone   Highly mineralized connective tissue with an excellent blood supply and fewer collagen fibers producing a rigid structure.

calcaneus   Lies inferiorly to the talus; forms the heel of the foot.

cancellous bone   Porous bone beneath the cortical bone that is composed of a framework of strong, small, irregularly shaped trabeculae that allow the bone to remain lightweight.

canine   One of four tooth types; also called the cuspid, used for puncturing.

carpals   Eight small bones of the wrist.

carrier   An individual who possesses one copy of a recessive allele that is not expressed due to complete dominance of another allele.

cartilage   Connective tissue with a poor blood supply and more collagen and elastic fibers than bone.

cartilaginous joint   Point of connection between bones that is held together with cartilage and is somewhat moveable.

caudal   Directional term used to indicate that an anatomical feature is more toward the tail than another anatomical feature.

Ceboidea   One of three superfamilies of Anthropoidea that includes all non-human primates in the Americas.

cell   The structural and functional basic unit of life for all organisms.

centromere   Constricted area on a chromatid that separates the chromatid into arms.

Cercopithecoidea   One of three superfamilies of Anthropoidea that includes all Old World monkeys.

cervical vertebrae   Vertebrae of the neck; numbered C1–C7; smallest and lightest vertebrae of the body.

chromatid   One half of a double-stranded chromosome.

chromosome   Long, thread-like material found in the nucleus of the cell; contains DNA and proteins; usually single stranded, but become double stranded for cellular reproduction.

circumduction   Movement of a bone in which the proximal end remains stable while the distal end outlines an imaginary circle.

cladistics   Method of evolutionary classification that groups together all organisms that have descended from the same common ancestor and is based heavily on shared, derived characters.

clavicle   Anterior bone of the pectoral girdle; commonly called the collar bone.

cline   Gradient of genotypes over geographical space.

clinal variation   Adapted differences found in human populations due to different, local environments that do no follow simple continental boundaries.

codominance   A genetic situation in which both alleles are fully expressed.

codon   Series of three bases in RNA that code for an amino acid.

cold adaptations   Specialized morphological characteristics of Neanderthals that permit them to live in glacial climates.

common name   Familiar term used in everyday speech to identify organisms.

common perception   Assumption that states all humans observe events through their senses in the same way, although cultural associations may vary.

compact (cortical) bone   Smooth and uniform type of bone that is found on the outer surface of a bone.

complementary base pairs   The bases of nucleotides that join in a very specific manner: adenine (A) with thymine (T) and cytosine (C) with guanine (G); form the rungs of DNA's double helix.

compound temporo-nuchal crest   Horizontally placed bony ridge on the lateral and posterior surface of the skull, found in some australopithecines.

control variables   Conditions or events of an experiment that the researcher attempts to keep the same.

controlled experiment   An experimental situation designed by a researcher, often occurring in a laboratory, in which the researcher can alter one variable in order to observe its effects on other variables; must contain an unaltered group for comparison.

coronal or frontal plane   Imaginary line drawn through the body that runs vertically, dividing the body into front and back parts.

coxal bones (os coxae)   Two bones forming the pelvic girdle.

C/P3 hone or honing complex   Dental arrangement found in apes that maintains the sharpness of the edges of the upper canine and lower first premolar.

cranial   Directional term used to indicate that an anatomical feature is more toward the head than another anatomical feature.

cranial buttressing system   A series of thickened ridges or buttresses that serve as a biomechanical adaptation for absorbing stress on the cranium.

cranial capacity   Estimated brain size of an organism.

cranial landmarks   Universally accepted points of reference or features on cranial bones that are used for taking cranial measurements.

cranium   Portion of the skull that includes the face and the encloses the braincase.

crossing over (recombination)   An event during meiosis in which genetic information containing genes for the same trait is exchanged between homologous chromosomes.

crown   One of three areas of a tooth; portion of the tooth that is visible above the gumline and is covered with enamel.

culture   The learned rules of a society that govern the behavior of the individuals of that society.

deciduous teeth   First set of teeth that is shed during childhood; commonly called baby teeth.

deep   Directional term used to indicate that an anatomical feature is internal to another anatomical feature.

dens or odontoid process   Vertical prominence on the body of the axis; acts as a pivot allowing the head to rotate from side to side.

dental formula   The count of the number and types of teeth in each quadrant of the mouth.

dependent variable   The condition or event being studied through experiment that may change due to the independent variable.

diaphysis   Shaft of a long bone.

diastema   A space between consecutive teeth.

dihybrid cross   A study examining the transmission of two traits.

diphyodont   Having two complete sets of teeth, such as deciduous and permanent.

diploe   Cancellous bone separating the inner and outer tables of a bone of the skull.

diploid   Characteristic of a cell that contains a full complement of chromosomes.

distal   Directional term generally referring to placement along the limb; used to indicate that an anatomical feature is further away from the trunk than another anatomical feature.

DNA (deoxyribonucleic acid)   Double stranded molecule that contains genetic information and is stored in the nucleus of a cell.

DNA fingerprinting   Determining an individual's specific base pair sequence as a means for identifying that individual.

dominance hierarchies   Form of ranked, organized social structure based upon the level of dominance exhibited by individuals.

dominant   Characteristic of an allele to mask or hide the expression of the other allele at the same locus.

dorsal   Directional term used to indicate that an anatomical feature is more toward the back side than another anatomical feature.

dorsiflexion   Movement of the ankle joint so that the toes are raised while the heel remains in contact with the ground.

double helix   Twisted ladder-like structure of DNA.

East African Rift Valley   Geologically active 1,200-mile long valley that runs through Ethiopia, Kenya, and Tanzania and contains millions of years of exposed strata and contains a wealth of fossil hominid remains.

ecology   Field of study that examines the interconnectedness of animals to their physical environment.

enamel   Hard, highly mineralized substance that covers the crown of a tooth.

epiphyseal plate (line)   Thin area of cartilage between the diaphysis and the epiphysis that provides for longitudinal growth of a long bone.

epiphysis   End of a long bone.

equilibrium   Situation in which the allele frequencies of a population remain constant, generation after generation.

estrus   Time of a female's peak fertility.

ethmoid   Bone of the cranium that is located between the frontal and sphenoid.

Eugene Dubois   Discoverer of the earliest found fossilized remains of *Homo erectus*, which were found in Indonesia in the 1890's.

eukaryotic   Cells with a true nucleus.

eversion   Turning the sole of the foot away from the midline.

evolution   A change in allele frequencies in a population over time.

evolution of sexual dimorphism   The development of sex-specific differences between males and females.

evolutionary taxonomy   Method of evolutionary classification that places importance on change that may occur along a lineage.

extant   Currently alive in this time period.

extension   Movement that increases the angle of a joint.

femur   Bone of the leg; commonly called the thigh bone.

fibrous joint   Point of connection between bones that are held together by short, tough fibrous tissue and is immovable.

fibula   Lateral bone of the lower leg.

fitness   An individual's ability to produce offspring; also called reproductive success.

flexion   Movement that decreases the angle of a joint.

folivore   An animal who has a specialized diet consisting mainly of leaves.

fontanelles   Gaps separating the bones of the cranium that allow room for brain growth prior to complete fusion of the cranial bones.

foramen magnum   The large hole in the basicranium through which the spinal cord passes, connecting the head to the vertebral column.

forensic anthropology   A subfield of biological anthropology that uses biological anthropological methods to analyze human remains from a medico-legal context.

founder effect   Type of genetic drift that can occur when a new population is established by a small, non-random sample that is separated from the larger population.

frontal   The bone of the braincase that forms the forehead and superior portion of the eye orbits.

frontal or coronal plane   Imaginary line drawn through the body that runs vertically, dividing the body into front and back parts.

frugivore   An animal who has a specialized diet consisting mainly of fruit.

gametes   Haploid cells that contain the genetic information required for reproduction; reproductive cells.

gene   Segment of DNA that codes for specific traits.

gene flow   Change in the allele frequency of a population due to migration.

genetic drift   Change in allele frequency of a population due to random chance.

genetically conservative   Characteristic of a trait or feature indicating that it tends to maintain its structure and does not easily evolve over time.

genotype   The genetic composition of an organism; the alleles present in an organism.

grooming   A very important affiliative behavior during which an individual picks parasites off of another individual while finger-combing through the hair of another individual.

grooming claw   Claw found on the second digit of the foot of many strepsirhines.

hallux   The first digit of the foot; commonly called the big toe.

haploid   Characteristic of a cell that contains one half of the complement of chromosomes.

Haplorhini   Suborder of the primate order based on a more modern scheme that includes tarsiers, monkeys, apes, and humans.

hard object feeding   Diet with an emphasis on heavy chewing, especially of hard seeds and nuts.

Hardy–Weinberg Principle   Proposal stating heredity alone cannot cause changes in the frequency of alleles in a population.

hemizygous   Genetic state in which an individual expresses a recessive genetic trait while only possessing one allele for that trait.

heterozygous   Genetic state in which an individual possesses different alleles for the same trait on both members of a pair of homologous chromosomes.

Hominidae   Primate family that includes modern humans and extinct ancestors since the divergence from the last common ancestor with chimpanzees.

hominids   Members of the taxonomic family Hominindae.

Hominoidea   One of three superfamilies of Anthropoidea that includes all apes and humans.

homologous characters   Traits shared by organisms that were inherited from a recent common ancestor.

homologous pair   A pair of chromosomes that carry genes for the same traits.

homozygous   Genetic state in which an individual possesses identical alleles for the same trait on both members of a pair of homologous chromosomes.

honing complex or C/P3 hone   Dental arrangement found in apes that maintains the sharpness of the edges of the upper canine and lower first premolar.

humans   Members of the Hominidae family.

humerus   Bone of the arm.

hybrid   Offspring of parents who are true-breeding for alternate forms of a genetic trait or characteristic.

Hylobatidae   One of two ape families that includes gibbons and siamangs.

hyoid   Small, horseshoe-shaped bone located in the throat above the larynx.

ilium   Large, flaring, superior portion of the os coxa; one of three bones that fuse to form the os coxa.

incisor   One of four types of teeth, most anterior teeth in the jaws, commonly used for biting and chopping.

incomplete dominance   Genetic situation in which one allele is not completely dominant to another.

independent variable   The condition or event being studied through experiment.

index   The ratio of one value to another, shown as a percentage.

inferior   In humans, directional term referring to placement along the transverse plane of the body; used to indicate that an anatomical feature is below another anatomical feature.

inferior nasal conchae   Found inside the nasal cavity; also called turbinate bones.

inner table   Smooth compact bone on the inner (endocranial) surface of a bone of the skull.

intermembral index   A calculation helpful for determining primate locomotor patterns, the humerus and radius lengths are added in the numerator and divided by the sum of the femur and tibia lengths in the denominator.

inversion   Turning the sole of the foot toward the midline.

ischial callosities   Thickened calluses used for sitting found on the rumps of Old World monkeys.

ischium   Thick, inferior portion of the os coxa; one of three bones that fuse to form the os coxa.

"Java Man"   Several crania of *Homo erectus* discovered on the Island of Java.

joint   Point of connection between bones.

karyotype   Photographic image of an organism's chromosomes that have been stained.

KNM-ER 1470   A relatively complete fossilized cranium of *Homo habilis* found at Lake Turkana with a larger cranial capacity and relatively larger face and teeth.

KNM-ER 1813   A relatively complete fossilized cranium of *Homo habilis* found at Lake Turkana with a smaller cranial capacity and relatively smaller face and teeth.

KNM-ER 3733   A famous skull representative of *Homo erectus* found in East Africa.

KNM-ER 3883   A famous skull representative of *Homo erectus* found in East Africa.

knuckle-walking   Specialized form of quadrupedialism wherein the hand is held in such a way that the weight of the body is placed on the middle phalanges, seen in chimpanzees and gorillas.

k-selected   Organisms whose life strategy is to produce few offspring and invest an extensive amount of time caring for their young.

lacrimal   Tiny paired bone of the face found in the medial portion of the eye orbit between the maxilla and the ethmoid.

lateral   In humans, directional term referring to placement along the sagittal plane of the body; used to indicate that an anatomical feature is further away from the midline than another anatomical feature.

Law of Independent Assortment   Mendel's second law that states during meiosis, the members of different pairs of alleles assort independently into gametes (especially so if they are on different chromosomes).

Law of Segregation   Mendel's first law that states during meiosis, the chromosome pair separates, so that each newly formed gamete receives one chromosome.

lemurs   Group of primates that live only on the island of Madagascar and includes such groups as true lemurs, dwarf lemurs, the indri and sifaka and the aye-aye.

Levallois technique   One method employed to refine Acheulean flaked stone tools.

ligament   Tough, strap-like fibrous tissue that connects bones to each other.

Linnaeus   Swedish naturalist who developed the system of scientific classification for organisms that is still in use today.

longitudinal arch   Curvature of the foot that runs from heel to toes.

lorises   Group of primates that live in tropical Africa and Asia and include animals such as the slow loris, slender loris, potto and bushbaby (or galago); all are nocturnal and most are solitary.

"Lucy"   Nickname of the fossilized remains of a young adult female *A. afarensis* that was found by Johanson, Taieb, and White in 1976 and is approximately 40% complete.

lumbar vertebrae   Vertebrae of the lower back; numbered L1–L5; largest of all vertebrae and they carry the weight of the upper half of the body.

mandible   The lower jawbone.

manubrium   Somewhat triangular shaped bone and is the most superior of the three bones that fuse together to form the sternum; articulates with the medial ends of the clavicles.

marrow/medullary cavity   Hollowed out central region of a long bone containing yellow and red blood marrow.

masseter   Laterally placed muscle that assists in chewing by raising the mandible.

maxilla   The bone that forms the lateral and inferior portions of the nose, the innermost and inferior edge of the eye orbit, the anterior base of the cheek, and houses the upper teeth; articulates with every bone of the face.

maximum length   Measurement of the long bones that records the longest distance from one end to the other.

maximum length of the tibia   Measurement of the tibia taken diagonally, from the lateral condyle to the medial malleolus.

medial   In humans, directional term referring to placement along the sagittal plane of the body; used to indicate that an anatomical feature is more toward the midline than another anatomical feature.

meiosis   Specialized cell division occurring in the testes and ovaries which produces gametes, each receiving half the genetic complement.

metacarpals   Five bones of the palm of the hand.

metatarsals   Five bones of the arch of the foot.

mitosis   The process of simple cell division during which one somatic cell divides into two identical daughter cells, each receiving a complete set of genetic information.

molar   One of four types of teeth; used for crushing and grinding.

monogamy   Type of social structure in which one adult male and one adult female (and any dependent offspring) live together; common among gibbons.

monohybrid cross   A study examining the transmission of one trait.

Mousterian stone tool culture   Characteristic stone tool manufacturing of Neanderthals and some early modern humans that includes modifications of early stone tools as well as the development of blade tools and microliths.

mRNA (messenger RNA)   One type of RNA that is formed from a DNA template inside the nucleus which carries a DNA message out of the nucleus that is used for protein synthesis.

Multiregional Model   Hypothesis stating that modern humans arose in different places and at different times throughout the Old World and were interconnected by gene flow at all times.

mutation   An actual change in the genetic material of an organism at the DNA or chromosome level.

Nariokotome Boy or WT 15000 or Turkana Boy   Skeleton of a young male *Homo erectus* about 11 years of age that is approximately 80% complete.

nasal   Tiny paired bone inferior to the frontal bone; forms the bridge of the nose.

natural causality   Assumption that states all events in nature are the result of natural causes.

natural experiment   An experimental situation in which the researcher has little to no control over any of the variables.

natural selection   Evolutionary factor that allows some individuals who possess certain variations to survive and reproduce more than other individuals, perpetuating more of their genes in the population; also called differential reproductive success.

Neanderthals   Group of specialized hominids who lived in Europe, Western Asia, and the Middle East between approximately 130,000 and 25,000 years ago.

neck   One of three areas of a tooth; the constricted portion of a tooth found at the gumline.

New World monkeys   Found in the Americas; all are arboreal and diurnal, except the owl monkey; some have prehensile tails.

nondisjunction   A failure of the chromosomes to segregate properly during cell division.

nonrandom mating   Situation in which individuals show a strong preference for certain mates over others.

nuchal (occipital) torus   Horizontally placed thickened ridge of bone across the occipital bone.

nucleotides   Basic building block of DNA, each containing a phosphate, a sugar (deoxyribose sugar) and a base group.

nucleus   Internal, membrane bound structure that contain DNA and are found inside eukaryotic cells.

occipital   The bone of the braincase that forms the posterior wall and base of the cranium.

odontoid process or dens   Vertical prominence on the body of the axis; acts as a pivot allowing the head to rotate from side to side.

Old World monkeys   Monkeys of Africa and Asia; live in a variety of habitats.

Oldowan stone tool complex   The first group of stone tools and are comprised primarily of cores and flakes as well as hammerstones.

one male polygyny   A harem type of social structure in which one (or two) adult breeding males and several adult females (and any dependent offspring) live together; common among gorillas and Hanuman langurs.

opposability   The ability to use the thumb or big toe to touch all other four digits of the hand or foot, respectively.

os coxae (coxal bones)   Two bones forming the pelvic girdle.

osteometry   The measurement of skeletal remains.

outer table   Smooth compact bone on the outer (exocranial) surface of a bone of the skull.

palatine   Small, paired bone posterior to the palatine process of the maxilla; form the posterior-most portion of the palate.

parabolic dental arch   Arrangement of the tooth rows in a rounded, curved formation.

parietal   Paired bone of the braincase; forms the top and sides of the cranium.

patella   Small, triangular bone that lies immediately anterior to the distal end of the femur; commonly called the knee cap.

pedigree analysis   A diagram depicting family relationships over several generations that is used for tracing the transmission of a genetic trait.

"Peking Man"   Several crania of *Homo erectus* discovered in China, but lost during World War II.

pelvic girdle   The bony structure comprised of the right and left os coxa and the sacrum.

periosteum   Tough membrane covering the outside surface of a bone except for the articular ends.

permanent teeth   Second set of teeth that replaces the deciduous teeth; commonly called adult teeth.

phalanges   Fourteen bones of the digits of the hand or foot, singular = phalanx.

phenotype   The physical characteristics of an organism; the expression of an organism's genetic composition.

phylogeny   A classification scheme indicating evolutionary relationships between organisms.

plane   Imaginary line, section or cut drawn through the body wall.

plantarflexion   Movement of the ankle joint so that the heel is raised while the toes remain in contact with the ground.

polyandry   Type of social structure in which one adult female and two to three adult males (and any dependent offspring) live together; common among marmosets and tamarins.

polygyny   Type of social structure in which multiple adult males and females (and any dependent offspring) live together; common among anthropoids, especially baboons and chimpanzees.

Pongidae   One of two ape families that includes orangutans, gorillas, chimpanzees and bonobos.

population   A group of potentially interbreeding individuals within a species.

population bottleneck Loss of genetic variation within a population.

population specific Term indicating that the amount of difference of certain physical characteristics is dependent upon the population being studied.

post-orbital bar Partial enclosure of the eye orbit.

posterior In humans, directional term referring to placement along the frontal or coronal plane of the body; used to indicate that an anatomical feature is more toward the back than another anatomical feature.

prehensility Grasping ability.

premolar One of four tooth types, considered posterior teeth or "cheek" teeth, used for slicing and grinding.

prokaryotic Cells without a separate nucleus.

pronation Movement of the palm downward.

Prosimii Suborder of the primate order based on a traditional scheme that includes lemurs, lorises, and tarsiers.

protein synthesis One of the main functions of DNA during which proteins are made.

proximal Directional term generally referring to placement along the limb; used to indicate that an anatomical feature is more toward the trunk than another anatomical feature.

pubic symphysis Area of articulation between the right and left pubic bone; can be used for age estimation.

pubis Most anterior portion of the os coxa; one of three bones that fuse together to form the os coxa.

Punnett square A diagram used to determine all the possible results of the mating of two individuals.

quadrumanual Specialized form of suspension utilized by orangutans, whose feet and hands are indistinguishable from each other and both are used extensively for climbing.

quadrupedalism Type of locomotor pattern that involves the use of four limbs to support the body above the ground or a tree limb.

race Term used to indicate an individual's ethnicity or ancestry; its use is complicated and controversial in biological anthropology.

radius Lateral bone of the forearm.

recessive Characteristic of an allele whose expression is masked or hidden by a dominant allele.

recombination (crossing over) An event during meiosis in which genetic information containing genes for the same trait is exchanged between homologous chromosomes.

reduced prognathism Lessened facial projection.

repeatable Something that can be observed more than once.

Replacement Model Hypothesis suggesting that modern humans arose in Africa and then migrated out into the rest of the Old World, completely replacing all other hominids without interbreeding.

reproductive strategies The behavioral approaches or physical limitations of an organism that affect its ability to produce and raise offspring.

rhinarium Wet nose, found on all strepsirhines.

ribosome Organelle in the cytoplasm which is the specific site of protein synthesis.

RNA (ribonucleic acid) Single-stranded molecule with a structure similar to that of DNA.

root One of three areas of a tooth; portion of the tooth that lies below the gumline, anchoring the tooth into the alveolar region of the maxilla and mandible.

rotation Movement of a bone around its vertical axis.

r-selected Organisms whose life strategy is to produce many offspring and invest little time caring for their young.

sacrum Large, somewhat triangular shaped bone composed of five vertebrae that fuse together during adulthood; articulates with the os coxae (coxal bones) to complete the pelvic girdle.

sagittal crest Medially placed bony crest on the top of the skull that runs anteriorly to posteriorly.

sagittal keel Thickened area of bone along the sagittal suture, seen in some members of *Homo erectus*.

sagittal plane Imaginary line drawn through the body that runs vertically, dividing the body into left and right parts.

scapula Posterior bone of the pectoral girdle; commonly called the shoulder blade.

Science   Method of gaining knowledge through the use of critical observation and experiment.

scientific method   A process for empirically testing possible answers to questions about natural phenomena in ways that must be repeatable and verifiable.

scientific name   Universally accepted term used for identifying an organism and is specific to that organism.

scientific theory   The concluding results of rigorous and exhaustive testing through experiment that is supported by a significant body of data and whose validity is not seriously doubted by the scientific community.

self-replication   One of the main functions of DNA which occurs when the cell is about to divide.

semi-brachiation   Specialized form of suspension that involves a combination of arm swinging and leaping; seen in both New World and Old World monkeys.

sex-linked   Characteristic of genes that occur on the sex chromosomes.

sexual dimorphism   Term describing differences due to sex, usually indicating that males are larger than females.

shovel-shaped incisors   Incisors that have vertical ridges on the lateral edges of the lingual surface of the tooth.

slow-climbing   A slow, specialized form of suspension that involves a combination of climbing and swinging; exhibited by the great apes.

social race   A category representing an individual's ethnic ancestry, but strongly based on social constructs or identity and not on genetics.

sociobiology   Field of research that examines the impact of natural selection on behavior.

solitary   Type of social structure in which the adults live independent of each other, although adult females will also have their dependent offspring; common among prosimians.

somatic cells   Diploid cells that make up the body of an organism, often called body cells.

species   A group of potentially interbreeding organisms found in nature that are capable of producing fertile offspring.

sphenoid   Butterfly shaped bone of the cranium; is the cornerstone of the skull as it connects the cranial base to the face and the face to the braincase.

stature   Height of an individual.

sternal body   Somewhat rectangular shaped bone that forms the middle section of the sternum.

sternum   Most anterior and superior portion of the thorax; articulates with the first seven pairs of ribs and is composed of three bones that fuse together (manubrium, sternal body, and xiphoid process).

Strepsirhini   Suborder of the primate order based on a more modern scheme that includes lemurs and lorises.

superficial   Directional term used to indicate that an anatomical feature is external to another anatomical feature.

superior   In humans, directional term referring to placement along the transverse plane of the body; used to indicate that an anatomical feature is above another anatomical feature.

supination   Movement of the palm upward.

supraorbital torus   Prominent brow ridge above the eye orbits.

suspension   Type of locomotor pattern that involves supporting the body using the forelimbs to hang beneath a tree branch.

synovial joint   Point of connection between bones that is surrounded by a fluid-filled, fibrous capsule and is freely-movable.

talus   The largest of the tarsal bones; articulates the with distal tibia to form the ankle joint and carries the weight of the body.

tarsals   Seven small bones of the ankle and foot.

tarsier   Type of primate classified as both a haplorhine and prosimian; represents a link between the higher and lower primates; nocturnal; live on the islands of Southeast Asia.

Taung   South African site of the first australopithecine discovery.

taxon   Generalized term to indicated any level of the hierarchical system of classification developed by Linnaeus.

taxonomy   The science of classification and nomenclature.

temporal   Paired bone of the cranium; found inferior to the parietal and forms part of the lateral wall of the braincase; also houses the sense of hearing.

temporalis　Muscle on the lateral surface of the skull that has an important role in chewing.

tendon　Tough, strap-like tissue that connects muscles to bones.

thick enamel　Increased thickness of the tooth enamel which is associated with tougher diets.

thoracic vertebrae　Vertebrae of the torso; numbered T1–T12; articulate with the ribs.

threat displays　Behaviors which are intended to intimidate others; used to exert control and often decrease tension among group members.

tibia　Anterior and medial bone of the lower leg; commonly called the shin bone.

tool use　Physically manipulating an object for a specific purpose.

tooth comb　Specialized grooming tool formed by the lower incisors and canines of some strepsirhines.

trabeculae　Small, irregularly shaped bars of bone that are very strong and provide the framework for cancellous bone.

transcription　Formation of mRNA (messenger RNA) from a DNA template.

translation　Process during which mRNA (messenger RNA) is translated into a strand of amino acids that will eventually form a protein.

transverse arch　Curvature of the foot that runs from the inside of the foot to the outside of the foot.

transverse plane　Imaginary line drawn through the body that runs horizontally, dividing the body into upper and lower parts.

tRNA (transfer RNA)　One type of RNA that resides at the ribosome and carries an amino acid during the process of protein synthesis.

true brachiation　Specialized form of suspension referring to traditional arm swinging and is very fast; exhibited only by the Hylobatidae.

Turkana Boy or WT 15000 or Nariokotome Boy　Skeleton of a young male *Homo erectus* about 11 years of age that is approximately 80% complete.

typical vertebrae　Vertebrae containing common features found on all vertebra; these features include a body, a vertebral arch, transverse processes, and a spinous process.

ulna　Medial bone of the forearm.

uniformity in space and time　Assumption that states all naturally occurring events occur the same, regardless of where or when they may happen in the universe.

universal donor　An individual possessing type O blood.

universal recipient　An individual possessing type AB blood.

valgus knee　Type of knee formation in which the femur meets the tibia at an angle due to the inward angle of the femur from the hip to the knee.

VCL　Type of locomotor pattern called vertical clinging and leaping in which the body is held in an upright position while the animal grasps onto the vertical trunks of the tree.

ventral　Directional term used to indicate that an anatomical feature is more toward the belly side than another anatomical feature.

verus knee　Type of knee formation in which the femur is in line with the tibia due to the lack of a femoral angle because the femur drops straight down from the hip to the knee.

vertebral column　Row of uniquely shaped bones that function to protect the spinal cord as it runs the length of the back.

vomer　Thin, sheet-like bone that forms the inferior nasal septum.

WT 15000 or Nariokotome Boy or Turkana Boy　Skeleton of a young male *Homo erectus* about 11 years of age that is approximately 80% complete.

xiphoid process　An irregular shaped bone that is the most inferior of the three bones that fuse together to form the sternum.

zygomatic　Paired bone of the face; lies between the maxilla and the temporal; commonly called the cheekbone.

zygote　A fertilized egg.

Bibliography

Arsuaga JL, Martines A, Garcia A, Lorenzo C. 1997. The Sima de los Huesos crania (Sierra de Atapuerca, Spain): A comparative study. *Journal of Human Evolution* 33:219–281.

Arsuaga JL, Martinez I, Lorenzo C, et al. 1999. The human cranial remains form Gran Dolina Lower Pleistocene site (Sierra de Atapuerca, Spain). *Journal of Human Evolution* 37:431–457.

Bass WM. 1995. *Human Osteology: A Laboratory and Field Manual.* Special Publication No. 2. Columbia, MO: Missouri Archaeological Society.

Brooks ST, Suchey JM. 1990. Skeletal age determination based on the os pubis: A comparison of the Ascadi-Nemeskeri and Suchey-Brooks methods. *Human Evolution* 5:227–238.

Broom R. 1947. Discovery of a new skull of the South African ape-man, *Plesianthropus. Nature* 159:672.

Brunet M, Guy F, Pilbeam D, et al. 2002. A new hominid from the Upper Miocene of Chad, Central Africa. *Nature* 418:145–151.

Buikstra JE, Ubelaker DH. 1994. *Standards for Data Collection from Human Skeletal Remains.* Research Series 44. Fayetteville: Arkansas Archaeological Survey.

Clark WEL. 1975. *The Fossil Evidence for Human Evolution.* Chicago: University of Chicago Press.

Dart RA. 1925. *Australopithecus africanus:* The man-ape of South Africa. *Nature* 115:195–199.

Fleagle JG. 1998. *Primate Adaptations and Evolution*, 2nd ed. San Diego, CA: Academic Press.

Gill GW, Rhine S. 1990. *Skeletal Attribution of Race.* Anthropological Papers No. 4. Albuquerque, NM: Maxwell Museum of Anthropology.

Goodman M. 1999. The genomic record of humankind's evolutionary roots. *American Journal of Human Genetics* 64:31–39.

Goodman M, Porter CA, Czelusniak J, et al. 1998. Toward a phylogenetic classification of primates based on DNA evidence complemented by fossil evidence. *Molecular Phylogenetics and Evolution* 9:585–598.

Groves C. 2001. *Primate Taxonomy.* Washington, DC: Smithsonian Institution Press.

Hardy GH. 1908. Mendelian proportions in a mixed population. *Science* 28:49–50.

Holliday TW. 1995. Body size and proportions in the Late Pleistocene western Old World and the origins of modern humans. PhD dissertation, University of New Mexico, Albuquerque.

Jantz RL. 1992. Modification of the Trotter and Gleser female stature estimation formulae. *Journal of Forensic Sciences* 37:1230–1235.

Johanson DC, Taieb M. 1976. Plio-Pleistocene hominid discoveries in Hadar, Ethiopia. *Nature* 260:293–297.

Krings M, Geisert H, Schmitz RW, et al. 1999. DNA sequence of the mitochondrial hypervariable region II from the Neandertal type specimen. *Proceedings of the National Academy of Sciences* 96:5581–5585.

Krogman WM. 1962. *The Human Skeleton in Forensic Medicine.* Springfield IL: Charles C Thomas.

Laidlaw SA, Kopple JD. 1987. Newer concepts of the indispensable amino acids. *American Journal of Clinical Nutrition* 46:593–605.

Larick R, Ciochon RL, Zaim Y, et al. 2001. Early Pleistocene ^{40}Ar/^{39}Ar ages for Bapang Formation hominids, Central Java, Indonesia. *Proceedings of the National Academy of Science* 98:4866–4871.

Leakey LSB. 1959. A new fossil skull from Olduvai. *Nature* 184:491–493.

Leakey LSB, Tobias PV, Napier JR. 1964. A new species of the genus *Homo* from Olduvai Gorge. *Nature* 202:7–9.

Leakey MG, Feibel CS, McDougall I, Walker A. 1995. New four-million-year-old hominid species from Kanapoi and Allia Bay, Kenya. *Nature* 376:565–571.

Lovejoy CO, Meindl RS, Mensforth R, Barton TJ. 1985. Chronological metamorphosis of the auricular surface of the ilium: A new method for the determination of adult skeletal age at death. *American Journal of Physical Anthropology* 68:15–28.

Mayr E. 1942. *Systematics and the Origin of Species.* New York: Columbia University Press.

Mayr E. 1963. *Animal Species and Evolution.* Cambridge, MA: Harvard University Press.

Mayr E. 1981. Biological classification: Towards a synthesis of opposing methodologies. *Science* 214:510–516.

Meindl RS, Lovejoy CO, Mensforth RP, Walker RA. 1985. A revised method of age determination using the os pubis with a review and tests of accuracy of other current methods of pubic symphyseal aging. *American Journal of Physical Anthropology* 68:29–45.

Phenice TW. 1969. A newly developed visual method of sexing the *os pubis. American Journal of Physical Anthropology* 30:297–302.

Pickford M, Senut B. 2001. "Millenium Ancestor," a 6-million-year-old bipedal hominid from Kenya: Recent discoveries push back human origins by 1.5 million years. *South African Journal of Science* 97:2–22.

Ruvolo M. 1997. Molecular phylogeny of the hominoids: Inferences from multiple independent DNA sequence data sets. *Molecular Biology and Evolution* 14:248–265.

Sarich VM, Wilson AC. 1967. Immunological time scale from hominid evolution. *Science* 158:1200–1203.

Schick K, Toth N. 1993. *Making Silent Stones Speak: Human Evolution and the Dawn of Technology.* New York: Simon & Schuster.

Schmitz RW, Serre D, Bonani G, et al. 2002. The Neandertal type site revisited: Interdisciplinary investigations of skeletal remains from the Neander Valley, Germany. *Proceedings of the National Academy of Sciences* 99:13,342–13,347.

Stanford C, Allen JS, Antón SC. 2006. *Biological Anthropology: The Natural History of Humankind.* New Jersey: Prentice-Hall.

Stewart TD. 1979. *Essentials of Forensic Anthropology.* Springfield, IL: Charles C Thomas.

Swisher CC, Curtis GH, Jacob T, et al. 1994. Age of the earliest known hominids in Java, Indonesia. *Science* 263:1118–1121.

Todd TW. 1920. Age changes in the pubic bone: I, the male white pubis. *American Journal of Physical Anthropology* 3:285–334.

Trotter M. 1970. "Estimation of stature from intact long limb bones." In *Personal Identification in Mass Disasters*; ed. Stewart TD. Washington, DC: National Museum of Natural History, Smithsonian Institution.

Trotter M, Gleser GC. 1952. Estimation of stature from long bones of American Whites and Negroes. *American Journal of Physical Anthropology* 10:463–514.

Trotter M, Gleser GC. 1958. A re-evaluation of estimation of stature based on measurements of stature taken during life and long bones after death. *American Journal of Physical Anthropology* 16:79–123.

Walker AC, Leakey RE, Harris JM, Brown FH. 1986. 2.5-myr *Australopithecus boisei* from west of Lake Turkana, Kenya. *Nature* 322:517–522.

White TD, Suwa G, Asfaw B. 1994. *Australopithecus ramidus*, a new species of early hominid from Aramis, Ethiopia. *Nature* 371:306–312.

Williams GC. 1966. *Adaptation and Natural Selection.* Princeton, NJ: Princeton University Press.

Wilson EO. 1975. *Sociobiology: The New Synthesis.* Cambridge, MA: Harvard University Press.

Chapter 2: **13**, Figure 2-3, Photo Researchers, Inc.

Chapter 10: **135**, Figure 10-1, From *Biological Anthropology: The Natural History of Humankind* by C. Stanford, J. S. Allen and S. C. Antón (Figure 7.9, p. 175). Copyright © 2006 by Pearson Education, Inc., Upper Saddle River, New Jersey 07458. Reprinted by permission of Pearson Education, Inc.; Figure 10-2, Craig Stanford; **136**, Figure 10-3, Joseph Van Os/Image Bank/Getty Images; **136**, Figure 10-4, Animals Animals/Earth Scenes; **137**, Figure 10-5, Corbis/Bettmann; **138**, Figure 10-6, Craig Stanford, Animals Animals/Earth Scenes; **139**, Figure 10-7, Craig Stanford; **140**, Figure 10-8, Craig Stanford; **142**, Figure 10-9, Craig Stanford, Corbis/Bettmann; **145**, Craig Stanford/Jane Goodall Research Center; **146**, Craig Stanford; **147**, Animals Animals/Earth Scenes.

Chapter 11: **150**, Figure 11-1, Craig Stanford/Jane Goodall Research Center; **151**, Figure 11-2, Joseph Van Os/Image Bank/Getty Images; **151**, Figure 11-3, Craig Stanford; **155**, Figure 11-4, Copyright (c) Zoological Society of San Diego, San Diego, California, U.S.A. All rights reserved; **156**, Corbis/Bettmann; **163**, Animals Animals/Earth Scenes; Craig Stanford.

Chapter 12: **165**, Figure 12-1, Craig Stanford/Jane Goodall Research Center; **167**, Figure 12-2, Craig Stanford.

Chapter 13: **179**, Figure 13-4, From *Paleoanthropology,* 2nd edition, by M. Wolpoff (Figure 38). Copyright © 1999. Reprinted by permission of The McGraw-Hill Companies; **192**, Institute of Human Origins, Arizona State University; **193**, Jeffrey K. McKee.

Chapter 14: **195**, Figure 14-2, Kenneth Garrett Photography; **198**, Figure 14-4, Kenneth Garrett Photography, Susan C. Antón; **200**, Figure 14-6, Kenneth Garrett Photography; **203**, Copyright Susan C. Antón; **204**, Copyright Susan C. Antón; Kenneth Garrett Photography.

Chapter 15: **207**, Figure 15-3, Kenneth Garrett Photography; Courtesy of and copyright by Eric Delson; **208**, Figure 15-4, Prof. Milford H. Wolpoff, John Reader/Science Photo Library; **211**, Figure 15-6, Photo Researchers, Inc.; **212**, Figure 15-8, Randall White; **213**, Figure 15-9 (a & c), Randall White, Figure 15-9 (b), Kenneth Garrett Photography; **214**, Kenneth Garrett Photography; Prof. Milford H. Wolpoff/University of Michigan.